Membranes

MEDICINE & CULTURE

Sander L. Gilman
SERIES EDITOR

Robert Michaels, M.D., Linda Hutcheon, Ph.D., and
Michael Hutcheon, M.D.
EDITORIAL BOARD

Georges Minois, *History of Suicide: Voluntary Death in Western Culture,*
translated by Lydia G. Cochrane

Jacques Jouanna, *Hippocrates,* translated by M. B. DeBevoise

Laura Otis, *Membranes: Metaphors of Invasion in Nineteenth-Century Literature,
Science, and Politics*

Membranes

*Metaphors of Invasion in
Nineteenth-Century Literature,
Science, and Politics*

L A U R A   O T I S

The Johns Hopkins University Press

BALTIMORE AND LONDON

Printed in the United States of America on acid-free paper
2   4   6   8   9   7   5   3   1

The Johns Hopkins University Press
2715 North Charles Street
Baltimore, Maryland 21218-4363

The Johns Hopkins Press Ltd., London
www.press.jhu.edu

Library of Congress Cataloging-in-Publication Data will be
found at the end of this book.
A catalog record for this book is available from the
British Library.

ISBN 0-8018-5996-4

To Elissa Sue Spinner (1962–1990)
A Healer, an Artist, a Friend

CONTENTS

ACKNOWLEDGMENTS

First, I would like to thank the National Endowment for the Humanities and the American Council of Learned Societies for the fellowships that allowed me to bring this study together through intensive research at the University of Chicago libraries during 1997–98.

I am also grateful to the Wood Institute for their support of my research at the Philadelphia College of Physicians in June, 1997. Without it, I would never have obtained the appreciation of S. Weir Mitchell's physiology and neurology that I eventually did. I thank Charles Greifenstein for acquainting me with the S. Weir Mitchell archive at the College of Physicians in August 1996 and January 1997. My thanks to the Library of the College of Physicians of Philadelphia for permission to quote from S. Weir Mitchell's unpublished letters and autobiography. I also thank the Estate of Dame Jean Conan Doyle for permission to quote selections from the Sherlock Holmes stories by Sir Arthur Conan Doyle.

I am deeply grateful to the Deutscher Akademischer Austauschdienst, whose summer fellowship allowed me to explore the Virchow Nachlaß in Berlin. This powerful learning experience helped me gain an understanding of Virchow, Koch, and their German culture that I could never have obtained here at home. In Berlin, I would like to thank Professors Wenig and Klaus at the Archiv der Berlin-Brandenburgischen Akademie der Wissenschaften, Herr Donath at the Robert Koch Museum, Herr Gerber at the Robert Koch Institut, Professor Schneck at the Institut für Geschichte der Medizin at the Humboldt Universität, Professor Winau at the Institut für Geshichte der Medizin at the Freie Universität, and Herr Kriech at the Institut für Pathologie at the Charité Hospital.

I am likewise indebted to the National Endowment for the Humanities and the Programa Cooperativo entre las Universidades Americanas y el Ministerio de Cultura Española for making possible my study of Ramón y Cajal's early scientific papers at the Biblioteca Nacional and the Instituto Ramón y Cajal in Madrid during the summer of 1993, another period that was as enriching culturally as it was intellectually.

I would like to express my deep appreciation to the administrators and librarians of Hofstra University for their unflagging enthusiasm for my investigations.

I could not have written this study of boundaries and connections without the valuable input of my colleagues, and I am deeply grateful to all those scholars who have helped me investigate the identity issue. I would especially like to thank Katherine Arens for her cogent advice as a writer and critic and the tremendous support she has provided for my interdisciplinary work. I thank Larry Rothfield for helping me to rethink my understanding of metaphor, and Thomas Brock for our pleasant afternoon discussing Robert Koch and microbiology. I am grateful to T. J. Reed for his comments on my analysis of *Death in Venice*. I am also grateful to Dale Pratt, Francisco LaRubia Prado, and Tomás Casas-Arruti for the insight they offered me into Spanish literature and culture. I am indebted to my colleagues at Hofstra University, especially JoAnn Krieg, Neil Donahue, and John Bryant, for their suggestions concerning the project. Most of all, I would like to thank Sander Gilman, whose confidence and pragmatic advice have allowed me to develop as a scholar.

Membranes

Introduction

It was 3 AM in the Stryker lab, and the grad students were straining to hear a response. One slowly waved a flashlight so that a bar of light swept across a screen; the other advanced an electrode, micrometer by micrometer, and waited. Then, it came: pop. Pa-pop. Connected electronically to a loud-speaker, the electrode was recording the firing of neurons in the anesthetized cat's brain. Pop. Pa-pop. It sounded like popcorn. Unconscious, but with its eyes open, the cat was "seeing" the bar of light, its cells reacting to the sweeps across the screen.

I was a biochemist, a mere visitor to the lab, but I learned an important lesson that night. The eye, and the regions of the brain that interpret visual information, respond only to changes, to borders between light and dark. There are cells that fire only when a bar of light moves horizontally, and cells that fire only when it moves vertically. There are cells that fire only when it moves from left to right; others, only when it moves from right to left. There are even cells that respond only to diagonal sweeps, but there are no cells that respond to a uniformly illuminated screen, with no movement, no edges, and no borders. The human eye likes to dart about, requiring frequent changes to maintain its flow of information. If you are forced to focus on a single object for thirty seconds without glancing away, you will watch the object dissolve into little gray flecks and disappear before your eyes. To create meaning from what it sees, indeed, for there to be vision at all, the eye needs borders, differences that distinguish one object from another.

Fresh from the lab, I learned the same lesson in Jonathan Culler's introductory course on literary theory. Explaining Saussure's idea of how words were paired with objects, Culler proposed that we define concepts not based on what they are, but on what they are *not*. When defining something, we typically compare it to something similar and then, like the eye, focus on the way it differs from the concepts most closely related to it. A cow, for instance, has four legs like a horse, but it is fatter. There is no natural match between a word and the thing it represents; no positive assertion of a thing's identity, just as there will be no firing in response to a blank screen, even when it is brightly lit. Like our visual system, we create meaning only through the differences we perceive and the boundaries we believe are present.

What had struck me in the lab as natural and quite reasonable devastated me in the classroom. Perhaps I had hoped that nature and culture worked differently, or that the humanities offered a different perspective from that of the natural sciences. How could there be truth, I wondered, and how could there be meaning, if we defined our ideas only negatively? What were our thought and our vision worth if we perceived the world only in terms of boundaries, arbitrarily drawn? I found these thoughts most disturbing when I applied them to our notions of personal identity, to our concept of selfhood. To what extent did people need borders, separating the "me" from the "not me," to define themselves as individuals? Could we ever construct a positive notion of what we were, or only specify what we were not, what we wanted to keep out?

It has been more than ten years since that class and that night in the lab, and in that time I have come to regard the division between the humanities and the natural sciences as another boundary arbitrarily drawn. Scholars on both sides of the line want to answer the same questions, and we express ourselves through metaphors provided by a common culture. If we exaggerate our differences and take pride in our technical dialects, it is because our identities, as we perceive them, rely on these differences. To communicate effectively with one another, to live with one another, we need to rethink these identities, focusing not on the semipermeable membranes that separate us but on our permeability and on our mutual connections.

When I approached the problem of selfhood, I deliberately ignored these disciplinary "membranes." I cared equally about what scientists, creative writers, and philosophers had had to say about identity, and I wondered what their writing would have in common. I found that people, like ideas, did not fall easily into categories. I discovered that authors whose stories fascinated me had been doctors, and that scientists whose ideas intrigued me had written fiction. Why not, I thought, explore the issue of identity through the work of physician authors, who could approach the problem of individual identity from many perspectives simultaneously?

The fiction and scientific writing of authors who excelled in both fields seemed to me the best possible terrain on which to study how literary and medical representations of selfhood cross-pollinated one another. While this choice allowed me to "control" for individual style, comparing the creative and analytical descriptions of particular writers, it also, unfortunately, restricted my choice of authors. In the nineteenth century, people who achieved success both as scientists and as authors were almost exclusively Western, middle class, and male. I am painfully aware of the exclusion of female and non-European voices from this study, especially since the authors I examine erect their model of selfhood in opposition to feminine and foreign forces. The concept of identity that emerges from cell theory and its fictions—I shall call it the "membrane model"—is based on exclusion. To maintain a truly interdisciplinary focus in my analysis, I am forced to exclude some of what this boundary-dependent model excludes. Because of the relative absence of nineteenth-century voices challenging the membrane model, I call extra attention to the sexual and cultural assumptions inherent in this concept of identity. I also try to point out the contradictions and tensions in its descriptions by its advocates. Of the five major authors I consider, two openly challenge it, and none embraces it unreservedly.

The writers I consider, like the notions of selfhood that they grapple with, defy classification as "literary" or "scientific." To see how language and culture affected the identity issue, I purposely selected writers from as many different empires as possible: Germany, the United States, Spain, Great Britain, and Austria. In their respective languages, all of these physician-authors confront their cultures' demands for borders, and they express and challenge them through common metaphors and maneuvers. This coincidence suggests that imperialistic culture, which offers the same metaphors to scientists and novelists, shapes both biology and literature by shaping the language through which they express themselves. By studying these authors' works in parallel, simply as writing, one can learn more about what identity meant during these years than one can by studying the works of bacteriologists or novelists alone. The relationship between literature and science is one of mutual feedback and suggestibility, each contributing to and drawing upon the "culture medium" out of which it grows. Culture, however, does not "determine" science or literature any more than science and literature determine culture; personal vision persists, despite all indoctrination and all scientific training. A government can influence but never fully control what its people see.

The Spanish neurobiologist Santiago Ramón y Cajal (1852–1934), whose science fiction stories I examine in the third chapter, stands out for his unique visual powers. As a neuroscientist, I had studied his exquisite drawings of brain cells, still the best available after a hundred years. There is nothing more beautiful than a highly branched neuron waiting for inputs, and both as a scientist and as an artist, Cajal inspires respect for this beauty. Cajal won the Nobel prize in 1906 for proving that neurons were intact, independent cells. He and Camillo Golgi, who shared the prize with him, stared at the same extraordinary tangles of neuronal processes and argued for years over whether the neurons merged into a net or, as Cajal insisted, were distinct individuals, intricately intertwined. Since Golgi invented the staining techniques that Cajal used, both must have seen similar images under their microscopes. What was it, I wondered, that drove Cajal to keep looking, determined to resolve boundaries between cells when there appeared to be no boundaries to resolve?

To answer this question, I begin my first chapter by considering the first scientists who proposed that all living things were made of individual cells, exploring the forces that shaped their scientific vision. Robert Hooke observed cells in cork in the late seventeenth century, but no one thought to assert that all plants and animals were constructed the same way. These claims came only after technical improvements in the microscope in the 1820s. Brian Ford, however, who has extensively studied the capacities of single-lens microscopes, denies that the perfection of achromatic compound microscopes in the mid-nineteenth century led directly to the development of cell theory and germ theory. Many scientists who made key discoveries in pathology did not use microscopes at all (Ford 1973, 97). The realization that microorganisms cause diseases, he argues, could easily have been made with Leeuwenhoek's lenses in the 1670s (1985, 130). Many factors besides the essential technical ones affect what one sees under a microscope, or at least the way one describes it. It has been proposed, for instance, that late eighteenth-century German philosophy, with its stress on individual perception, inspired people in many fields to conceive of life in terms of independent living units (Rothfield, 97). How might politics and culture have shaped the cell theory?

As I focused on the years 1830–1930—from the time scientists first proposed that individual cells composed all living things until they began developing vaccines for the most threatening contagious diseases—I noticed an affinity between political and biological thinking. Rudolf Virchow (1821–1902), who argued that doctors could understand diseases only by seeing how they affected individual cells, illustrates the absolute interdependence of science and politics. In the first chapter, I study the ways his medical and social interests inspired one another. Cell theory relies on the ability to perceive borders, for to see a structure under a microscope means to visualize a membrane that distinguishes it from its surroundings. Germ theory, the idea that infectious diseases are caused by living microorganisms, encourages one to think in terms of "inside" and "outside" to an even greater extent. If one believes that invisible germs, spread by human contact, can make one sick, one becomes more and more anxious about penetration and about any connection with other people—the same anxieties inspired by imperialism.

Politically, the years 1830–1930 mark the peak of European colonialism, particularly that of England and France. Germany, which seized its colonies only in the 1880s, and Spain, which had long been in decline as an imperial power, are special cases. The aggressive acquisition of colonies during these years transformed the way that European nations defined themselves. The colonial powers simultaneously claimed vast new territories as "theirs" and labeled these territories' cultures, peoples, animals, and diseases as "not theirs." They attempted to engulf and control as "self" what they excluded as "not self," destabilizing their traditional identities. Imperialism opened the borders, both geographical and cultural, on which Europeans had relied for their knowledge of who they were.

While they were happy to expand outward, Westerners became horrified when the cultures, peoples, and diseases they had engulfed began diffusing, through their now permeable membranes, back toward their imperial cell bodies. Politically, in the nineteenth century, Europeans became increasingly aware of their vulnerability and relied ever more on these illusory "membranes," of which they were more and more conscious, to define themselves in terms of what they were not. They presumed that they had a right both to expand their boundaries and to exclude from their identities the new elements they had taken in.

Bacteriology served this imperialist ideology, the scientific and colonial powers sending forth "microbe hunters" to aid in their expansion (LaTour, 141). "Microbe hunter" is Paul de Kruif's descriptive term for Koch, Pasteur, and other scientists who identified the microorganisms that cause diseases. As Donna Haraway puts it, "expansionist Western medical discourse in colonizing contexts has been obsessed with . . . hostile penetration of the healthy body. . . . the colonized was perceived as the invader" (Haraway, 223). Medical and cultural thinking combined to present aggression as defense; to depict the invaded as the invaders. I conclude my first chapter by analyzing the way politics and science mingled in the career of Robert Koch (1843–1910), discoverer of the tuberculosis and cholera bacilli and an enthusiastic "microbe hunter" in Germany's colonies.

All of the physician-authors I have selected had some training in bacteriology and incorporated, on many levels, its commands to visualize hidden threats and to think in terms of "inside" and "outside." The American neurologist S. Weir Mitchell (1829–1914), on whom I focus in the second chapter, studied medicine in the late 1840s and adopted the belief in living, external threats from his father, an early advocate of germ theory. Mitchell, like the later physician authors, approaches the mind with the perspective of germ theory: it must protect itself by developing a strong "will" to screen dangerous impulses from within and dangerous suggestions from without. When people failed to fend off these threats on their own, Mitchell believed, the physician must step in, temporarily, and control their mental lives for them.

The late nineteenth-century passions for colonialism, bacteriology, and hypnotism coincided more than chronologically. Arthur Conan Doyle (1859–1930), concerned with infiltration on both social and psychological levels, depicts British society as permeated by foreign criminals "passing" as respectable citizens (Rothfield, 140). In my fourth chapter, I argue that Sherlock Holmes, his hero, acts as an immune system—and like a bacteriologist—to identify them and render them innocuous.

Infectious foreign bacteria threatened to penetrate and destroy individual bodies, and it occurred to many physicians in the 1880s that infectious thoughts might destroy an individual mind in an analogous fashion. Watching hypnotized subjects lower their mental "barriers" and respond to suggestions like automata was a very frightening experience. Like germ theory, it stressed people's disturbing openness to outside forces. Arthur Schnitzler (1862–1931), whose early writings I explore in the fifth chapter, took a particular interest both in hypnosis and in the bacteria that caused syphilis, and he came to accept people's openness to germs and to suggestions as a fact of life. His literary works show the futility and the risks involved in defining oneself by exclusion when so much of one's identity consists of words and roles suggested by others.

By 1900, even writers with no medical training were concerned with infectious microbes and thoughts and the unreliable boundaries people had constructed to exclude them. To illustrate the extent to which "membranes" preoccupied all early-twentieth-century Europeans, in my sixth chapter I analyze their representation by a writer with no scientific background. Thomas Mann (1875–1955), who learned of germ theory principally through its cultural interpretations, writes about cholera with phrasing strikingly similar to Doyle's and Koch's. In Mann's *Death in Venice*, as in Schnitzler's works, the attempt to deny one's connections to undesirable forces proves disastrous. Like the people that empires reject, these repressed forces will take their revenge.

Reflecting both scientific fears of infection and nationalistic fears of infiltration, the membrane model bases identity on resistance to external forces, many of which are projections of undesirable internal drives. Penetration of one's "membrane," whether by bacteria or by foreign ideas, represents an insult, a subversion of selfhood. Sexually, it represents an unmanning, the humiliating assumption of a passive sexual role. Julia Epstein has noticed how frequently contemporary writers claim that AIDS is "rending the fabric of society." This metaphor, she believes, suggests "the rending of coverings in general, from the drapery that hides private fissures in the body's surfaces to the epithelial membranes whose intactness signals innocence and, therefore, safety from infection" (Epstein, 18). Not simply individual identity, she argues, but the identities of social classes rely upon boundaries people have constructed and maintained. AIDS does not recognize these boundaries. By violating these illusory protective layers, by challenging their value and their existence, AIDS "rends the fabric" of society as viewed by the privileged, ripping through their protective "clothing."

The sexual paranoia inherent in the membrane model—a paranoia still very much in evidence in notions of identity today—has its basis in two interrelated cultural prejudices: (1) depreciation and misreading of female sexuality as passive penetrability, and (2) exaggerated esteem for the intact hymen, whose rupture initiates one into the realm of the passive, the penetrated, and the impure. Today this realm is occupied by the HIV positive; a hundred years ago it encompassed the "weak-willed," those with insufficient resistance to bacteria, subversive suggestions, emotional impulses, or foreign saboteurs. Our fears of "leakage" and desires for containment, today centered around HIV, are a continuation of nineteenth-century terrors that our membranes—and with them, our identities—will be ruptured (Epstein, 159).

We are still living in an imperial age, and our quest for defining edges and anxiety about penetration persist a hundred years after Koch's journeys to Africa. As we begin to recognize the cultures and the lives so long denied as closely related to our own, we must accept that the social and political borders we see are not "natural," not a phenomenon grounded in external reality. The eye seeks boundaries, and language constructs divisions that are not really there. They create these differences so that there may be vision and communication, but these differences vary from eye to eye and from language to language. In my anxiety about what this reliance on arbitrary boundaries does to truth, I reassure myself that vision works beautifully. If only, in our quest to understand what we are, we can see as well as our eyes.

ONE

Virchow and Koch

The Cell and the Self in the Age of Miasmas and Microbes

Every widespread disease in the nation, be it mental or physical, therefore shows us the life of the population under abnormal conditions, and all we need to do is recognize this abnormality and signal it to the statesman so he can dispose of it. . . . Do we not always find the diseases of the populace traceable to defects in society?

—Rudolf Virchow

We only need to make a blood preparation and examine it microscopically; then we find the malaria parasites in it and thus have the irrefutable evidence that the person in question is concealing the infectious material inside of himself. . . . If all carriers of parasites in a given area are freed from their malaria parasites, then the area is rendered malaria free. . . . We must be prepared, first, to detect the infectious material easily and with certainty, and second, to destroy it.

—Robert Koch

During the second half of the nineteenth century, both cells and bacteria became known as well-defined, independent entities. As pathologists focused on the cell as the locus of disease and on the microbe as its cause, the blame for diseases shifted from physical environments to the people who inhabited them. This change in perspective indicates an increasing tendency to conceive of life and disease in terms of units with distinct boundaries. The idea that all life forms consist of individual, largely independent cells developed only gradually, emerging from the observations of seventeenth- and eighteenth-century microscopists (Duchesneau, 345). As the European middle class increased its political and economic power in the 1830s and 1840s, however, the bourgeois ideal of the free, responsible, and "self-contained" individual began to express itself in medicine as a model of good health.[1] Cultural historian Michel Foucault argues that in the nineteenth century, "the action of the illness rightly unfolds in the form of individuality" and that doctors, now focusing on their particular patients' bodies to understand the nature of disease, sought "the forbidden, imminent secret: the knowledge of the individual" (Foucault, 169–70). This perspective expressed itself on a microscopic as well as a macroscopic scale. While on a practical level, microscopists began seeing cells in plants because of improved achromatic lenses, they also saw cells because, as their own descriptions indicate, the idea of a bounded individual as the unit of life became culturally acceptable and appealing. This study explores nineteenth-century cell theory and germ theory as a culturally motivated enclosure movement evident in scientific, literary, and political writing.

Zooming in on Life and Disease

The human body is distressingly vulnerable, disturbingly open to its environment. Hippocrates' call for doctors to consider "winds, waters, site, soil, and diet" still seems reasonable considering people's intimate relationship with their physical surroundings (Riley, ix). Well into the nineteenth century, the earth itself was thought to emit fever-producing vapors, so that fissures, cracked foundations, and recently plowed fields became terrifying threats (Corbin 1986, 23). Air, which "entered into the very texture of living organisms," was most suspect (11). In the eighteenth century, while still holding the earth and atmosphere responsible for disease, Europeans began to lose their fatalistic acceptance of miasmas and to conceive of the environment and the diseases it caused as something that could be controlled (Riley, x). Even early hygienists began to think not just in terms of physical environments but of personal environments—of individual space and individual air.

As chemical knowledge increased, scientists became more ambitious in their desires to "fix" and control the elements of which people were composed, viewing disease as "the dissolution of individuals and the self" (Corbin 1986, 21). While chemists like Boyle and Lavoisier studied the composition of air, physicians worried about the relationship between internal and external atmospheres, whose competing pressures were revealed through exhalations, belches, and flatulence (11). One's personal odor, which "revealed the inner identity of the 'I,'" could be permeated, diluted, invaded (143). Social historian Alain Corbin argues that the "rise of the concept of the individual," developed through the philosophy of Kant and Fichte, may have promoted the "privatization of human waste" in the late eighteenth century (61).

Not all people qualified as "individuals," however, just those whose financial means let them control their personal space. Following the cholera epidemics of the 1830s, health officials seeking harmful vapors shifted their focus from public places, where people intermingled as odoriferous equals, to the dirty, overcrowded houses of the poor. The smell of human waste became associated with slum dwellers as "the bourgeois projected onto the poor what he was trying to repress in himself" (Corbin 1986, 144). Since odors revealed identity, the poor became one with the filth amid which they lived.

Declaring that "everything that stinks does not kill, and everything that kills does not stink," conservative physician Paul Brouardel proclaimed that after the general acceptance of microbial theory in the early 1880s, the miasmatic approach was dead (Corbin 1986, 223). Such a view, however, oversimplifies the dynamic field of hygiene, and philosopher of science Bruno LaTour is more accurate in arguing that germ theory actually served hygienists' needs. Even within the nineteenth-century miasmatic movement, among those who believed that places caused disease, there was an increasing tendency to examine "private space" and bad-smelling individuals in seeking the origins of disease. The belief that individuals are to blame for transmitting diseases does not begin with the acceptance of microbes or even with the acceptance of cells. It begins in 1780 with the Edict of Villers, which ordered each private citizen to "look after his own shit" (60). By the nineteenth-century, a concept of the individual had emerged that required people to take responsibility for their own emanations and guard themselves against the excretions of others.

Contagionism, the belief that diseases are transmitted from one person to another, predates the idea of a bounded, independent self and can trace its roots to classical times. It was advocated in the sixteenth century by Fracastorius and Paracelsus and in the seventeenth by Kircher, who, with his microscope, saw tiny "worms" in the blood of plague victims (Ackerknecht 1948, 565; Genschorek, 35–36). For centuries, contagionism and anticontagionism (miasmatism) had been competing as explanations for diseases. By the 1830s and 1840s contagionism had reached a low level of repute, regarded as an old and unsubstantiated idea with no practical hygienic applications. The liberal hygienists who opposed it, regarded today as medically backward, were fighting for adequate water supplies, waste disposal systems, and clean, ventilated living quarters; they feared that conservative governments would seize upon contagionism as an excuse to cancel their public works projects. These anticontagionists saw themselves as advocates of modern medicine and may well have saved more lives than the bacteriologists who succeeded them (Ackerknecht 1948, 567). As had happened with cell theory, germ theory displaced miasma theory in the second half of the nineteenth century not just because of innovations in microscopy or because of Pasteur's and Koch's technical ingenuity, but because cultural developments made the idea of infectious germs believable.

The growth of industrialism and colonialism in the nineteenth century greatly increased contact between nations and cultures. If diseases were contagious, commercially crippling quarantines had to be established, so political beliefs inevitably affected people's opinions as to whether disease spread through foul air or human contact. Anticontagionist reformers, largely liberals and radicals, fought for scientific, commercial, and individual freedom simultaneously, regarding the three as inseparable (Ackerknecht 1948, 589–91). While the middle class stood to benefit from free trade, the landed gentry and other traditionalists had nothing to fear from embargoes that favored national interests. Contagionism consequently attracted conservatives, officers and bureaucrats who thought that centralized power structures, not individual citizens or local authorities, should control policies affecting public health. Historian of science Erwin Ackerknecht finds that "the ascendancy of anticontagionism coincides with the rise of liberalism, its decline with the victory of the reaction" (589). Politics thus shaped medical opinion, but simultaneously, scientific discoveries influenced political thinking.

Bichat, Turpin, Schwann: The Emergence of Cell Theory

In France, which led Europe both in hygiene and in social theory at midcentury, the socialist Etienne Saint-Simon reported being "strongly influenced" by the scientist Xavier Bichat (1771–1802). Bichat, who described the body as a conglomerate of tissues, did not use a microscope or discuss individual cells, but Schwann, Virchow, and most other developers of cell theory cite him as an inspiration. Although Bichat's vision of the body had its precedents in seventeenth- and eighteenth-century visions of cells and fibers, his forceful arguments that one could understand life and death only in terms of local tissues fascinated scientists and philosophers alike (*DSB* 2:122–23).[2] Michel Foucault, intrigued by Bichat's "clinician's eye," regards him as a central figure in the shift to a medical epistemology privileging "the surface gaze" (Foucault, 129).

In the preface to his *General Anatomy* (1801), Bichat introduces his vision of the body by opposing it to that of vitalism. He absolutely rejects "one sole, abstract, and ideal principle, whether it be under the name of soul, archaeus, etc." Instead, careful observation reveals the body as a collection of tissues, "each hav[ing] its particular organization as it has its own life." He tells readers that he aims "to analyze with precision the properties of living bodies; to demonstrate that every pathological phenomenon is derived from their increase, their diminution, or their change" (1824, 1). Local transformations explain both life and death.

Seeing himself as an empiricist dispelling romantic fantasies about the body, Bichat stressed the importance of direct observation. Never one to trust lenses, he scanned tissues with the naked eye, selecting very thin, almost transparent layers that were free from fat and easy to scrutinize (Ford 1973, 96). To determine the properties of tissues, he manipulated them by stretching them, blowing on them, or saturating them with various fluids. The practices used by unscrupulous butchers to inflate their meat appear to have given him many ideas. One question that particularly interested Bichat was whether the tissues were independent of or in communication with one another. To find out, he injected fluids into tissues and checked their neighbors for penetration. In one experiment, he deprived dogs of water and then "compelled them to drink a great quantity" (Bichat 1824, 42). He found that tissues around the stomach and intestines contained no more water than those in other parts of the body (47). Most often, he observed that healthy tissues permitted little access to their neighbors; in terms of their permeability, the tissues he examined exhibited considerable independence. Only when damaged did tissues became increasingly permeable to external fluids.

Bichat's famous statements in *Physiological Researches on Life and Death* (1800): "Life consists in the sum of the functions, by which death is resisted" and "the measure of life in general is the difference which exists between the effort of exterior power and that of interior resistance," suggest that an inside/outside dichotomy underlies his scientific vision (1827, 10–11). Life, for Bichat, is "resistance," and his conception of the body encourages doctors to scrutinize the dying individual because the selective destruction of largely independent tissues helps to reveal their individual roles. With Bichat, Foucault is convinced, medicine became a "science of the individual" (Foucault, 197). While Bichat's vision of diverse tissues seemingly contradicted the idea of organic wholeness, it directed the pathologist's attention to the individual body because diseases could be understood only by studying individual cases. Such an outlook invited scientists to explain illness and health in terms of smaller and smaller living units.

Since the 1660s, when Robert Hooke had observed "cells" in cork, scientists had been reporting that plant tissue consisted of individual subunits, but no one had proposed such a division as a universal structural principle. By the 1820s, however, the French botanist P. J. F. Turpin felt enough confidence in his enhanced microscopic vision to argue that all plants, even unicellular organisms, consisted of independent vesicles of globulin. While the globules he observed were most likely artifacts, "hazy circles" of light created around the smallest points his imperfect lenses could resolve, Turpin's colorful descriptions impressed Theodor Schwann, who would propose a decade later that animal tissues consisted of cells (Ford 1973, 95).

To the naked eye, Turpin proposed, plant tissue appeared to consist of "globulin" of various types. However, under the microscope, he found that globulin from plants invariably revealed itself to be a "collection of distinct individuals," the units that composed multicellular organisms closely resembling independent unicellular organisms (Turpin, 33). He concluded that "the entire tissular mass of plants is nothing but an agglomeration . . . of smaller globular, univesicular plants, each one having its vital principle of action, organization, and reproduction" (49).[3] For Turpin, the presence of these bounded individual vesicles explained the affinities and differences between the species of plants he studied.

When Schwann proposed in the late 1830s that animals, like plants, were composed of individual cells, he had no intention of fragmenting organisms by drawing boundaries between and within them. On the contrary, he hoped to demonstrate that common structural and developmental principles united all living things.[4] Since Turpin and Schleiden had already convinced biologists of the cellular structure of plants, the revelation of cells in animal tissues would "prove the most intimate connexion of the two kingdoms of organic nature" (Schwann, ix). Like Turpin, who had studied animal as well as plant tissues, Schwann had great difficulty seeing animal cells, because their membranes are infinitely finer than the thick cell walls of plants. His conviction that cells existed in all animal tissues could be substantiated initially only by observations of bounded units in epithelial tissue and cartilage which other scientists dismissed as secretions. As Koch and Cajal would later, he persisted because he wanted to see these boundaries. Schwann's *Microscopic Researches* (1838) suggests that he sought cells in animal tissues for philosophical reasons. He could conceive of higher organisms as cellular because the German philosophical tradition "stressed the importance of forces and elements that exceeded or bypassed human embodiment" (Rothfield, 97).

In Schwann's case, the belief in universal natural forces and structures led him to two arguments for animal cells. First, like most romantic biologists and philologists, he felt that to understand the true essence of existing forms, he must study their development. In mature animals, with body plans based on circulatory vessels, the "elementary particles . . . exhibited the greatest variety" and did not look anything like plant cells (Schwann, x). The developing embryo, however, which did not yet have vessels, showed "plant-like growth" and had cells that could be readily observed (x). Schwann proposed that because animals developed out of cells and because cells existed in some of their tissues, cells formed the basis of their bodily plan. His comparison of plant and animal cells confirmed his conviction that "one common principle of development forms the basis for every separate elementary particle of all organized bodies" (ix). If cells were a universal rule of nature, all life forms became more interesting and meaningful in their affinity to each other.

Schwann's second argument, reinforced through his association with physiologist Johannes Müller, was that animals were intimately related not only to plants but also to inorganic matter through their common subjection to physico-chemical laws. Schwann's numerous references to crystals have led to misunderstandings and have caused many to underestimate his contribution to cellular theory. Schwann never stated that cells were crystals or that they were formed by crystallization. He merely said that crystallization provided the "nearest analogue" to the formation of cells (Schwann, 201). Clearly the processes were distinct, he indicated, since crystals grew only by apposition, whereas new cells could always arise between existing cells. His comparison of cells with crystals was just a reminder that organisms develop according to physiological laws, not predetermined abstract ideas. This belief ties him to those who developed cellular theory throughout the century.

Since the earliest observation of cells, biologists had commented on their seeming "independence." In animal tissues the first sightings of cells occurred in epithelial preparations. Turpin argued that the structures he observed in vaginal discharges were real cells, pointing out that each was "living *individually* of its own account" (Schwann, xii). Schwann wrote that "each cell is, within certain limits, an Individual, an independent Whole. . . . Each cell remains distinct, and maintains an independent existence" (2, 5–6). Although every cell interacted with others and was subjected to the conditions provided by the organism, Schwann believed that "we must ascribe to all cells an independent vitality" (192). These descriptions suggest a tendency to think of individual cells as individual people, and historically, the vision of the body as an association of cells coincides with the vision of society as an association of autonomous individuals. While Schwann's achievements reflect biological reality, technological improvements, and his persistence as a scientist, the cell theory developed in part because Schwann *wanted* to see cell membranes, a cultural as well as a scientific desire.

Virchow as Politician: Reform through Local Action

The career of Rudolf Virchow provides the clearest possible evidence that nineteenth-century science and politics were intimately related. Born into a lower-middle-class family in Pomerania in 1821, Virchow was able to study medicine only because of a military fellowship. During his training at the Friedrich-Wilhelms Institut (the Pépinière) in Berlin, Virchow worked with the rigorously empirical physiologist Johannes Müller, who permanently influenced his scientific outlook (*DSB* 14:39–44). Virchow received his degree in 1843 and then served at the Berlin Charité Hospital, involving himself increasingly in the turbulent political conflicts of the day. In 1848, he fought at the barricades along with students and workers. When sent to observe a typhus epidemic in Silesia, he was appalled by Prussian peasants' living conditions, and he began promoting public health as a political issue, positing the doctor as the best agent for social reform. Alarmed by his powerful speeches and essays, the Prussian authorities dismissed him from his post in Berlin in 1849.

Luckily a new chair in pathological anatomy had just been created in Würzburg, which Virchow was able to assume (*DSB* 14:41). While teaching there, he developed his theory of cellular pathology, arguing that microscopic observation of cellular changes provided the only real means of understanding disease. After the publication of his enormously influential textbook *Cellular Pathology* (1858), Virchow achieved international fame; and, hoping that he had finally been cured of his revolutionary ways, the Prussian government invited him back to Berlin as director of a new Pathological Institute. Virchow returned to Berlin, where he worked for the rest of his life, but authorities' hopes that he would cease his demands for social reform were soon dashed.

Appointed to the Berlin City Council in 1859, Virchow immediately began agitating for a modern sewer system, a project realized over the next decade largely because of his indefatigable campaigning for financial support. In 1861, he founded the German Progressive Party and was elected to the Prussian House of Representatives, where he continued to serve until his death in 1902. He also served in the German Reichstag, the national congress, from 1880 to 1897. For more than twenty years he maddened Bismarck with his noisy opposition to military spending and his demands that tax money be spent on public health projects instead of arms.

Bismarck tried, unsuccessfully, to split the liberals, but he could not silence the little professor of pathological anatomy, whose constituents repeatedly elected him with overwhelming majorities. Seeing that freedom from disease depended as much upon government funding as on scientific discoveries, Virchow gradually withdrew from his laboratory interests and increased his political involvement. His knowledge of pathology remained formidable, however, and during the 1880s and 1890s, as Koch's and Pasteur's discoveries changed the way people regarded infection, he continued to assert that diseases could only be understood through local analyses of cell damage and of social conditions.

Because Bismarck hoped to establish a unified Germany—under Prussia's direction—as a major world power, most tax money collected was earmarked for a military buildup. Virchow's became one of the most strident voices opposing the Minister's plans. In one session of the Prussian House of Representatives, Virchow remarked sarcastically that one didn't know whether the Prussian Kriegsminister was actually the Minister of War or the Zollparlament (an association that levied customs and duties). Instead of improving its weapons, Virchow maintained, Germany should be improving the health and education of its people, not just for humanitarian reasons but for practical economic ones. He used this argument repeatedly in lobbying for an expensive modern sewer system, declaring that every sick or dead citizen represented an economic loss to the state. Opponents of his sanitation projects argued that their cost was excessive and even accused him of taking financial kickbacks, but ultimately his view that "saving human lives is the best financial investment for the state" prevailed (Virchow 1985, 2:196).

As a liberal, Virchow believed that genuine reform could only occur at the local or individual level, and he saw threats to individual freedom and local authority from both the left and the right. In the same speech in which he compared the Minister of War to a tax collector, he asserted that "the German policies of Prussia will only really contribute to the national security when they base themselves on the development of freedom. . . . We do not wish that in self-administration such high positions be created as a sort of Oberpräsidium (presiding chair), but from the bottom up, self-administration should be created from the small circles of the people."[5] At the same time, however, he shared Bismarck's fears of the socialists, declaring that their ultimate goal was "to use the state as a great police institution in order to determine the destiny of every single citizen" (Virchow 1878, 10).[6] Throughout his life, Virchow never really changed the opinion he had formed after observing the poverty and suffering of the peasants in 1848: society as a whole could improve only if individual people improved their own lots, provided they were granted a modern education and fair working conditions. "We oppose the centralization of life in the hands of a supreme state with all our might," he wrote in "Diseases of the People." "Only in the greatest possible liberation of the individual conscious of itself do we see that variety, that richness of individual life, which we recognize as the aim of humanism" (1985, 1:120).

Such unflagging opposition to centralized power so enraged Bismarck that, in 1865, he challenged Virchow to a duel. Debates in the Prussian House of Representatives—as usual, about military spending—provoked the incident. Bismarck, attempting to build up the German fleet, wanted to lend money to the Austrians, who were in financial need and could provide military support; the Progressive Party opposed the move because the deal promised to create new conflicts. As the debate grew heated, Virchow said that if Bismarck had really read the report in question, "he did not know what he should think of [Bismarck's] love of truth."[7] Bismarck demanded satisfaction; Virchow naturally refused, and the professor received letters and petitions from all over Germany thanking him for setting a good example for the nation's youth. The press supported Virchow and welcomed the opportunity to ridicule Bismarck, celebrating the scientist as a modern hero who rejected barbaric, outdated means of proving one's heroism: "A man like him, who, in his calling as a doctor must look death in the face every day, has no need, through subjection to a dumb and brutal prejudice, to demonstrate that he has courage. Whoever must be resigned, daily, hourly, to give his hand to typhus, to cholera, to smallpox, and whatever all these scourges of humanity are called, truly has no need to place himself before the barrel of a pistol or the point of a dagger to show the world that he is a man."[8] In the end, the outraged minister had to settle for intimidating the professor by placing a chain of police officers along his route from the House of Representatives to the Charité Hospital, from his political to his scientific office.

Despite his objections to Prussia's centralized, imperialistic governmental style, Virchow was a patriotic German and a supporter of Prussia, and he responded when called in 1870 to place his hygienic and medical expertise at the military's disposal. The Franco-Prussian War, which motivated both Koch and Pasteur (on opposite sides) to accelerate their studies of diseases, created insuperable tensions between French and German scientists for decades. As a liberal and a scientist, however, Virchow had difficulty viewing the French as his enemy. "Let us not forget in this war," he writes, "that we are fighting with those people who, after ourselves, have made the greatest sacrifices for the freedom of humanity" (Virchow 1870, 5).[9]

Still an admirer of the French Revolution in 1870, Virchow respected the French for their cultural advocacy of individual rights and free thinking. His scientific and political writing always illustrates a belief in individual initiative. In both medicine and politics, he opposed centralized, authoritarian power systems, conceiving of the free, individual unit as the basis for all activity. Historian of science Renato Mazzolini, who has systematically studied Virchow's analogies between cells in the body and individuals in the state, finds that Virchow would have encountered such analogies more often in political than in scientific writing. Virchow's scientific essays and debates often assume the tone of political polemics (Mazzolini, 81, 14). Virchow's political concept of the independent individual, which he took with him to Würzburg in 1849, served him not merely in a descriptive sense but actually helped him to abandon Schwann's crystallization analogy for cell formation and to develop his own view that cells could only come from other cells (117–19). In Virchow's own words, "As an investigator of nature, I can only be a Republican" (49).[10] His desires for medical and social reform were inseparable, and his belief in individual rights, action, and responsibility unified his political and scientific views (Ackerknecht 1953, 43).

While Virchow openly acknowledged his indebtedness to Schwann and Bichat, it is less obvious which philosophers and political theorists may have shaped his vision of free, independent, living units as the basis of social and physiological activity. Because of Virchow's emphasis on freedom and individual perception, some scholars have argued that he was influenced by Kant, Schelling, and Hegel (Ackerknecht 1953, 52). Schelling had lectured at the University of Berlin from 1841 to 1846 while Virchow was working at the Charité and beginning to involve himself in the political reform movement. In describing both cells and individual people, Virchow frequently uses the term *Selbstthätigkeit* (self-motivated activity), and Renato Mazzolini points out that Virchow's teacher Johannes Müller, strongly influenced by Schelling, also conceived of the body in terms of "Activität" (activity) (Mazzolini, 67). Virchow cites Schelling in an article of 1885, "The Struggle between Cells and Bacteria" as a thinker who reinforced his idea that "a cell . . . yes, that is really a person and in truth a busy [*thätige*], an active [*active*] person" (Virchow 1885, 3). Preparing an essay on nutrition and the foci of disease in 1852,

Virchow reports that he "took as a point of departure an essay of Schelling's about life" in which he discovered an old statement about the nature of plants: "It lives from within, for itself alone it prospers, for itself alone it lives, nothing from outside judges or acts on it" (1885, 3). Virchow finds that the same is true for animal cells and that "such an idea is not mysticism, but pure realism"(1885, 3)[11] Schelling's vision of the organic unity of life encouraged him to see the independent cell as a more realistic version of the "life force."

Virchow showed his awareness of earlier analysts of individual perception and freedom (as well as his national bias) when he stated that the French philosophical movement of 1849, which greatly interested him, had its source in Kant, Hegel, and Luther. He asserted that "its basis is free thought removed from subservience to authority. . . . But mental freedom cannot exist apart from that of the body" (1985, 1:115). Both as a doctor and as a politician, Virchow aimed to improve the health, the living conditions, the working conditions, and the education of all people so that they might be free to help themselves. Until they could take responsibility for their own well-being, there could be no real solutions to social problems. His political and his medical goals were thus inseparable.

Virchow as Scientist: The Independent Cell

Virchow's observation of the Silesian typhus epidemic in 1848 shaped his scientific as well as his political ideas. From a poor rural region himself, he responded angrily to deaths that could only be attributed to poverty and squalor. Virchow's "Report on the Typhus Epidemic in Upper Silesia" (1848) reveals the miasmatic grounding of his socio-political approach to disease. It opens with a detailed account of the geography, geology, architecture, culture, and religion of the region, gradually "zooming in" from statistics on latitude and elevation to descriptions of life in particular homes. Generally, six to fourteen people shared a log-and-mud hovel with a cow or two, and "the effluvia of so many people and of the cattle" quickly produced a headache in those not accustomed to it (Virchow 1985, 1:217). The people lived on potatoes, milk, and sauerkraut and placed boards on the floor rather than remove the inch of water that had accumulated when the snow melted. Virchow did not blame the peasants, however, for their unhygienic living conditions.

Instead, he blamed the government for failing to educate them. Virchow described Prussia sarcastically as a "Paper State," in which the centralized laws and administration had no effect on real people's lives. In addition, he blamed the owners of newly built factories who viewed their workers only as "hands." The worker must have "not merely his subsistence," he wrote, "but also the opportunity of creating his livelihood by his own efforts [*durch Arbeit seine Existenz selbst zu begründen*]" (Virchow 1985, 1:316). In the short term, the epidemic could be fought by removing the cows and the water from the houses and by seeking water supplies free from human waste; in the long term, one could only eliminate typhus by teaching the people to do this themselves. Social reform was the doctor's responsibility.

As a physician, Virchow prescribed "full and unrestricted democracy," writing that the only possible solution for Silesia was "education, with its daughters liberty and prosperity . . . our task [*unsere Aufgabe*] now consists in the culture of one-and-a half-millions of our fellow citizens who are at the lowest level of moral and physical degradation [*Gesunkenheit*]" (Virchow 1985, 1:311). Only when each person was "free from within [*innerlich frei*]" could there be any hope of freedom from epidemics.

Virchow thus attributed disease to unhygienic living conditions, as did almost all doctors and public health officials in 1848. In his report he painstakingly analyzed the causes, symptoms, and spread of typhus. Most physicians of the day believed peasants "caught" this illness from bad air and water—not from each other—after they had been weakened by malnutrition. Like them, Virchow attributed the disease to "a change in the blood, its poisoning by noxious substances," shunning the "zoological parasites" proposed by Henle as the cause of disease (Virchow 1985, 1:269). Had Virchow attributed the disease to living germs, it would have been much more difficult to link the elimination of disease to the social reforms he wanted so badly.

On the level of practical hygiene, miasma theory and germ theory were difficult to distinguish. Koch would have agreed completely with Virchow that damp, dark, unventilated living quarters and water supplies contaminated with fecal matter caused disease. Both scientists associated diseases with particular places, but for different reasons. To Virchow, such places "poisoned" the inhabitants with "tainted air"; to Koch, they provided ideal living conditions for pathogenic bacteria, which could be associated with specific areas because as living organisms, they had natural habitats.

The implications of these theories begin to diverge only when one moves from practical hygiene to social action. Bruno LaTour points out that hygienists prior to Pasteur suffered from an excess rather than a dearth of knowledge; if diseases had many causes (foul odors, tainted water, unknown factors in the soil), then they had no cause (LaTour, 20). If Henle were right and diseases had a single cause, an identifiable living germ passed through human contact, it would be much more difficult to convince governments to finance public works projects. Any quest for the cause of an epidemic would focus on people themselves as the source of the disease. Although governments did want healthy workers and soldiers, they might respond to epidemics simply by "sealing off" entire segments of their societies. If diseases were associated with the poor rather than with poverty itself, the health of the bourgeoisie might be safeguarded simply by minimizing their contact with the lower classes. Virchow, who saw all too clearly what was at stake, asked why "all of these thousands of proletarians [had] to fall by the way, while the well-to-do classes of the nation got away with only token sacrifices?" (Virchow 1985, 1:116). For him, the fact that the poor had died while the rich lived proved that disease must be related to living conditions. In a statement for which he became famous, Virchow defined disease as "the expiration of life under altered conditions" (*der Ablauf der Lebenserscheinungen unter veränderten Bedingungen*) (1847b, 1).[12]

Reviewing the goals and achievements of cellular pathology in 1891, Virchow wrote that "the ultimate goal of investigation in cellular pathology is the localization of the disease." Alterations of the tissue were most informative because "they show conclusively where the points of attack for the virulent material lie."[13] In his essay "Krankheitswesen und Krankheitsursachen" (The essence and causes of disease) (1880), Virchow recalled, "I posited the living cell as the only essence of disease, or . . . I defined the sick cell as the pathological entity" (5).[14] Although Virchow's descriptions of cells as independent, living beings opened him to charges of reviving vitalism, he insisted that his idea represented not an outdated notion of "life force" but life and disease as they really were.

Even among pathological anatomists, Virchow was not the first to suggest that investigators focus on cells; Lebert—whose microscopical studies Weir Mitchell would admire—along with Vogel and Wedl had preceded him (Rather, vii). Schleiden and Schwann had also compared cells to individuals before Virchow (Mazzolini, 73). Virchow's innovation lies in his personal style, in the forcefulness with which he expressed his ideas, and in the way he recreated pathology as an epistemological system privileging the microscopic. In "Krankheitswesen und Krankheitsursachen" Virchow wrote that "what the individual is on a grand scale, the cell is that and perhaps even more on a small one. . . . Every cell is, as such, an enclosed unit, which has taken up in itself the foundation, the principle of its life, which bears in itself the laws of its existence, and which possesses in relation to the rest of the world a certain autonomy" (Virchow 1880, 6, 185).[15]

If cells resembled individual people in their activity and relative independence, then the body, as an association of cells, must be regarded as a society. Virchow's frequent comparisons of the body to a state tie his thinking to a metaphorical trend that has existed since classical times. For Virchow, society could only be compared to a multicellular organism because it was a collection of free individuals, and his criticism of the traditional "Staatsorganismus" idea gives his analogies their force and originality (Virchow 1875, 20; Mazzolini, 54–55, 76, 102). In a multicellular organism, as in a society, there is no such thing as a truly independent unit of life, since individuals rely on one another to maintain their existences. Virchow created a fascinating analogy to show that in a body, as in society, the individual living unit is responsible for the health of the whole: "A historian is very inclined, in the abstraction of his study, to forget the individual living persons, of whom a country or a people is composed. And thus all action is in the parts, and the life of a people is nothing more than the sum of the lives of the individual citizens. So it is also in the little country, which the body of every plant and every animal represents" (Virchow 1856, 36).[16] In studying a person's disease, one must remember that the person is composed of other, smaller, individuals.

Such analogies reveal the consistency of Virchow's political and scientific thinking; to him, the idea of centralized control was anathema in the body as it was in the state. He openly associated his predecessors' and rivals' theories with authoritarian political beliefs. Stahl's vitalism, with its concept of a soul, Virchow called the "monarchical principle in the body" (Virchow 1847a, 216). Rokitansky's humoral pathology and Henle's neuropathology, two perspectives that offended him the most, he described as "a despotic or oligarchical conception of the organism insofar as they represent the aristocracy and the hierarchy of blood and nerves" (Mazzolini, 50).[17] Virchow even compared the centralized control systems featured in other theories of pathology to the functioning of a police state, the term he had used for the Prussian administration of Silesia in 1848. In 1847, he wrote: "Pus formation is no longer the struggle of the organism to heal itself, by filling up this or that hole; the corpuscles of pus are no longer the *gendarmes* whom the police state orders to escort over the border this or that foreigner who has entered without a passport; scar tissue no longer builds an imprisoning wall, in which such a foreigner is enclosed, when it pleases the Police-Organism" (1847a, 216).[18] The very idea that some higher power should oversee the body or the state, imprisoning foreign invaders and imposing order on its constituents, offended him both as a politician and as a scientist. Even though no cell could be regarded as truly independent, Virchow insisted that pathology must base itself on their individual activities and rights.

The relative independence of the cells, in Virchow's mind, was based on their individual functions, their freedom to form associations, and above all on the membrane that made them visible under his microscope and defined them relative to one another. When he first begins discussing cells in his textbook, Virchow states that "what really constitutes a cell is the presence within a non-nitrogenized membrane of nitrogenized contents differing from it" (Virchow [1859] 1971, 31–32). Anatomically, a membrane defines a cell's form; in essence, microscopists knew that cells existed because they could see their boundaries. More important, though, the membrane plays a key physiological role. Discussing vitalism in 1858, Virchow wrote that the fundamental quality of life was simultaneous independence [*Selbstständigkeit*] and dependence [*Abhängigkeit*], a quality epitomized by the bounded cells he observed: "Life consists of an exchange, but it would stop being life, if this exchange did not have certain limits. These limits establish certain standards of moderation and regulation, as much in the simple cell as in the organism composed of cells. In the cell we have come to know the membrane and the nucleus as the regulators and moderators."[19] The membrane defined the cells not only because it made them visible and set their limits in a physical sense but also because it let them regulate their own inputs and outputs. While these semipermeable membranes never entirely sealed cells off from their environments, they allowed cells to resist them and to "select" the molecules that could enter.

The concept of self-boundedness, the distinction between inside and outside, would assume even greater significance in germ theory. Virchow, often incorrectly identified as an opponent of germ theory, at first objected to the new perspective because he felt it placed undue emphasis on factors outside the cell and the body. Pasteur's and Koch's discoveries in the 1880s made many believe that each disease had a corresponding microbe and that the discovery of the microbe explained the disease. A French writer in 1885 appalled Virchow by proclaiming:

Cellular pathology has lived. Our body is no longer that "republic of cells, each one living its own life." That was the beloved republic of the German professor Virchow. Dethroned, your cellular republic, great Master . . . She succumbed to the verdict of the parasitic style. Down with the cells, long live the independent beings, infinitely small, but prolific . . . coming from outside, penetrating the organism like a horde of Sudanese, ravaging it for the right of invasion and conquest. (1885, 8–9)[20]

Such politicized proclamations, which compared bacteria to the natives whose lands the Europeans were invading, alarmed Virchow, for they distracted both scientists and the public at large from the central issues of disease.

Pathology, he reminded doctors, was best understood at the cellular level. He saw no real contradiction between cellular pathology and germ theory, only a disagreement about emphasis.

Bacteria, whose existence and pathological role he acknowledged, were for Virchow the causes but not the essence of disease. The microbe, the external cause, created harmful activity in the cells and tissues, the internal cause; new converts to germ theory were overlooking this internal cause (Ackerknecht 1953, 112). Both the bacteria and the cells produced the disease, but the reaction of the tissues did not "depend *in essence* [*wesentlich*] upon outer influences" (1880, 10). Virchow feared a "mixing up" [*Verwechselung*], a "total confusion" [*völlige Verwirrung*] of the concepts of cause and essence, one that had recurred continually since ancient times. Defining his position in 1885, he wrote that the cells "are still there, and they are still the main issue." Once a microbe had been indisputably linked to a particular disease, he predicted, researchers would return to the techniques of cellular pathology. "First the discovery of the parasite," he wrote, "then the investigation of its etiology, then the question: how does it give rise to the disease?" (1885, 9).[21] Cellular pathology and bacteriology were complementary, not contradictory.

It is thus an error to view Virchow as an enemy of germ theory; he merely insisted that social conditions and constitutional factors still played a role in causing disease (Ackerknecht 1953, 117). It is equally wrong to consider him an enemy of Robert Koch, as he has sometimes been depicted. In 1878, Koch—still a country doctor—visited Virchow in Berlin and showed him his microscopic preparations. Virchow received him coldly and told him that "anything he couldn't see with a dry lens wasn't worth looking at" (Brock, 82). Later, however, he treated Koch respectfully and acknowledged the importance of Koch's discoveries.

As Virchow had predicted, the rapid association of diseases with microorganisms in the 1880s led to no immediate cures, and Europeans in the 1890s continued to die of cholera and tuberculosis by the thousands. In 1890, when Koch announced that he had developed a cure for tuberculosis, Virchow became one of his most skeptical examiners. The bacteriologist, whose "cure" was not ready for testing in humans, had been forced by government ministers to announce it prematurely so that German scientific achievements could eclipse all others at an international scientific meeting in Berlin (Brock, 195–213; Genschorek, 100–108). Most scientists, including Virchow, sympathized with Koch, knowing the pressure to which the normally prudent bacteriologist had been subjected.

Virchow demanded to know how Koch's "cure" affected the cells and the tissues. He personally autopsied patients who had died under treatment, and he confirmed everyone's suspicions: in most cases, the "cure" did not work. While it did selectively attack tissue infected with the tuberculosis bacteria, it did not kill the bacteria themselves; instead, its loosening of infected tissue actually spread the disease in the lungs. The press, which had been promoting Koch as a hero of the empire, accused Virchow of jealousy, for he also objected to the construction of an expensive new Institute of Infectious Diseases for Koch on the basis of the dubious "cure."

On the floor of the House of Representatives, science and politics merged. Virchow, always cautious about the allocation of tax money, challenged conservatives, who upheld Koch as a paragon of German imperial scientific achievement. Factions quickly formed along party lines. Count Eberfeld rose to praise Koch's work, acknowledging Virchow's along with it. Virchow rejected the compliments and contested the count's right to discuss a "cure" for which he had no evidence. Eberfeld replied that all doctors agreed about the cure's scientific meaning, and Virchow cried, "Say, then, what the scientific meaning is!" The count answered that he could not say, but that there was no doubt about it. "All phrases!" exclaimed Virchow angrily. Taking the last word, the count proclaimed that "The phrases have been pronounced by good authorities, so in my appraisal I find myself in good company," and applause rang out from the right.[22]

Even when the voice of central authority could outweigh scientific evidence, Virchow defended the ideas of the 1840s: in science, the strictest empiricism; in politics, respect for individual rights and local authorities; in both, a conviction that only individual activity could produce genuine change. The difference between Virchow and Koch is both generational and ideological. Both were cautious scientists, demanding the most rigorous and irrefutable microscopic evidence before endorsing any idea. Both were patriots, but whereas Virchow loved the Germany of 1848 that had fought off Napoleon and forged its own constitution, Koch, twenty-two years his junior, loved the Germany of 1870, the Germany of the Kaiser. Like Virchow's, his science and ideology are one.

Henle and Pasteur: Living Germs

Jakob Henle's certainty, in 1840, that diseases were caused by living parasites shows that a scientific idea can never be linked absolutely to a historical period or political outlook. The idea had been recurring since classical times; it is its reception, not its origin, that ties it to the imperialist politics of 1870–1914.

Henle, Koch's teacher, did not argue that living germs caused all diseases, only some. Here he concurred with the hygienists who opposed him. He distinguished epidemic from endemic diseases, writing that "the difference is simply that, with the epidemic, the causes of the disease seek out the individual; with the endemic, the causes of the disease, bound to particular places, are sought out by the individual" (Henle, 12).[23] Even in this early articulation, one senses the anxiety germ theory aroused by depicting living organisms actively "seeking out" their victims.

In his controversial text, *On Miasmas and Contagia and Miasmatic-Contagious Diseases* (1840), Henle submits that "the material of the contagion [is] not only organic, but also *alive*, and indeed endowed with individual life, which stands in relation to the ailing body as a *parasitic organism*" (25).[24] Suppose, he writes, you prick a person's finger with a thorn, then prick a second person's finger with the same thorn, so that the disease is transferred from the first to the second. "Here, what would be transferred by the thorn is not the disease, nor any product of the disease, but the stimulus that brought it forth," he explains. "Not the disease, but the thorn is the parasite" (26).[25] While he never fully disowns the miasmatic theory of disease, his vision of tiny, independent life forms penetrating much larger ones anticipates Pasteur's and Koch's descriptions three decades later.

It is a challenge to trace, in Pasteur's career, the conviction that living organisms cause disease. He embraced the idea long before he could prove it; it is really the idea that motivated him to seek the proof (Dubos, 233). Although he valued empirical evidence as highly as Koch or Virchow did, he believed that "at the start of any investigation one must have a preconceived idea as guide" (*Oeuvres*, 6:493).[26] Beginning as an organic chemist, Pasteur had moved on to studies of fermentation after ten years (1847–57) of studying how organic substances rotated polarized light (Dubos, 90). By 1858, he had convinced himself and many other scientists that "ferments, properly called, are living beings, . . . the germs of microscopic organisms abound on the surface of all objects, in the atmosphere and in the water" (*Oeuvres*, 6:112).[27] Pasteur produced strong evidence that living organisms caused fermentation. When he washed grapes and examined the liquid under the microscope, he saw "many little organized bodies . . . simple, transparent, colorless cells" (1879, 153). If he grew vines under glass, isolating them from microorganisms in the air, in the soil, or on other grapes, the grapes the vines produced proved incapable of fermentation. He concluded that when brewers throw yeast into wort, "[they] are sowing a multitude of minute living cells, representing so many centers of life" (1879, 144).

Associating microorganisms with fermentation was one matter; tying them to infectious diseases was another. Even in 1859, however, Pasteur declared that "everything indicates that infectious diseases owe their existence to similar causes" (Dubos, 233). The glass that had isolated some vines from yeast cells, preventing their grapes from fermenting, reminded him of the European quarantines that had so often proved fruitless. Such barriers worked well if erected at the right time but were useless if the germs were already present: "similarly, the quarantine measures effective against cholera, yellow fever, or plague are of no avail against our common contagious diseases" (235). Many philosophers and physicians had preceded Pasteur in making this analogy between fermentation and disease, as indicated by vernacular descriptions of fevers as "ferments" in the blood, but Pasteur's ingenious strategies for making the germs visible to his society made his comparison infinitely more plausible (Ford 1973, 106–7).

The very idea that one might erect a barrier against germs, successfully or unsuccessfully, encouraged people to view them as a living force. Like most advocates of germ theory, Pasteur associated health with the maintenance of just such a barrier, writing in 1879 that "the human body in a state of health is closed to all of these organisms" (*Oeuvres*, 6:498).[28] In some ways, it was comforting to associate specific diseases with specific organisms, since if one knew the microorganism's life cycle and nutritional needs, one knew much more about the disease than if one associated it with the soil, the water, or the weather. Unlike the vapors of the hygienists, microbes could be visualized. Once they were unveiled, scientists could study their movement and distribution and eventually control the spread of the disease. The main purpose of bacteriological laboratories in the 1880s and afterward was to "render visible these invisible agents" (LaTour, 63). Pasteur boasted in 1879 that "the three diseases of which I have just spoken, anthrax, blood poisoning, and chicken cholera, all exist in the state of germs enclosed in a bunch of flasks in my laboratory" (*Oeuvres*, 6:495).[29] If one could see germs, one could confine them.

While Pasteur's perspective made the causes of disease easier to visualize and comprehend, it also made them more frightening, for people, not places, became the reservoirs of disease (Dubos, 270). He warned that "the human body and those of animals can harbor certain microscopic organisms" (*Oeuvres*, 6:497).[30] The old miasma theory had dictated that one could avoid a disease by avoiding a particular neighborhood, city, or region. But if people themselves contained the organisms that caused disease, and one could not tell who was infected, one risked penetration and destruction through all human contact. It was Koch, not Pasteur, who introduced the notion of the healthy carrier, but Pasteur's writing clearly posits people as the vehicles by which disease is spread. In 1879, he grew impatient when Hervieux described puerperal fever in terms of miasma theory. Interrupting him, Pasteur declared: "The cause of the epidemic is nothing of the kind! It is the doctor and his staff who carry the microbe from a sick woman to a healthy woman!" (Dubos, 262).[31] Diseases were spread by people, and it was people who had to be scrutinized and controlled.

Such control became increasingly difficult as European nations expanded their commercial connections and imperial boundaries. In 1907, introducing Koch at a scientific meeting, Andrew Carnegie reported that the French now named Pasteur as the greatest Frenchman who had ever lived; in the past it had been Napoleon (Brock, 272–73). In the microbial age, scientists assumed the heroic role of soldiers, the creators and the defenders of empires.

Koch as Doctor: Identifying the Culprits

In 1882, in his classic paper on the tuberculosis bacillus, Robert Koch declared the victory of the germ theory of disease over the miasmatic one, making a deliberate dig at Virchow's view: "It was once customary to consider tuberculosis as the manifestation of social ills. . . . But in the future, the fight against this terrible plague will no longer focus on an undetermined something, but on a tangible parasite, whose living conditions are for the most part known and can be further investigated" (Koch 1987, 95). Like Pasteur, Koch had believed that living germs caused disease long before he could ever demonstrate it definitively. At last he had unshakable proof.

The third of eleven children of a German mining engineer, Koch studied medicine in Göttingen from 1862 to 1866. Henle, his most influential professor, taught him anatomy and encouraged him in some early microscopical studies (*DSB* 7:420–35; Genschorek, 18). Koch longed to continue his research in the natural sciences and to travel around the world, and he considered working as a ship's naturalist or doctor. Financial needs, however, forced him to work from 1866 until 1880 as a general practitioner in a series of small towns. Koch liked healing people and was extremely popular with his patients. In his later travels he wrote that "it really is a wonderful thing, when people seem to have fallen hopelessly into the clutches of death, to be able to tear them away from this fate. Then it is really a joy to be a doctor" (Genschorek, 184).[32]

Koch's motivation as a bacteriologist reflects this strategy of aggressive intervention in the interest of saving lives. While working as a doctor, he began investigating bacteria in an amateur laboratory he had constructed in his own home. A systematic thinker, a tireless worker, and a brilliant technician, he always focused on improving his techniques, with a single goal in mind: the association of specific microorganisms with specific diseases (Brock, 28).

As a doctor, Koch realized that by linking a disease to a microbe, he would provide a foolproof means of diagnosing and identifying it in every case. This could be accomplished only by knowing the appearance of a microorganism as thoroughly as possible, studying all of its variations and identifying their common features. Germ theory would be clinically valuable only if a single species of microorganism, not a collection of microbes of different shapes and etiologies, caused a single disease, since it was on this one-to-one specificity that its diagnostic worth depended. In a report on malaria—a disease caused by protozoa, not bacteria—he announced with pleasure that "their form is so characteristic, that the detection of a single parasite suffices to diagnose the disease with certainty" (Koch 1900, 2).[33] Identifying the invasive microbes was the first step toward curing the patient.

To identify a microbe as the cause of a disease, one had to know not only its appearance but also its life cycle. Koch loved the natural sciences and kept a menagerie of animals in his house, and his knack for investigating the etiology of microscopic organisms may have been due to his great interest in larger ones. His 1876 paper on anthrax, which provided the first irrefutable evidence that a particular microorganism caused a disease, was entitled "The Etiology of Anthrax, Based on the Life Cycle of the Bacillus Anthracis" (Brock, 34). Pasteur had declared decades earlier that microorganisms caused disease, but he would always focus more on developing antisera than on definitively identifying microbes (he successfully inoculated cattle against anthrax in 1881).[34] Koch selected anthrax not to cure it but as a means to an end; even in 1876 he was seeking a system of techniques that would detect the living *Erreger* (causative organisms) of any disease as rapidly and indubitably as possible (31).

So that others could compare their microscopic observations to his, Koch perfected photomicrography, his wife standing guard to warn him when passing clouds might ruin his developing images of bacteria. The introduction of photography to bacteriology, he believed, would take the subjectivity out of microscopic investigations, and he wrote, "I am absolutely certain that a bad photograph of a living organism is a hundred times better than a misleading or possibly inaccurate drawing" (Brock, 65). Scientists must develop a system for objectively identifying bacteria.

Using his assistant's wife's fruit jelly recipe, Koch developed the plate culture technique, which allowed bacteriologists to grow a given species of microorganism in isolation from all others. Pasteur, who made serial dilutions, would multiply a given sample of bacteria by transferring a few drops, successively, to new flasks of sterilized culture medium. He could never guarantee a pure culture because he could never be sure of the content of the original sample. Koch, who believed that "the pure culture is the foundation of all research on infectious disease," could guarantee purity because the colonies of bacteria he grew on solid plates arose from single microbes. Any contamination was immediately visible (Brock, 94–104).

Armed with these techniques, Koch devised criteria a researcher must fulfill to prove that a microorganism caused a disease: (1) one must be able to detect it in all cases of the disease, (2) one must be able to purify it in culture, and (3) one must be able to create the disease by introducing this pure culture to a healthy animal. The criteria, still known as Koch's Postulates, had been proposed by Klebs and implied by Henle, but Koch succeeded in fulfilling them in some cases because of his painstaking attention to methodology (Brock, 29).

Gaining renown in the scientific community, Koch moved to Berlin in 1880 to a position at the Imperial Department of Health. In 1882, his discovery of the tuberculosis bacillus brought international fame, and in 1885 he was named chair of hygiene at the University of Berlin and director of a new hygiene institute (*DSB* 7:425). Koch finally visualized the unusually small and stain-resistant bacillus when so many had failed before him because even after months of negative results, he believed that the techniques, not the theory, were at fault (Brock, 118–25). By focusing all his energy on a system of visualization, he identified the cause of Europe's deadliest disease.

Always conscious of his role as a German scientist, Koch saw himself as a servant of the Reich. Rejected for nearsightedness when he volunteered for the army in 1870, he insisted on serving as a field doctor. While he may have seen the war as a welcome opportunity for travel and adventure, several of his comments make his patriotism explicit. After his discovery of the tuberculosis bacillus in 1882, he reported, "I even had the privilege of explaining bacteria to the crown prince" (Brock, 139). He told his daughter that the medal he had received for identifying the cholera bacillus in 1884 was his favorite award "because it had been given to him personally by the Kaiser and because he could wear it like a military decoration" (167). Koch never got along well with Pasteur, although each built on the other's work. His inadequate knowledge of French created serious conflicts between them in the 1880s, provoked principally by antagonism on Koch's part (173–75). Because of his loyalty to the Kaiser and his administration—whose institutions made his work possible—Koch slipped easily into the role of imperial emissary, extending his quest for pathogenic bacteria as Germany extended its colonial empire.

In Germany, imperialism and bacteriology coincide to a remarkable degree; both Koch's key discoveries and Bismarck's grudging establishment of "protectorates" occur in the early 1880s. By 1884, Germany was in a state of "colonial fever," and Bismarck ceded to the repeated calls from German merchants for "protection" in Africa when he saw an opportunity to fill the Reichstag with conservative, procolonial delegates who would support his other policies (Simon, 84; Wehler, 274,466). So intense and so interrelated were the imperial and the bacterial drives in the 1880s that they expressed themselves in each other's languages. One writer found that "the 'colonial dreamers' have fallen victim to a true 'colonial fever bacillus' " (Wehler, 474).[35] In France, a new culture of bacilli was announced in the press as "the new French colonies" (LaTour, 98).

Koch as Microbe Hunter: Defending the Empire

Between 1890 and 1910, Koch traveled frequently to Africa representing the German government. To ensure continued funding for his research, he had to please the Kaiser's administration, and records indicate that he was often told, not asked, to go. His own lifelong love of travel and adventure also motivated his bacteriological missions. His descriptions of his quests, however, suggest that while he deplored the destruction of foreign cultures, he supported for the colonial drive and sympathized with the imperial mentality. Just as the establishment of colonies provided economic opportunities for Europeans, it provided him with opportunities as a scientist. In a letter to his assistant Gaffky in 1903, Koch wrote: "I consider it my duty to travel and work where I can use my scientific abilities to the best. . . . Out here in Africa, one can find bits of scientific gold lying on the streets" (Brock, 237). Comparing himself to imperial adventurers scrambling for gold, he envisioned himself as seizing an opportunity to acquire new knowledge. Koch loved Africa, and he occasionally spoke out against imperialism, finding it "really a shame, that the European culture is so mercilessly wiping away what before made the land so interesting" (Genschorek, 171).[36] At bottom, however, he saw it as his duty to identify and destroy the microbes that hindered European settlers in Africa and Asia or—worse yet—threatened to return home with them.

Colonial medicine was not for black Africans. Because of the Europeans' superior weaponry, microorganisms, not people, became the primary enemies restricting their expansion. As the French bacteriologist Roux wrote in 1915, "the identification and movement of each parasite made it possible to advance further" (LaTour, 141). Doctors in Africa became analogous to soldiers, defending the empire against its tiny enemies and providing "ways of protecting parasites (white-skinned macroparasites) against parasites (microparasites in the form of miasmas or centers of infection)" (95). Robert Koch's reports to the government and his speeches to the Colonial Society illustrate exactly this mentality.

Koch expressed his relation to malaria, for instance, in territorial and military terms. In 1900 he declared that "for the struggle against malaria, it is of the greatest significance to inform [orientieren] oneself quickly about the presence and strength of the enemy." He concluded that as one eliminates malaria from colonial territory, "gradually one will be able to occupy ever more territory and extend the basis of operations" (Koch 1900, 15, 25).[37] In 1908, proposing strategies to combat sleeping sickness, he argued that the best way to prevent the disease in Europeans was to separate them, physically, from the natives. The primary goal was to keep the foreign settlers free from the parasite: "In Muansa the houses of the Europeans lie right in the middle of the natives' huts. This is a terrible mistake, because then the Europeans, despite all the care that they devote to hygiene in their own homes, are placed in the same danger as the natives. It must thus be seen to, that the European settlements be widely separated in space from the living areas of the natives" (Koch 1908, 45–46).[38] Although Koch did examine native victims of the disease, he did so primarily to gather intelligence. Eventually, he hoped to free all people from tropical diseases, but he undertook his colonial missions as a researcher, not a physician; and medical attention for the natives ranked third after gathering information and maintaining the Europeans' health. The natives, in fact, provided a good means of studying the disease.

Koch's first quest for a foreign microbe occurred in 1883–84, when cholera broke out in Egypt and threatened Europe. The French organized a team of bacteriological investigators, and the German government, in a competitive spirit, ordered Koch to direct a rival one. Neither group succeeded in isolating the microorganism, and Koch wrote in apparent disappointment that "cholera has almost disappeared in Alexandria, which for our purposes is too early. . . . Thus, I am afraid that we are without either cholera patients or cholera victims" (Brock, 150–51). Although it appeared unlikely the epidemic would reach Europe, Koch requested permission to proceed to India, long regarded as the "Heimat" (homeland) of cholera, to seek the microorganism at its "source." Once in Calcutta he achieved a pure culture in only a few days (159).

It was the third postulate, the production of disease in a healthy experimental animal, that was the most challenging to fulfill at home and abroad; such animals were difficult to obtain and, when injected with microbes, often did not develop the same symptoms as human beings. Experimenting with people was, of course, out of the question, but in India, observing the way that natives used the same tanks for drinking water, washing laundry, and sewage disposal, Koch wrote that "we are thus dealing here, to a certain extent, with an experiment conducted on people, brought about by accident, which in this case replaces the need for an experiment on animals" (Genschorek, 115).[39] Koch's identification of the cholera bacillus made him an imperial hero, and on returning to Germany he was received by the Kaiser.

In the growing German Empire, the goal of healing European settlers sometimes took second place to maintaining the colonies themselves. Koch noted in frustration in 1898, in a speech to the Colonial Society in Berlin, that as soon as malaria-stricken settlers in German East Africa "had barely regained their strength, they gave up their life as farmers, and traveled back to Europe on the next steamer" (Koch 1898, 282). As a doctor, he needed to keep German settlers not only healthy but also confident enough to maintain their presence, and this meant the elimination of disease not just from their bodies but from entire territories. "I am convinced," he continued, that we will not be happy with our colonial possessions, until we succeed in becoming masters of this disease" (1898, 283). He requested that well-trained doctors, specifically taught to combat malaria, be sent to the colonies and concluded that "when we truly become the masters of this disease, this will be synonymous with the peaceful conquest of the most beautiful and fruitful lands of the earth!" (1898, 314).[40] He received thunderous applause.

The struggle against microbes, even in the colonies, was viewed as a defensive more than an aggressive project, driven by fear that tropical microorganisms would reach Europe and colonize the colonizers. In 1884 Koch wrote: "It is . . . inconceivable that the cholera could originate in Europe without the comma bacilli having first been conveyed here." And for him there was no doubt how it was conveyed there, since "if one carefully examines the origin of individual epidemics, it is clear that the disease is always transported by people" (Koch 1987, 165, 164). With his techniques for identifying microorganisms largely in place, Koch began developing systems for eliminating diseases altogether. Just as his achievements with anthrax and tuberculosis had established his methods for identifying bacteria, his experiences with cholera and malaria in the colonies suggested a strategy for removing diseases permanently from given geographical areas: first, identification; then, elimination (*Ausrottung*) and destruction (*Vernichtung*).

In Stephansort, a small German tobacco town on the New Guinea coast, Koch carried out what he described as a "war of annihilation" (*Vernichtungs-krieg*), testing the blood of every inhabitant and treating with quinine the 157 persons revealed as carriers of the parasite. The *Vernichtungskrieg* succeeded, and the residents thanked Koch. He concluded that "our attempt illustrates further, that we with our investigative method have in fact detected all of the parasites, and with our method of treatment have also really destroyed them" (Koch 1900, 19).[41] He had identified the disease-causing agents by rendering them visible; he could eliminate diseases only if people themselves were equally available to his gaze. He recommended that the Stephansort procedure be implemented everywhere.

Since people carried diseases, they all became suspect. Bruno LaTour suggests that the triumph of microbial theory in the 1880s redefined the concept of individual liberty, making it acceptable for governments to investigate citizens and restrict their movements, since no individual had the right to contaminate others (LaTour, 123). Koch certainly held this view, writing that "every person, who bears in himself the disease-causing agent is a danger to his healthy surrounding area" (Genschorek, 186).[42] He acted on this idea in 1902, using the methods he had developed in New Guinea to fight a typhus epidemic in Trier. Because their reports focus on the same disease and because their arguments contrast so sharply, it is useful to compare Koch's typhus article to the one Virchow wrote in 1848.

The reports were written fifty-four years apart, and certainly, if Virchow had had Koch's evidence that microorganisms caused the disease, his recommendations might have been different. What is so striking, however, is the different ways the two doctors view their patients as individuals. "In the past one took a more *defensive* attitude," wrote Koch, referring to miasma theory. "We have now moved away from this defensive point of view and have seized the *offensive*. . . . We must be prepared, first, to detect the infectious material easily and with certainty, and second, to destroy it" (Koch 1903, 8, 10).[43] For Koch, taking the offensive meant actively seeking the parasites not only in those obviously ill but also in those "suspected" of carrying them (*die Verdächtigen*) and in "the apparently healthy." By implementing mandatory testing, he discovered 72 carriers of typhus, 52 of whom were children, even though only eight cases had been reported. Koch found that the cases could be traced through "chains" (*Ketten*) between people, and he determined to "place the typhus victims under such circumstances, that they could create no further infection" (18).[44] He concluded by suggesting, once more, that the aggressive program of detection and treatment be applied to other diseases in other areas.

What distinguishes Koch's thinking from Virchow's is Koch's confidence in central control. For Koch, it was not problematic to order citizens in for treatment, to examine each person's blood systematically, or to regard each as "suspicious." Response to such an order was simply one's civic duty, just as it was his to travel to Africa whenever the Kaiser requested it. Such systematic annihilation was for him the most thorough and efficient way to eliminate disease and thus was ultimately a humane action.

Sent to investigate a cholera epidemic in France after he had returned from India in 1884, Koch grumbled that "whether in the houses the waste of the sick and the dirty linen are destroyed (vernichtet) or properly disinfected is left more or less up to the good will of the people" (Koch 1912, 2:859).[45] As opposed to what? one wonders. He continued by recommending that competent doctors be dispatched immediately to take charge of the situation. In a popular monograph on the proper care of the lungs, written in 1902, he suggested that prospective tenants consult the police to learn the "history" of an apartment, for if someone had died there of tuberculosis, it could be made safe only by "a proper disinfection directed by the police or by a doctor" (1902, 61).[46] Koch believed that the best way to eliminate a disease was a systematic program under central command, for his experiences both as a doctor and as a citizen of a growing empire told him that this was what worked.

Virchow, who trusted "the good will of the people," recommended that only education, economic support, and regulations ensuring personal freedom come from the government. His experiences as a hygienist, microscopist, and liberal politician had shown him that only individual activity could improve society. The positions of the two scientists overlap, of course—Virchow could not have built his sewer system without money and direction from the central government—but their approaches to typhus illustrate a fundamental ideological difference. For Virchow, it was each citizen's duty to maintain his own boundaries; for Koch, the empire maintained its boundaries and those of its citizens by violating those boundaries itself.

Both Virchow and Koch saved millions of lives: Virchow with his sewer system, and Koch with his identification of microbes. Although Koch's discoveries never guaranteed cures in and of themselves, they allowed future bacteriologists to develop antibiotics in the decades ahead. While his ideology differed from Koch's, Virchow's concept of a bounded self provided a foundation for germ theory by suggesting that to preserve one's identity, one must defend one's boundaries.

S. Weir Mitchell

Identity as Resistance

It is impossible to imagine a body wholly isolated in
nature. It would no longer be real because there would be
no relation to manifest its existence.   —Claude Bernard

Nowhere do I think as fluently and with more sure result
than on a swift train. Here I feel secure from invasion. I am
guarded by the immense average of silent reserve attained
by an American.   —S. Weir Mitchell

"I stood still for a moment, feeling that I was losing intelligent self-control,"
recalls S. Weir Mitchell's character Victor St. Clair, describing to his cultured
New England friends his entry into the exotic Cobra City.

By degrees I made them out, an army of serpents, gray, inert forms pendent from
bough or rock-ledge, slowly moving loops, or on the ground gray tangles of lazily stir-
ring, intricate coils. . . . They stood erect, their heads some two or three feet above
their anchoring coils. . . . The cobra is apt to sway from side to side, and now the hedge
of poison-bearers swung thus to and fro, as if moved by some monotonous mechanism. . . . It was noiseless and regular, and seemed to murmur, 'Death and life, death
and life.' . . . I half turned to go back, when, as if this were a signal, all the slowly gliding
or hanging or inertly coiled tangles acquired individuality, and came, not swiftly, but
as if deliberately, toward me, gray, sinuous lines, convergent. (*DN*, 336–37)[1]

St. Clair realizes that he can pass unharmed through the thousands of deadly
coils as long as he controls his own terror. One cobra has entwined itself
around his arm, and he knows that "if in what I must call the agony of a too
long enfeebling emotion I should let go my grasp, release it, I [am] lost" (340).

Instead of attacking him, the cobras turn on a tiger who has been stalking him, and the normally impulsive St. Clair survives the Cobra City because he has charmed the serpents within him, his own emotions.

Fantastic as it may seem, S. Weir Mitchell's fictional account of the Cobra City epitomizes his concept of selfhood. Neurologist, physiologist, novelist, and poet, Mitchell conceived of mental health in terms of resistance and control. He investigated snake venom for years and continued to brood on its mechanism even after he had given up laboratory work. Mitchell's novels, as well as his scientific writings, refer often to poisons and to snakes, tentacles, and coils. In his imaginative depiction of the Cobra City, he represents internal, psychological threats as external, physical, and foreign ones. These dangers to selfhood in the healthy person, he believed, were the forces that reigned unchecked in the unwell: fear, anger, instinctive behaviors, selfish desires, and sexual drives. Healthy individuals, to Mitchell, were people in whom a strong will carefully controlled irrational drives, which forever threatened to coil themselves around them. A strong will masters snakes; a sick will is squeezed to death; and uncontrolled emotion is poison. Because instinctive fears and desires are common to all people and to many animals, one's identity includes the charmer but not the snakes.

In Mitchell's works, where mental health means maintaining defensive lines, much remains unspoken. His fantasy of the Cobra City, unquestionably sexual in nature, expresses great admiration for what the narrator finds most terrifying: "One single beautiful cobra in his pride of power with his mantle spread is a splendid fear" (DN, 339). Defined in opposition to the tentacles it must fend off, individuality for Mitchell is a front along which one combats internal and external threats. Penetration of this line, synonymous with illness, means an unmanning, a humiliating loss of autonomy. The Cobra City episode expresses perfectly the instability of his model of identity and pathology: one is most drawn to what one must exclude, and it reaches out, simultaneously phallic and feminine, to wrap itself around the person it will poison or squeeze to death the moment it is admitted.

Infection and Suggestion: Mitchell's Medical Background

Son and grandson of a physician, S. Weir Mitchell learned the most about medicine from his father, J. K. Mitchell, who argued that fungi caused contagious diseases and that animal magnetism had a real, physical basis. An intelligent but unmotivated student, Mitchell despised the mediocre professors, who beat the boys, and focused his energy instead on outdoor sports and adventure stories. He particularly enjoyed tales of exploration and conquest, like Garcilaso de la Vega's account of Spanish actions in Peru and Bernal Díaz de Castillo's history of the conquest of Mexico (A, 57–61).[2] Mitchell began studying medicine at fifteen at the University of Pennsylvania but was forced to withdraw in his senior year because of his father's failing health. He was able to resume his studies at Jefferson Medical College in 1848 and took his degree in the spring of 1850. While Mitchell forced himself to study at first, he soon became genuinely interested in the way the body worked. He was especially attracted by experimental medicine and in particular by microscopy, which was promising to yield vast information about physiology and pathology. He came to believe that if he, who had no apparent predisposition for medical study, could make himself a successful doctor, any man—Mitchell thought that medicine was generally unsuitable for women— should be able to do the same. As he put it, "I had won power to use my own mental machinery" (97). Mitchell's own life convinced him that anyone could discipline and reform himself, and he incorporated this belief into his medical thinking.

In November 1850, Mitchell's father sent him to Paris to learn the newest medical trends and techniques. One of his first acts upon arriving was to buy a microscope. On 3 April 1851, he wrote to his father: "I examine all the specimens I can meet with, and when I meet with anything new to me I draw it."[3] Dutifully attending the courses on surgical technique that his father had recommended, Mitchell confessed that he "liked better the lessons of Bernard in physiology and Robin in microscopy" (A, 103). He found himself attracted to microscopy because it was a new, exciting technique as yet relatively unexploited by American scientists, but principally he was impressed by his father's long interest in the field (Earnest, 25). "Every other evening," he wrote to his father, "I go to Robin's course on microscopy. I hear that you expect me to rival you at this. I fear not" (15 February 1851). Many of his letters home during his stay in Paris mention medical texts, particularly on microscopy and animal magnetism, that he intends to mail home to his father. In the early spring of 1851, he was working with the microscope four to five hours per day. Throughout his career, Mitchell would retain his faith in microscopy as the most reliable technique for assessing pathological changes to the tissues. Even after his specialization in neurology, he continued, like Virchow, to think small, looking to local and minute disruptions for the causes of disease.

Ironically, Mitchell lost a good deal of his precious time to study medicine in Paris because he got sick. In December 1850 he caught smallpox while taking the pulse of a patient in Paris. In the spring, incapacitated by the flu, he wrote bitterly, "it seems I can escape nothing" (April 1851). Death and disease followed him closely throughout his career, reinforcing his developing awareness of people's vulnerability. Even when giving anecdotal accounts of his experience with disease, Mitchell represents infection as an attack or invasion. In *Doctor and Patient* (1888) he recalls: "A little girl coughed in my face a hideous breath of membraneous decay. I felt at once a conviction of having been hit. Two days later I was down with her malady. She herself and two more of her family owed their disease to the overflow of a neighbor's cesspool, and to them—poor, careless folk—Death dealt out a yet sterner retribution" (1904, 62–63). While Mitchell studied medicine before germ theory became accepted, both his father's early advocacy of the idea and his own personal encounters with disease predisposed him to see illnesses as violations against which the body must be on guard.[4]

It is significant that both J. K. Mitchell and Oliver Wendell Holmes, who did the most to shape Weir Mitchell's ideas about disease, believed that many diseases were caused by living germs, probably fungi. A good friend of S. Weir Mitchell as well as his father, Holmes had joined Semmelweis in the 1840s to argue that childbed fever was caused by microorganisms. Like Holmes, Mitchell's father was interested in microscopes because they were so essential for studying the "fungi" he was convinced caused many diseases. In publishing "The Cryptogamous Origin of Malarious and Epidemic Fevers" (1849), J. K. Mitchell took a great risk in defending what was then regarded as an antiquated view of disease. While his idea of microbes differs considerably from Koch's or Pasteur's, what is so striking in J. K. Mitchell's essay is the *way* he discusses germs, stressing their role as external, independent organisms with a disturbing power to spread and promote decay. He calls them "dubious beings" that undergo "astonishing modifications," and he emphasizes, as Koch would later, that their power to infect may reside in their resemblance to human cells (J. K. Mitchell, 36). Organisms that resemble the cells of other life forms, he hints, defy the boundaries by which those life forms are classified and are most likely to be able to penetrate those other life forms. When he describes the fungi's abilities to hide and to spread, his Biblical rhetoric reveals a fear of these infectious organisms as a generalized evil: "The close cavities of nuts afford concealment to some species; others, like leeches, stick to the bulbs of plants and suck them dry; . . . they attach themselves to animal structures and destroy animal life. . . . Where then are they not to be found? Do they not abound, like the Pharaoh's plagues, everywhere? Is not their name legion, and their province ubiquity?" (43). J. K. Mitchell's vivid images of insidious parasitism have a literary quality, and they arouse strong emotion, as they were designed to do, against these secretive organisms that suck the life out of healthy living things. The physician who visualized these creatures under the microscope was thus performing a heroic task of revelation and detection, studying potential invaders and killers so as to anticipate and thwart their attacks.

There can be no doubt that J. K. Mitchell's belief in infectious living organisms influenced his son's medical views. S. Weir Mitchell's descriptions of deadly, invasive bacteria tie his thinking in the field of hygiene to his concepts of mental health and pathology. In a speech honoring the new Institute of Hygiene at the University of Pennsylvania, he proclaimed: "One disease after another has been traced to its parent cause in some tiny agent of mischief. A row of culture-tubes in a laboratory, with their bright-colored organisms, represents a Pandora's box of pathological disaster" (S. W. Mitchell 1892, 8).[5] The reference to Pandora's box identifies the chaos and decay wrought by the bacteria as a feminine evil, a force to be contained and controlled. The term *mischief*, one of the words Mitchell uses most frequently to describe pathology, associates these tiny, invasive agents with a group of children or an unruly mob, adding a political dimension to his call for containment. Very early in his career, then, Mitchell became convinced that disease resulted from a failure of containment and a violation of personal boundaries, a paradigm upon which he would rely as a neurologist.

J. K. Mitchell combined his interest in infectious germs with an interest in infectious suggestions, then known as animal magnetism or mesmerism. Each of the physician authors considered in this study, S. Weir Mitchell, Santiago Ramón y Cajal, Arthur Conan Doyle, and Arthur Schnitzler, would combine these same interests. To a certain degree, this coincidence results from the years in which the four were trained and practiced medicine. In the 1880s, with the work of Koch, Pasteur, Charcot, Bernheim, and Forel, both germ theory and hypnotism became scientifically respected fields. In the 1840s, however, both were considered antiprogressive, the territory of quacks (Ackerknecht 1948b, 567). J. K. Mitchell's interest in the two and his writings about each reveal how intimately the two fields are related on a thematic level. Each area—one biological, the other psychological—attempts to describe and gain control of entities (either microorganisms or suggestive thoughts) that penetrate living systems and disrupt their normal functions.

J. K. Mitchell had a knack for hypnotizing people. S. Weir Mitchell, who undoubtedly witnessed some of his father's hypnoses, distrusted the technique as a means of therapy but seized upon the idea that by exercising one's will, one could defend one's ideals and one's identity against outside suggestions. One encounters his association of suggestibility with weakness both in his medical essays and in his fiction. In Mitchell's novel *Characteristics*, Dr. North—who often expresses the author's medical views—asserts that "the subject of hypnotism is very apt to be the victim of suggestion, and to have set free that imitative instinct which we usually keep under control" (122–23). The imitative instinct, in Mitchell's eyes, was one of those internal serpents that must be controlled by force of will. In *Doctor North*, in part a novel of manners, the author invokes cultural rules of etiquette in reminding readers of the thoughts that abound in society and that can rudely burst into people's minds if they are not on their guard: "Some thoughts seem to step in thus from the outside without so much as the ceremony of knocking" (158). Those who imitate automatically, without thinking through the ideas they adopt, reveal their immaturity and lack of will. Vincent, a character in *Characteristics* and *Dr. North* whom Mitchell presents in a consistently positive light, proclaims that "colonies have no adult life. They are overgrown children. They are simply imitative, and imitation implies weakness" (*DN*, 151). As in the Cobra City episode, irrational human drives are associated with the colonies and are presented as forces to be controlled. Here again, Mitchell's negative attitude toward suggestibility may have its roots in his own experiences. Reportedly, he was a "highly suggestible child," and his overcoming of his own nature—if, indeed, he did overcome it—again led him to believe that others could and should do the same (Poirier 1983b, 18). Just as cryptogamous organisms could disrupt a body, suggestions from a hypnotist could disrupt a mind, but only if one let them in.

In a 1908 article assessing his rest cure for nervousness, Mitchell acknowledges the inadequacy of the term *suggestion* to describe a phenomenon so broad and so much a part of the human experience. He compares the French definition of suggestion, "*insinuation mauvaise,*" with Samuel Johnson's British one of "private hint, intimation, insinuation" and finds them very different. The French synonym, *instigation*, associates the uncontrolled spread of ideas in the mind with political disorder, the agitation of the discontented. Mitchell's own definition of suggestion, "getting into a man's mind an idea or order which becomes influential without conscious thought on his part," combines the British and French interpretations, reflecting fears at once political, cultural, and sexual (S. W. Mitchell 1908, 2035). He finds, however, that both the French and English concepts of suggestion lead smoothly into "persuasion, counsel, and many forms of appeal," a definition so broad that *suggestion* would have to encompass most forms of human interaction (2035).

Even in 1851, when Mitchell attended Claude Bernard's lectures on physiology, the model of the body he encountered was one of interaction and
exchange. Bernard, who in the 1850s would work out many of the mechanisms involved in digestion, advocated physiological experimentation on live
animals, and he left a deep impression on Mitchell. In one encounter, when
the young American declared "I think so and so must be the case," Bernard
replied, "Why think when you can experiment? Exhaust experiment and
then think" (A, 103). When the young doctor was in Paris, Bernard was
performing the experiments he would describe in *Lectures on the Nervous
System* (1858). It is quite possible that the French physiologist inspired Mitchell's interest in neurology (Mettenry, x).

In his *Introduction to the Study of Experimental Medicine* (1865), Bernard
distinguishes active experimentation from passive observation, arguing for
the superiority of the former. He proposes that the physiologist needs instruments to "penetrate inside of bodies, to dissociate them and to study their
hidden parts" (1949, 5). Declaring that "the experiment is just an observation
produced for the purpose of control," he writes that the experimenter "forces
nature to unveil herself by attacking her with all manner of questions" (20,
23). Mitchell's friend Oliver Wendell Holmes went Bernard one better, telling naturalist Louis Agassiz how he loved "to see a relentless observer get hold
of Nature and squeeze her until the sweat broke out all over her and Sphinc-
ters loosened" (Burr, 83). Mitchell's later attitude toward his female patients,
his determination to cure them in spite of themselves, often reflects this
aggressive point of view.

An even more important influence on Mitchell's medical thinking was
Bernard's notion of the *milieu interieur*, his conception of the body as simultaneously dependent on the external environment and capable of creating its
own internal environment. Vitalists had argued incorrectly, he maintained,
that living things differed from inorganic matter in their independence from
external forces. While life functions appeared to be independent of the external environment, they were actually regulated by the internal one, which
responded both to the cells within and to the conditions outside. Life, by its
very nature, could never be associated with hermetic boundaries or the exclusion of external forces. "It is impossible to imagine a body wholly isolated
in nature," he concludes. "It would no longer be real because there would be
no relation to manifest its existence" (Bernard, 71). When Mitchell admits
the universality of suggestion and the futility of excluding all social influence,
he recalls Bernard's vision of life as interaction and exchange.

While Mitchell's notion of healthy life as resistance might at first seem incompatible with Bernard's concept, the two are closely related. Resistance presupposes interaction; warm-blooded animals, for instance, interact with cold environments but would die if they failed to keep out the cold. Mitchell's model of physical and mental health, emphasizing exclusion and control, is simply an interaction in which the victory must always fall to one side. One must dominate and not be dominated by one's environment and impulses.

Although forced to abandon experimentation early in his career, Mitchell never gave up the perspective of physiology. His father wanted him to become a surgeon, but here Weir failed him, finding that he had "neither the nerve nor the hand" (A, 108).[6] In the end Mitchell compromised, seeing patients by day and devoting his evenings—from 4 PM until 1 AM—to the research that he preferred, investigations of how poisons kill their victims.

Snake Venom: Penetration and Pathology

Mitchell liked snakes. For many reasons, he found himself intrigued by the mechanism of rattlesnake venom. As Bernard had taught, poisons revealed the relations among bodily functions by selectively destroying them. Above all, what attracted Mitchell to snake venom was the surprising lack of knowledge about it and the dearth of other investigators in the field, the "reluctance of other men to attack a problem" (Rein, 19). As far as he could see, no one in a hundred years had done any significant studies on how snake venom worked, possibly because of people's feelings of repulsion for snakes and their irrational fears of them (A, 153). "M. Bernard, alone," he comments, "of all the recent writers, seems to be aware of our lack of knowledge in this direction" (1861, 5). Although he eventually engaged in research in many areas, he called his study of snake venom "one of the most important works of my life" (A, 144). Other scientists agreed with his assessment. His obituary in *Nature* calls his 1860 study of rattlesnake venom "a perfect model of what an investigation into the physiological action of a poison ought to be" (8 January 1914). His rattlesnake studies, particularly his 1881 discovery that the poison had multiple components, laid the foundation for future studies in the field (Burr, 74).

Mitchell's studies of snakes are thorough, painstaking, and systematic, explaining in detail the handling, behavior, anatomy, chemistry, and physiology involved so that the reader can picture it. He mentions, for instance, that snakes do not eat in captivity and that he therefore has to force-feed them, a process that foreshadows his force-feeding of nervous women twenty years later.[7] Like Bernard, Mitchell was fascinated by poisons because they revealed both the body's own exquisite regulatory mechanisms and its sensitivity to outside forces. He defined a poison in the same way his father had described the fungi that caused fevers: "an agent which has no normal existence in the body of a man" (S. W. Mitchell 1868, 295). When he discusses rattlesnake venom, he concentrates on the interplay of internal and external forces, always considering what "poison" really means. His most valuable discovery in his investigation of snake venom came more than twenty years after his initial investigations, when he found in 1881 that the poison consisted of several chemical components that worked in combination: a peptone, a globulin, and an albumen. His account of how he discovered the separate effects of each on the body, step by step, reads like a detective story (1883).

As he had known since the 1860s, the venom kills its victims by causing a breakdown in circulation at the local level, and he declared, "the remarkable power possessed by this poison to cause putrefaction in the living tissue in so short a time is astonishing" (S. W. Mitchell 1883, 12–13). Mitchell watched in horror as, under his microscope lens, capillaries collapsed, flooding the surrounding tissue with blood. His descriptions of poisoned tissue closely resemble his later ones of "poisoned" minds, both of which suffer from insufficient resistance. The poison causes, he wrote, "an absolute impairment of the texture of the part, so that they no longer offer a normal resistance to force. The vessels thus altered give way under a circulatory pressure" (1868a, 310). He describes the "mischief" wrought by the poison, using the same word he would later apply to bacteria and unhealthy suggestions (1868a, 297).

Even though rattlesnakes' venom destroyed tissue, Mitchell admired the snakes, both for their behavior and for their design. He found their "whole posture bold and defiant, and expressive of alertness and inborn courage," and he respected the way the snake "reserves his forces, judging wisely as to his own powers" (S. W. Mitchell 1868c, 453–54). As a physician, he appears almost to identify with the snakes. He calls the poison glands "the laboratory in which the serpent makes his potent medicine" and considers the two glands that produce it "as independent of one another as two rival drugshops" (454–55). The hollow tooth that delivers the poison is compared to a needle, an "exquisite instrument" that injects the venom as doctors inject their medications. While he respected the construction of the snake's fang, writing that "the point of this singular weapon is brittle, but of an exquisite fineness," what particularly struck him was the serpent's perfect control, its "power to restrain the flow of venom" (1860, 15–16). Sounding like Darwin, he praised the bite mechanism as "a wonderful example . . . of a series of complex acts following one upon another in ordered sequence" (1860, 20).

As a process of violent penetration, ejaculation, and withdrawal, the injection of snake venom closely parallels a sexual encounter, or more specifically, a rape. Despite his reluctance to discuss any sexual matter in his creative or scientific writing, Mitchell reveals his awareness of this parallel in his descriptions of biting. He expresses fascination for "the mechanism, through the agency of which the poison is ejaculated" and finds that the poison gland "resembles very strikingly, in section, the appearance of a small testicle" (S. W. Mitchell 1860, 6, 12). He writes admiringly that "the animal has the most perfect control over the movement of the fang, raising or depressing it at will" and observes that in snakes who have not bitten for months, "the first gush of their venom was sometimes astonishingly large" (21,27). When the serpent is finished injecting the venom, it has to "disentangle itself from its victim" (22). In light of these sexualized descriptions, Mitchell's tendency, as a physician, to identify with snakes becomes extremely disturbing. He looked upon penetration with horror, yet both he and the rattlers needed to puncture people to do their jobs.

Bodies in Pieces: Mitchell's Civil War Experiences

When the Civil War erupted in 1861, Mitchell had little time left for physiological research. Still thinking actively about how the body's systems interacted and responded to outside influences, the physiologist became a neurologist. The war left a permanent impression on Mitchell just as it did on his nation. As a doctor, Mitchell never saw military action, but he did explore the Gettysburg battlefield only a few days after the slaughter, "a sight I shall never forget" (A, 150). While on his first assignment at the Filbert St. Hospital, Mitchell became interested in nervous disorders, "about which little was then known" (146). As had been the case with snake venom, he was attracted by the lack of certain knowledge and by other physicians' unwillingness to explore a confusing field. Doctors who preferred not to handle nerve injuries began transferring cases to Mitchell's ward, and with help from Surgeon General William Hammond, he and his colleague George Morehouse founded what would become the Turner's Lane Hospital, a 400-bed facility for treating nerve injuries (146–47). Mitchell would go on to become America's premier neurologist, a founder of the Neurological and Physiological Societies. Always learning from his patients, he incorporated his experiences in the hospital into two of his most influential scientific works, *Gunshot Wounds and Other Injuries of Nerves* (1864) and *Injuries of Nerves and Their Consequences* (1872), and into his stories and novels.

Mitchell's choice to study pain—something that can be known only subjectively—with the rigorous methodology of science indicates that from the beginning of his career he combined the observational techniques of a scientist and novelist. In his Turner's Lane Hospital notes, it is clear how carefully he listened to his patients' descriptions of their pain. One patient reported a burning "like mustard," not relieved by the application of water; another, like Poe's Roderick Usher, found that any sound, even music, made his "screwing" pain unbearable.[8] A soldier told him that when hit, he had felt as if he had been struck in the back by a stick and had been so sure of it that he had turned around to accuse the man behind him (Mitchell, Morehouse, and Keen 1864, 14–15). Mitchell recorded anything his patients could tell him about their personal perceptions, valuing their comments, no matter how bizarre, as his only source of information. One of his highest achievements was to convince the scientific community that amputees' phantom limb pains had a real neurological basis. Although Mitchell sympathized with patients suffering chronic pain, he believed that overcoming pain—recovering a sense of oneself—required character.

By *character*, a word Mitchell used frequently, he meant the product of social education and a unique individual spark, a personal way of thinking and behaving. It is the outcome of long struggles between internal and imposed desires, the ability to respond to social demands while retaining one's own identity. Assessing his rest cure in 1880, he declared that "the whole mode of treatment rests on a study of character" (S. W. Mitchell 1880, 131). Mitchell sought to restore fragmented bodies and personalities by shoring up the boundaries of character when they threatened to collapse. Like Bernard, he relied on "poisoned" systems to show him how healthy systems worked. As Mitchell put it, "the man who has not known sick women has not known women" (*RB*, 113).

Mitchell's Concept of Selfhood: Resistance and Defense

One learns about the healthy self in Mitchell's works by examining the sick self; one learns what he values in individuals by hearing what is wrong with them. Mitchell's most revealing comments about character and identity are those he makes about himself, and often those qualities he most wants to eliminate in his patients and characters are those that he personally overcame. He confessed that, "I have always been a nervous, excitable person, needing to have a sudden grip on myself in danger or when wrath arises" (A, 81). Mitchell suffered at least two nervous collapses of which he was willing to speak little, referring to his attack in 1872 as "too personal for full record" (1908, 2035). He seems convinced, throughout his medical writings, that if he could overcome his own nervousness, anyone could, and he has no tolerance for patients who resist this view. Based on his own experiences, he believed firmly that one must learn to repress certain parts of oneself. All people, from the most despicable scoundrels to the most peevish hysterics, could develop their character, if given the appropriate education and "moral training" (Lovering, 158).

For Mitchell, good character meant strong will, self-discipline, self-restraint, and resistance to instinctive impulses and imposed suggestions. Excessive susceptibility or sensitivity to one's surroundings or to one's own feelings meant weakness, a weakness that had to be overcome. Underlying this model of selfhood is Mitchell's notion of disease as something that penetrates the body from the outside, resulting in a humiliating reversal of control in which the active experimenter becomes the passive object. Describing his bout with smallpox in 1850–51, Mitchell refers to "what I have been doing in the meanwhile, or rather what has been *done with me*. . . . I had begun a course on microscopy with Mr. Robin when the varioloid took it on himself to demonstrate a little on my own poor body" (14, 15 January 1851). To be so entered was an embarrassment as well as an inconvenience.

Although Mitchell recognizes the role of social interaction in personal growth, this exchange is largely a means to an end, training the individual to shut out undesirable influences later on. Openness to social encounters is safe only if one can control them. In a very revealing moment, Mitchell's character Dr. North suggests that this resistance to penetration has its roots in American culture: "Nowhere do I think as fluently and with more sure result than in a swift train. Here I feel secure from invasion. I am guarded by the immense average of silent reserve attained by the American" (*DN*, 138).[9] A matter of survival as well as politeness, this protective zone of "silent reserve" was necessary for those in Mitchell's culture to conceive of themselves as unique individuals.

How did one develop these personal barriers that thwarted both internal desires and invasive thoughts? One should begin, Mitchell suggests, by learning to control the internal forces, the earlier the better. In his "Clinical Lecture on Nervousness in the Male" (1877), he calls self-restraint "life's most urgent lesson," explaining that ordinarily a man's "hardening" education—in contrast to a woman's—"forc[es] him to repress emotion and to restrain the exhibition of feeling until restraint develops habit" (179). Any child, he believes, can be made nervous if overindulged, that is, taught to listen too hard to his or her own feelings and to value them too highly. Mitchell never doubts that a powerful external authority, imposed in childhood, will lead to a correspondingly powerful inner one in adulthood, and as a doctor he assumes that authority until he is satisfied his uncontrolled patients have internalized it.

Mitchell's writings consistently present the undisciplined mind as frightening and dangerous. Desire itself becomes threatening if unchecked, whether it arises in an hysterical female or a robber baron. Both, ultimately, want power, and Mitchell represents this selfish desire through references to the lower life forms with which he associates it. In Mitchell's fiction, self-centered characters provoke references to tendrils and tentacles, recalling the slithering bodies of his snakes. The narrator of *Dr. North* calls another character, Xerxes Crofter, who ruthlessly takes control of railroads, a "devouring octopus" (*DN,* 117). In the popular medical text *Doctor and Patient* (1888), Mitchell wrote that the relative who nurses a female invalid "is in the grip of an octopus" (126). In his novel *Roland Blake,* which appeared two years earlier, he brought this metaphor to life in the hideous character Octopia Darnell, who wraps her neurasthenic tentacles around her cousin Olivia.

It is when one compares Mitchell's medical case studies to his literary characters that this fear of uncontrolled desire emerges most clearly. In defining selfhood, both as a doctor and as a novelist, Mitchell attempts to exclude both internal impulses and external intrusions, identifying the "real" self as the force that works against them.

In 1888, Mitchell reviewed the history of Mary Reynolds (1793–1854), a case of "dual consciousness" in which his father had consulted. At eighteen, Mary fell into a deep sleep and awoke in a state of "unnatural consciousness." In her "second state," the suddenly fearless Mary rambled through the woods and, "attracted by the beauty" of a rattlesnake, tried to grab it by the tail. When warned of the dangers of the woods, she told her family, "I know you only want to frighten me and keep me at home" (S. W. Mitchell 1889, 9). In her original personality, Mary had avoided people and had spent most of her time reading her Bible; she now sought people out, planned elaborate practical jokes, and referred disparagingly to her wilderness home as the "Nocturnal Shades" (16). Periodically, Mary would fall into a deep sleep and awaken in one or the other of her two distinct personalities. She continued to alternate between the two until the age of thirty-six, after which she remained permanently in a slightly altered version of the second, extroverted state. Mary's uncle, who wrote the report on which Mitchell relied, regarded

Mary's first personality as her "true self," even though she spent more of her life in the second state. Mitchell's case studies and novels often make the same move, refusing to accept wild, defiant behavior as connected to the "real self."

A model of selfhood that represents envelopment and penetration as pathological may well have its origin in sexual fears, specifically in the fear of becoming female, of becoming a sexual object. While Mitchell fastidiously avoids references to sexuality both in his scientific writing and his fiction, he occasionally allows his characters to hint at sexuality. When the issue of dual consciousness arises in *Dr. North*, North's wife asks: "If I am two people, and one can pop up like a jack-in-the-box, I may be six people, and how can I be responsible for the love-affairs of five?" (294). They are discussing Sibyl May-wood, a girl who has developed a nervous disorder following her infatuation with St. Clair (discoverer of the Cobra City) and has been writing him love letters, unconscious of her own actions. North, following the precedent of Mary's case, explains, "in her sound state she is able to control herself . . . In these times of alternate consciousness she obeys her emotional nature. . . . The real Sibyl does not know that she wrote those letters" (293, 302). Like his creator, the fictional Dr. North identifies the "real" self as the controlling force, excluding the "eccentric boarder" who writes out her desire. Health means self-control, and a loss of control indicates a pathological state. For Mitchell, responsibility, an essential aspect of selfhood, rests on self-contain-ment, and the progressive fission that Sibyl is undergoing, the uncontrollable and sexually suggestive bursting of the jack-in-the-box, arouses horrifying possibilities of explosive and uncontrolled growth. In cordoning off certain aspects of consciousness when he constructs identity, however, Mitchell him-self initiates this fission. At the conclusion of *Dr. North*, seeing Sibyl's recov-ery, North declares that "the sick and the well are two people" (486).

Constance Trescot *(1905)*: *The Violence of Internal Drives*

Assessed by Mitchell as his finest character study and his best book, *Con-stance Trescot* follows the destruction waged by an uncontrolled personality and illustrates in an unforgettable way Mitchell's lifelong tendency to associ-ate primal desires with animals and to define human identity in opposition to them (Rein, 102). Raised by her uncle to have "no distinct creed," Constance is a "creature of instincts," and she "loves and hates with an animal fidelity" (*CT*, 11–12). Mitchell carefully points out the misjudgments in Constance's education: she was never punished, only reasoned with. Worse, she was never allowed to attend church, so that she might choose a religion actively when she came of age: "reasoning would do everything" (26). Constance's older sister Susan provokes thought when she asks her uncle why he doesn't let the girl wait and choose her manners and morals as well, rather than learning them as a child. Of course, Constance adopts neither religion nor reason; her love for her husband Trescot supplants both as a motivational force. The narrator explains that "she had been trained to certain habits which passed for duties; but being without any ultimate beliefs with which to test her actions when called upon by the unusual, the instincts of a too natural creature were apt to be seen in what she did or felt" (87).

The plot of the novel reminds readers of the economic chaos and need for healing following the Civil War, and it reflects the fragmentation and lack of control in the characters' consciousness. Constance's uncle in New England holds riverfront property in a small Missouri town, and the town desperately needs this land to revive its economy. To obtain the blessing of Constance's uncle and earn enough money to marry Constance without delay, Trescot accepts the thankless job of defending the uncle's interests in the former Confederate town. In contrast to his wife, Trescot is a controlled, rational, forgiving and religious man; and Mitchell describes his influence on Constance as one of doctor on patient. Trescot tells her, for instance, that "like the great rolling worlds overhead, we too are pulled by a hundred exterior forces and, like them, must keep our orbits steadily" (*CT,* 147–48). Under Trescot's "thoughtful guidance," Constance's mind is "slowly unfolding" (91).

Greyhurst, another of Mitchell's most interesting characters, is leading the town's fight to regain the riverfront. Eventually, he faces Trescot in court. Several times Mitchell mentions Greyhurst's "remote strain of Indian blood," offering a racial explanation for the emotionality he shares with Constance (*CT,* 168). While her animal tendencies result from a lack of education and his from "wild" blood, the characters are clearly two of a kind. By using similar metaphors, Mitchell creates a parallel between Constance and her husband's adversary, portraying them as a pair of untamed animals. Greyhurst is a "rude animal," a "brute," a "wild beast," and a "half broken, . . . ill-trained colt"; Constance is "some splendid animal tamed and stilled by the touch of a master" (150–51, 168, 145). Greyhurst fails at life because he is too sensitive, "too thin-skinned for friendship," too susceptible both to his own stormy passions and to the criticism of those around him. He has been living in the worst possible environment for an undisciplined man, the "wilder West . . . [where] the individualities of men were less conventionally governed" (168). In a rare lapse, to reinforce the reader's impression of Constance's wildness,

Mitchell refers directly to sexuality: she is "one of the rare women who, for good or ill, attract because of some inexplicable quality of sex . . . she who has [the quality] instinctively knows its power" (96). Constance and Greyhurst attract each other from the start, a drive that will catalyze the other emotions between them. The repeated references to emotions that threaten to break loose, of course, also recall the war, the devastation that can follow unrestrained anger.

Structurally, the novel follows both Constance's and Greyhurst's emotions, reaching its first climax the first time their passions burst loose. Greyhurst, "no master of himself," sees Trescot steadily gaining sympathy in court with his politeness, generosity, and careful argumentation, and he "los[es] the tranquillity which is needful for quick and perfect use of the mental mechanism" (CT, 217, 193). When Trescot wins, he approaches Greyhurst with the news that Constance's uncle has died, giving her control of the property, which she will gladly sell to the town. Greyhurst shoots him before he can tell it, and Constance suffers a nervous collapse.

Through the rest of the novel, Constance torments Greyhurst, her animal nature reigning triumphant once her paternal husband has been removed. The doctor who treats her observes that "there was something feline in her delicate ways, her grace of movement, her neatness, the preservation of primitive passions and instincts, her satisfaction in the chase and in torturing" (293). She pursues Greyhurst in a carefully designed campaign of revenge, tormenting him with guilt, ruining him financially, and even driving away his fiancée, his last chance for redemption. Her desire is finally fulfilled when he enters her house saying he has come to pay a debt, aims a gun at her, and then shoots himself.

Once her revenge has been accomplished, however, Constance has no motive for living. As the novel closes, she has become a selfish invalid, still attempting to control those around her because she cannot control herself. Perhaps more than any other of Mitchell's novels, *Constance Trescot* serves as a warning. The narrator's comment, "the passions are near neighbors," refers both to society and to the human mind (311). Mitchell's images of postwar suffering remind readers that one must learn to live with one's neighbors.

Despite the "Pandora's Box" of animalistic drives all people contain, Mitchell sees hope for humanity. The potential for salvation in his system lies in the very force that makes people unique: the individual will. Mitchell conceives of will in a literal, physical way; it does mean selfhood, but before this it means cerebral control of the voluntary muscles, the ability of the brain to command action. Explaining his use of electricity to revive muscles in

Gunshot Wounds, he writes that response to faradization is a good indicator of "future volitional control" and may even help the will to "reassert its dominion" (141). He refers elsewhere to the will as a "mandate" or "order" that is sent to the muscles (1880, 130). Control is the very essence of will and of selfhood, and when the will weakens or collapses, one loses one's identity as a unique living being.

In "Man, the Individual," a lecture delivered to the Society of Colonial Dames in 1902, Mitchell reveals the tremendous value he attributes to personal uniqueness. "Individuality," he begins, "or what I may venture to call the law of diversity, is of all natural conditions the most absolutely without exception" (2). In his experience, he continues, even organs, nerve cells, and blood cells show individuality, and he suspects that the principle may apply even to atoms.[10] He admits that "the trend of polite life and social training is to make men as to conduct outwardly similar," but he finds that people manage to retain their uniqueness anyway (9). Applying Darwinian theory to social development, he states that the encouragement of individuality reveals a well-developed civilization. A nation that exhibits "the largest amount of useful individual diversities is surely rising in the scale of development" (10). Here, again, one sees how cultural ethics are interwoven into Mitchell's literature and science. His model of selfhood incorporates the American belief in the "supreme worth of the individual," in Mitchell's era, the right of the upper-class entrepreneur to profit from the less individualized masses.

Social and Economic Concepts of Selfhood

A third-generation physician, Mitchell always identified himself with the American intellectual elite. His second wife, Mary Cadwalader, was a Philadelphia "aristocrat," and after his marriage to her in 1874, he moved among America's wealthiest and most influential people. Mitchell placed great value on the "manners" that he felt distinguished educated people, respecting workers only when they exhibited these same niceties. Generally he regarded them as a breed apart, discussing them with the same scientific distance he used when describing laboratory animals.

Class differences, seen from a medical perspective, emerge with particular clarity in *Constance Trescot*. Visiting a squatter's cabin, Constance observes "the crude business of death among the poor" (113). After Trescot's death, the squatter Coffin is struck by Constance's "complete pallor" and thinks, "The women of his own class wept and were natural." The narrator then takes over, explaining, "This woman had back of her two centuries of Puritan self-restraint, and the controlling reserve of a class accustomed to hide emotion" (238). Such were Mitchell's patients, and such were the people who developed nervous diseases. His view of health as restraint and resistance has its roots not only in cultural notions of sexual difference but also in concepts of class and economic difference.

Mitchell's writings do not subvert and rarely criticize the socioeconomic system under which he lived. On the contrary, his scientific theories of selfhood grow out of and reinforce the American capitalist tradition.[11] Mitchell's novels come close to challenging the tenets of Social Darwinism, particularly in his depiction of the ruthless and morally undeveloped Xerxes Crofter. In the end, however, even Crofter makes a positive impression as a character in the process of development, a man of raw courage and daring who risks his own life to save North's young daughter.

To rise in society, or to maintain one's position, Mitchell's writings suggest, one must look out for one's character, and here the best tactic is exclusion, cutting oneself off from negative influences. This ability to shut others out at will, Mitchell's character Clayborne proposes, indicates an increasing degree of civilization: "As you go down the social ladder toward cave life, somewhere the power to exclude your fellows ceases" (DN, 122). Mitchell's literary works complement his scientific ones in presenting the independent, controlled, and semipermeable individual as the healthiest living unit, a view perfectly compatible with American capitalism's cult of the individual.

When discussing the pathological conditions he has dedicated his life to studying and conquering, Mitchell repeatedly compares them to unworthy forms of government that deny individual freedom. A Republican, Mitchell believed in social control based on individual responsibility rather than centralized power, and, like Virchow, he conceived of the body in the same terms. Mitchell abhorred both despotism and anarchy and feared rule by a tyrant as much as he dreaded social chaos.[12] Applying his political views to the human mind, Mitchell viewed any drives that usurp control from the will as "tyrants" and "despots." He associates the will in an individual, that is, with the voice of the majority in a democratic state—the will of the educated male voters.

The external environment restricted this individual control whenever it affected behavior, and Mitchell believed that "the lives of men are lived under the limited monarchy of circumstance" (Rein, 58).[13] Most threatening to the will and to personal freedom were the internal "tyrants" of instinct and emotion. Constance Trescot tells Greyhurst, "it is hard for a man to escape from the tyranny of his own temperament." He agrees that he suffers from "despotism of temperament" and envies Trescot "his entire self-control." She asks, "Cannot a man make himself what he really wants to be?" "Can a woman?" he counters. "No," she replies (*CT,* 120).

A tyrant humiliates his subjects by robbing them of their freedom to act, and Mitchell stresses this humiliation in his metaphors. He despised slavery, and he was alarmed by the self-perpetuation of enslavement, whereby those enslaved by their own drives were apt to subjugate others. Those individuals most permeable or "open" to their own emotions, that is, were most likely to become both slaves and slave drivers. It is significant that his character Octopia Darnell, a slave to her selfish desires and a despot in her own right, loved having slaves and longs for a return to her old plantation life in Virginia. Octopia, who craves power, is herself powerless if one chooses, like Mitchell, to define her selfhood in opposition to her moods. Describing her mental state, he suggests that those who lose control of their emotions lose their very humanity and are reduced to puppets: "she was the puppet of her moods, which obeyed like an automaton the wires pulled by her emotions" (*RB,* 53). He uses the same metaphor for the pathetic Greyhurst, who suffers the same humiliation. After Greyhurst shoots Trescot and Constance has denounced him as a coward, the narrator tells us that "some unseen hand was jangling the wires of puppet memories—he a helpless looker-on" (*CT,* 224). Mitchell pities the people who lose control of their own minds, but he never loses faith that they can regain it. He despises his patients only when they make no effort to overthrow the "tyrant" and regain the power that is rightfully theirs.

Selfhood for Mitchell means fighting despotism, fighting for freedom and for self-control. His extensive use of the word *despotism* throughout his creative and scientific writing reveals the close relation between his political and his scientific views. First, he applies it to any natural law or instinct that limits an individual's potential to act. As always, it is the internal pull of these natural drives that proves most formidable, and Mitchell frequently describes instincts as despotic. Young Olivia of *Roland Blake,* condemned to wait on Octopia, is "nobly gifted with the yearning instincts which are of despotic force in the highest womanhood" (36–37). Such despotic drives and impulses compete directly with the will to control the thoughts and actions, and they often defeat it because of their singular intensity. The will can, however, match them in energy under the right circumstances. For Mitchell, environmental and instinctual forces influence but never determine behavior. Like poisons, they are challenges that shape character by demanding resistance.

The most harmful despots are those that reign longest, and as Mitchell sees it, some personalities invite them. Constance Trescot's long drive for revenge provides the best example: "It had become so despotic in its rule as to make all else secondary in value, and, as is the case with the domination of a fixed idea, to impair, in time, the competence of will and reason. Thought is then emotionally disturbed and, soon or late, mere indecision and indefinite craving replace resolute and well-considered plans of action" (*CT,* 340–41). Actions that are automatic, guided by emotion rather than reason, degrade the people who commit them. Yet even when an obsession has apparently seized total control, Mitchell retains hope that the "real individual," the force that resists both external and internal drives, can reassume command. In "Man, the Individual," Mitchell acknowledges the power of tyrants, but he then declares that "under such despotic environments, and for a time, the man's will, and his desire for independence, yield to the pressure, but he never completely loses his individuality and there is always a certain amount of resistance which may at any time reassure as to the indestructibility of the individual" (9). Comparing Mitchell's many uses of the term *despotism,* one infers that individual identity exists in spite of and in opposition to circumstances, instincts, habits, feelings, impulses, and basic drives. These forces do contribute to identity, but they do so because the will must have something to resist.

To Mitchell, for whom identity was so closely linked to control, there was something worse than a tyrant: the complete absence of mental government, or "moral anarchy." In his medical writings and in his novels, his political beliefs emerge when he describes unruly mobs and uncontrolled riots to depict the play of unchecked emotions. In these instances, he employs the term *mischief*—the word he used for the chaos created by bacteria—drawing associations to children and to the undisciplined masses. When he explains the value of rest and excessive feeding in *Fat and Blood,* Mitchell writes that the doctor is "slowly repairing mischief" done to the body by an oversensitive and uncontrolled mind (16). Woman's desire to compete with man intellectually, he finds, is "making mischief" by creating such exhaustion (1904, 13). The hysteric or neurasthenic who allows her body to fall into such a state is capable of a "mischievous emotional display," suggesting a breakdown of authority and the need—temporarily—to impose control from the outside.

Mitchell's concept of "mischief" often brings class into play. Reflecting on the spoiled Richard Darnell's mind in *Roland Blake,* the narrator proposes that "Minor motives . . . are like mischievous boys in a mob, and make half the trouble" (329). In this simile, the "mob" first has a "major motive"—in 1886, two years after the Chicago Haymarket Affair, perhaps higher wages or shorter hours. The boys, with the "minor motive" of excitement or love of disruption, turn the demonstration into a riot. Like society, Mitchell implies, the mind will find itself in chaos if it cannot constructively manage the desiring mob and exclude the minor motives.

In a mind unregulated by will, thoughts that would normally be rejected become little stinging demons, assailing both the mind and, eventually, the body. Octopia, for example, who is never in control of her own mind, finds that when her brother presses her for money, "a mob of liliputian motives assailed her" (RB, 251). The physician's task was not simply to restore order, however, but to train the patient's own "government" to reassume command. In his introduction to Doctor and Patient, Mitchell warned that "to read the riot act to a mob of emotions is valueless" (7). Patients open to every sort of impulse needed not just self-government but the right kind of self-govern- ment, one in which they could consider, judge, and resist the suggestions with which they were constantly bombarded.

For Mitchell, the body and mind retain all the complexity and sensitivity of a capitalist economic system, and he describes them as such. Particularly in his popular scientific works, the body accumulates "capital," "spends" ner- vous energy, and can become "impoverished" and run into "debt." In Wear and Tear, or Hints for the Overworked (1873), one of his most widely read books, Mitchell proposes that Americans living on the land for a few generations "store up a capital of vitality" (1874, 8). Considering the life that businessmen lead in the cities, however, with high stress, little exercise, and long work hours, Mitchell warns: "Are we not merely using the interest on those ac- cumulations of power, but also wastefully spending the capital?" (8).

Mitchell's Fat and Blood, which was also widely read, described accumu- lated fat not just as capital but as personal property, a marker for the general prosperity of the body. Fat allowed the physician to monitor the activity of centralized control systems, since weight gain or loss indicated the net out- come of conflicting forces. For Mitchell, loss of fat generally accompanies conditions that "impoverish the blood," whereas a "gain of fat" usually means a "rise in all other essentials of health" (16–17). In this last description, Mitchell might be discussing the stock market, and as an "investor," he tries to interpret changes so as to predict upcoming events. He admonishes those businessmen who are "making money fast and accumulating a physiological debt" (1873, 30). If the steady drain of funds continues, the result will be psychological and physical "bankruptcy," which are of course interdependent and express themselves in a nervous collapse. The doctor who comes to the rescue must take the whole system into account, never treating individual symptoms but instead the entire "digestive, assimilative, and secretive power in which the whole economy inevitably shares" (1884, 43). Here Mitchell follows Bernard, of course, who had proposed that the body worked not only like an economic system but also like a machine because of the intricate interdependence of its functions. As a neurologist, Mitchell was both an economist and an engineer, focusing his attention not so much on defective parts as on control systems, and intervening just enough to restore normal function.

The Rest Cure: Restoring Control by Imposing Control

Weir Mitchell today is best known for his infamous rest cure, perhaps because Charlotte Perkins Gilman, who underwent it herself, depicted its fallacies so chillingly in *The Yellow Wallpaper*.[14] The cure involved several weeks of absolute confinement to one's bed, a carefully regimented diet, massage, and electricity. Above all, the patient—almost always female—was to have no sympathetic audience and no opportunity of carrying out her own desires, which Mitchell believed were guided by caprice in the absence of a strong will (Rein, 95). To cure the body, the doctor would temporarily replace the patient's will with his own; the patient's would then regenerate itself once her body was restored.

Mitchell conceived of mental and physical strain in a literal, absolute sense: when he thought about exhaustion and overuse, he envisioned an actual breakdown of tissues and cells. With the rest cure, Mitchell aimed to intervene in a vicious cycle, in which the will had broken down because of an exhausted body, and the body could not restore itself because "mischievous" impulses reigned in the absence of a strong will. As is evident when he describes nervous exhaustion, his conception of neuropathology grew out of his early physiological training and his discoveries during the Civil War. In an early article, "Paralysis from Peripheral Irritation" (1866), Mitchell had proposed that an injury to a remote area could disrupt a nervous center by overstimulating it until it was exhausted. Excessive, unrelenting nervous activity, he believed, could kill the body supporting the mind.

The rest cure thus applied to the nervous system and the entire body the logic for treating a broken limb: stop using it so that it may heal. Designed for women in whom nervous disorders accompanied severe anemia and anorexia, the rest cure aimed to overcome the nervous condition by treating the entire "economy." Mitchell wrote proudly of the extraordinary quantities of food his patients consumed and of the weight they gained. He introduced massage and electricity to counteract effects of inactivity like circulatory problems and constipation. The massage, he believed, exercised the muscles "without the use of volitional exertion or the aid of the nervous centers" so that he could produce movement and maintain circulation without creating nervous fatigue (1884, 84). The electricity, whose use he had advocated in *Gunshot Wounds*, fulfilled the same purpose, stimulating the muscles while bypassing the patient's exhausted nerves. The regimen as a whole, of course, could work only on patients who genuinely suffered from exhaustion and poor nutrition. To those like Gilman, who had fallen ill because they could not live with the identities society imposed upon them, the rest cure was humiliation and bondage.

When Mitchell describes the recoveries, both of his characters and of his patients, one can infer what health means to him. The goal of the rest cure is the restoration of self-control, and a healthy individual is a restrained one. In hysterical patients, he envisions convalescence as a "self-conquest," a "slow, steady, hopeful training of the will" (S. W. Mitchell 1880, 69–70). Reviewing the logic of the cure in 1908, Mitchell wrote that "with the return of bodily vigor there is always an increasing power of self-control over emotion" (1908, 2036). By restoring physical health, Mitchell believes he is restoring the ability to think rationally, and his literary characters fulfill his wish. Sibyl Maywood in *Doctor North*, once isolated from the charismatic St. Clair, "swiftly gained health, and with it self-control" (212). This restoration of control allows a woman to return to her social duties, inevitably involving a restraint of her own desires.

In Mitchell's descriptions of his female patients, one hears the myth of Pandora's box. The nervous woman, he writes, "has acquired within herself a host of enemies" (S. W. Mitchell 1904, 131). Her mind is a leaky container, a dubious prison-fortress holding back a swarm of evil impulses. If the structure gives way, they will escape, and a woman is always more likely than a man to crack open the box. One "model" patient, whom Mitchell praised for her ability to carry out her duties despite excruciating pain, told him "if my mind gets weaker, I shall go to pieces—the bits would be worthless as the scattered bricks of a sound house" (89).[15] Interestingly, however, he attributes female penetrability—to Mitchell, synonymous with weakness—to the type of education women received rather than to their essential nature, wishing that girls as well as boys could be taught "the self-conquest of restrained emotion" (85).

As his phrasing suggests, Mitchell's model carries strong moral and sexual implications. It is significant that in his hygiene speech, in which he refers to bacteria as "a Pandora's box of pathological disaster," he presents physical health as a requisite for moral goodness. Perfect health is almost a virtue, he asserts, "essential to the attainment of that efficiency which makes duties easy and resistance to temptation a normal result" (1892, 4). On a more general level, "a population below the normal level of health is sure to be also below the norm of goodness" (5). To maintain one's moral health and resist the penetration of evil impulses, he implies, one must maintain one's physical health and resist the penetration of bacteria. In both cases, disorder results from being violated, from allowing oneself to be entered, like a woman.

Although he does not know why, Mitchell is certain that "character is more subject in women than in men to changes physiologically produced" (*RB*, 112). In both sexes the two are interdependent, he believes, but women's greater sensitivity to natural fluctuations makes them more vulnerable to nervous diseases. He speaks often of women's affinity for illness with a sarcastic and misogynistic tone, expressing it more strongly in his novels than in his scientific writings. North declares, in *Characteristics*, that how people bear illness is "a matter of temperament, of moral construction," and he finds that women bear it "too well"; it has been his experience that "to get a man into bed and a woman out of bed is almost equally difficult" (60).[16] In his depiction of Octopia Darnell, above all, Mitchell takes out his hostility against his obstreperous female patients (Rein, 116). Mitchell saw that illness gave some women power, and he sought to wrest this power from them.

Not just any doctor, in Mitchell's eyes, could cure women with nervous diseases. Because the physician had to impose his will upon them, replacing controlling forces that had either never developed or had broken down, the doctor required above all "force of character" (S. W. Mitchell 1884, 62). He was to be "a beneficent despot—beloved and feared" and was to be upheld as a moral authority to his patients (Poirier 1983a, 23; 1983b, 16). Mitchell warned doctors to be on the lookout for the hysterical patient "fatigued by what she hates but not what she likes"; such a woman was to be "control[led] with a firm and steady will" (S. W. Mitchell 1884, 55).

When the doctor tells a patient "you must," subjecting her to his will, she of course resists. Mitchell loathed his patients' ploys for power, and his proud descriptions of how he outwitted malingerers bear a striking resemblance to Doyle's accounts of Sherlock Holmes' triumphs. The ideal doctor, he writes, possesses "alertness in observation, with a never-satisfied desire to know even the trifles of a case" (S. W. Mitchell 1904, 38).[17] The patient who wanted to remain an invalid was both the greatest challenge and the most important one in whom to reconstruct the absent barriers to emotion and desire.

The rest cure aimed to eliminate in advance the patient's capacity for resistance. To restore order in the patient's body and mind, it was essential that she be cut off from all that was familiar and above all from anyone who might confirm her own perceptions of her body and the world around her. She must talk only to the doctor or to paid nurses who upheld his views so as to hear only his version of her life, her body, and her illness. As in traditional brain-washing, Mitchell hoped to alter her thoughts and personality by cutting her off from all intellectual and emotional support. The "cured" woman, constantly reminded of her lapses in duty to others, would arise from bed after gaining thirty pounds, and Mitchell concludes his case histories with triumphant references to marriages and pregnancies. "She has since had a child" stamps the case "closed."[18]

Conclusion: Is Selfhood Control?

Mitchell believed that in restoring their self-control, he gave his patients back the identities they had lost. Suzanne Poirier, however, asserts rightly that the rest cure "allowed for no individuality" (Poirier, 1983b, 35). Only by carefully examining the meaning of individuality and identity can we judge which perspective best describes the relationship between Mitchell and his patients. Mitchell's case studies often remind the reader of exorcisms, in which the doctor-priest struggles for power with emotion-demons that are running wild in a patient's consciousness. The disease, not the patient, is his foe (1983a, 25). If she opposes him, it is the demons talking, for he never associates the "real" identity of the patient with her emotions.

Individuality and identity, for Mitchell, depend on the limited capacity of the living unit to exclude, a property common to cells and to human minds. This exclusion does not mean the erection of an impenetrable barrier against one's surroundings; it means a constant process of interaction, scrutiny, and, when necessary, rejection. Dead or damaged tissue betrays itself through its permeability; just so the diseased mind allows harmful suggestions and its own dangerous emotions to "get through" and command actions that should be controlled by the reasoning will.

For Mitchell, selfhood means not the protective border but the activity at the border, the encounter with one's impulses and the decision of whether to translate them into actions. As a physician, he has no intention of robbing his patients permanently of their individuality, for he aims to teach them that "[they themselves have] some control over [their] symptoms" (S. W. Mitchell 1877, 183). The patients must then resume this controlling role when the doctor passes the burden to them.

If individuality includes the right to challenge social laws and conceptions of "duty," however, then Mitchell's "cure" does mean an extinguishing of individuality. His writings never really question the political and economic laws of his society; they express them in scientific and literary form. It is these laws, ultimately, that crushed the identities of workers, women, children, and non-Westerners during Mitchell's lifetime.

To his credit, Mitchell tried hard to establish a treatment that would take individual personalities into account, and he tried to avoid concocting "universal" laws, always stressing the limits of medical knowledge. In *Fat and Blood*, he wrote that it was "unwise . . . to lay down too absolute laws" (114). Skeptical of early psychological studies, he insisted that "no one can thus convey on paper any useful knowledge of the vast range of human individuality" (1908, 2037). Mitchell's avoidance of drugs, which may ultimately have been the most positive aspect of his rest cure, reflects this dislike of imposing a universal treatment on diverse patients. But the rest cure itself, of course, was largely a standardized regimen.

Besides associating identity with the will and the struggle for self-restraint, Mitchell associated it with the unknown element in people, for he is never certain, when faced with universal instincts and social pressures to conform, what it is that makes individuals differ. Mitchell, however, did not try very hard to probe this unknown element. In particular, he avoided examining the "repressed crude forces" in his patients and characters, most likely following the demands of his culture (Oberndorf, x). Creating from his Civil War experiences with nerve injuries a paradigm on which he would rely throughout his career, Mitchell sought physical causes for nervous disorders, if not obvious, then remote, and he particularly avoided sexuality as an explanation (Rein, 38). Mitchell paid little attention to dreams for the same reason he paid little attention to sexuality: they were a "private" or "personal" matter about which no one wanted to hear. "Dreams are very personal things," explains North in *Characteristics*. "My father always insisted to me when a child that it was bad manners to relate dreams" (15).

Born twenty-seven years before Freud, Mitchell developed a different concept of selfhood because he responded to different cultural needs. He was aware that there is "relief in confession" and even offered the provocative thought that "the mode of putting things is only one of the forms of self defense" (AQ, 10). Like Freud, he saw no sharp distinction between the sick and the well, confessing that "the elements out of which these disorders arise are deeply human, and exist in all of us in varying amount, while many of the determining and conditioning factors come from accidental, or, at least, external agencies" (1881, 51). He considered most of the ideas, in fact, that

Freud would develop into psychoanalytic theory, and he rejected them as unproductive and unscientific.

Raised in a culture that celebrated individuality while demanding self-restraint, self-control, and self-containment, and trained as a physiologist, Mitchell based his concept of selfhood and mental wellness on exclusion. His theory, like his notion of the healthy mind, represses emotions and instincts, and just as sexuality will emerge in a mind that rejects it, it emerges in his writing when he describes pathology as penetration. For Mitchell, to exist as an individual was to resist one's environment and one's own natural inclinations. While never shutting out the surroundings entirely, the borders of the self made identity possible. To be was to determine what one was not, and to reject it.

Santiago Ramón y Cajal

The Neuron and the Net

Man can defend himself only against the enemy that he
knows.   —Santiago Ramón y Cajal

Santiago Ramón y Cajal, Spain's Nobel Prize–winning neurohistologist, is
known for his vision. With his microscopes, Cajal[1] saw nerve cells as intact
morphological units when others did not, and in 1888 he provided the definitive evidence that each neuron was an independent entity. Like Koch, Cajal
succeeded in visualizing boundaries that other scientists could not see partly
because of his painstaking attention to staining and fixing techniques. Also
like Koch, however, he was motivated by an ideological perspective that
became a scientific attitude. Responding to his own experiences and to
Virchow's pathology, he believed that individual cells and human beings
represented the true origin of will, creativity, and regeneration.[2]

Throughout his career, Cajal opposed the theory of a nerve net in which
all neurons merged into a great mesh. He rejected this reticular hypothesis, he
asserted, because of his commitment to reporting scientific truth exactly as he
saw it. To "see" in microscopy, however, is no simple matter. One encounters
complex snarls of cell processes, and one can either accept them as continuous
networks or continue—as Koch did—to perfect one's techniques, presuming
there is more to be seen. The Italian neurobiologist Camillo Golgi, who
invented the staining technique on which Cajal relied, looked at the nerve
terminals and saw a net. Cajal looked at the same images and saw independent
cells. Why?

Cajal's comments suggest that personal values affected what he saw, feeding his desire to resolve structures by pushing the limits of human vision. Following a tradition that can be traced to Aristotle, Cajal believed that intelligence, reason, and memory were possible because of associations, or connections, between cells. But what exactly was a "connection"? Did it imply shared protoplasm, or could distinct, individual cells, separated by their own membranes, form their own associations? Even Virchow, who had led a generation of doctors to view pathology as an alteration of cellular activity, saw the nervous system as a special case in which cells were not physically intact. When Cajal examined vast tangles of processes in 1888, the heyday of the reticular theory, he relied entirely upon his own vision. Like Mitchell, he believed in interaction and resistance, and while he communicated extensively with other scientists, he never accepted their claims without testing them carefully or thinking them through. His stories and essays, like his articles, impart his vision of free, independent cells and people, always in communication yet always with boundaries that defined them as individuals.

As did Mitchell, Cajal believed in willpower and individual initiative because of his own experiences. Born in a poor village in Aragón in 1852, he was "a restless little devil, willful, and unbearable" who loved nature and resisted authority with a passion (Cajal 1989, 6–7). Cajal praises the "will-power" (*energía de voluntad*) of his father, a barber-surgeon who had walked to Barcelona, apprenticed himself, and lived for years in the greatest poverty in order to become a doctor (5). Like Mitchell's, Cajal's father steered him toward medicine, but the rebellious son, who loved art and drawing, resisted. The struggle between them lasted for years. Cajal's father took away the boy's paper and pencils, enrolled him in stricter and stricter schools, apprenticed him to a cobbler, and once even allowed him to spend several days in prison, desperate to impose some control on a boy who loved nature and defied authority. In his autobiography, Cajal presents himself as a "hero of the will" much as Mitchell did, proposing that if he, a rebellious boy and poor student from an impoverished background, was able to transform himself into an eminent scientist through willpower alone, almost anyone could (Tzitsikas, 100).

Cajal first became interested in medicine in 1868 when his father began teaching him anatomy by showing him cadavers, and gradually his interests in art and nature merged. Until this time Cajal—again like Mitchell—had been a poor student because he had seen no point in lessons that required one to memorize theories not grounded in observable facts. "Nature can be understood only by direct study [*contemplación*]," he wrote in his autobiography (Cajal 1989, 144). Never good at memorizing words alone, Cajal asserted that to learn, one must read things, not books. Throughout his career, he would reject any verbal expression that could not be linked to a "clear and vigorous visual perception" (146).[3]

As a young medical student, 1868–73, Cajal responded eagerly to Virchow's vision of the body as a population of individual cells, and this view led to arguments with his vitalist professors. He saw the body in terms of romance and struggle and was particularly interested in its ability to fight infection. After being licensed in medicine in 1873, he was drafted into the army and sent first to the Carlist campaign and then to Cuba. He returned in 1876 after a near-fatal bout with malaria. Working with his father in Zaragoza, he began preparing for the challenging competition for an academic chair in medicine. In 1877, inspired by the work of Maestre de San Juan and López García in Madrid, he set up his first microscopy laboratory. He obtained an academic position in Zaragoza in 1879 and in 1883 accepted a more prestigious chair of anatomy in Valencia (*DSB* 11:273–76).

During his years in Valencia, 1883–87, Cajal joined the quest to prepare vaccines against microbes that caused infectious diseases. In 1885 when a cholera epidemic broke out, he was asked to assess Ferrán's vaccine, which the Spanish bacteriologist had been developing ever since Koch had identified the comma bacillus (López Piñero, 18). It is significant that as he was drawn toward microbes, Cajal also became interested in hypnotism and suggestion. He turned away from both fields in 1888, however, to focus entirely on neuronal structure. He moved on to a chair of histology in Barcelona and finally, in 1892, to a prestigious chair in histology and pathological anatomy in Madrid, which he held for thirty years (*DSB* 11:273). He continued to refer to infection and suggestion for the rest of his life, however, often employing them to describe the dissemination of unwanted ideas.

While studying the transient forms of Koch's comma bacillus, Cajal wrote some imaginative stories. He had already used fiction to play with scientific ideas, composing two adventure novels in the early 1870s. One had involved a Robinson Crusoe–like protagonist who discovered an uncharted island; the other, an explorer who entered the bloodstream of gigantic beings on Jupiter and experienced their bodies from the perspective of a microbe. Unfortunately, both have been lost (Benítez, 29). During 1885 and 1886, Cajal wrote twelve *Cuentos de vacaciones* (Vacation stories), of which he decided to publish only five, in 1905. Bringing to life the problems of infection, suggestion, will, perception, and language, Cajal's stories raise issues that were already disturbing him in the laboratory but which would not be resolved or articulated in his scientific writing until much later.

Almost all of Cajal's stories explore the basis of personal identity, which is repeatedly associated—as in Mitchell's fiction—with fending off dangerous suggestions. For Cajal, as for Mitchell, the best defense against such invasions is the individual will, which can be developed only when a person overcomes outside influences and rallies his or her own mental forces. Written in scientific terms, yet with an irony inadmissible in scientific writing, Cajal's "Vacation stories" provide a "vacation" for the writer as well as the reader, a much-needed opportunity to play. Written two or three years before he proved neurons were independent, but edited seventeen years afterward, they offer a framework through which one can study his developing ideas on the cell and the self.

"For a Secret Offense, a Secret Revenge":
The Dangers of Infection

At the age of twelve, Cajal was locked in prison for one of his more dangerous pranks and found himself looking at a vermin-filled pile of straw on which he would have to spend the next several nights. "This effervescence of hungry life [*hervor de vida hambrienta*] filled my mind with dread [*pavor*]," he wrote in his autobiography (1989, 72). More than forty years later, describing diseases in the Gulf of Guinea, Cajal expressed this fear in much the same terms. The African colony, he wrote, was "a dense microbial hatchery, a promised land for all pathogenic agents. . . . an obstinately hostile environment, where everything is an enemy, because everything is life" (1910, 9–10).[4] Like the African natives, their very status as living beings presented a threat, since they might succeed in launching a "secret offense" of infection before the European invaders could develop the "secret revenge" of a vaccine. Cajal's writings, literary and scientific, express the horror that microbes aroused in their potential hosts, a horror of life that thoughtlessly devours life, of life that effortlessly violates the boundaries of the individual.

As a scientist trained during the microbial era, Cajal was passionately committed to the struggle against infectious diseases. In the preface to Vicente y Charpentier's *Desinfección doméstica* (1901), he presented the fight against germs as an all-out war. Expressing a particular concern for the workers of Madrid, he wrote that the dark, damp tenements in which they were forced to live provided ideal growing conditions for bacteria, so that they subsisted "in an environment teeming with enemies" (vi). The microbe, wrote Vicente y Charpentier, "surrounds the individual, pursues him without rest . . . introducing itself so easily into the organism" (Vicente y Charpentier, 2, 6).[5] Routinely, he used the word "invasion" for "infection." When microbes "invaded," they—the simplest form of life—could defeat the most highly evolved and complex.

Even though Cajal regarded microbes as a force to be resisted, his rich visual imagination allowed him to view the universe from the bacteria's perspective. His lost novel of 1871, written before Pasteur's theories were generally known and accepted, presented the explorer as an invasive particle in the body of a larger being. "Our explorer was only the size of a microbe," he wrote in his autobiography. "and was therefore invisible."[6] The protagonist eventually went on to the brain to discover "the secret of thought and of the voluntary impulse" (Cajal 1989, 182). Cajal's "Vacation stories" return to the microbial perspective to learn the same secret.

In Cajal's first story, "A secreto agravio, secreto venganza" (For a secret offense, a secret revenge), the eminent bacteriologist Max von Forschung (Max Research, in German) marries an attractive young American, Emma Sanderson. Discovering a new microbe every six months, or, in the absence of a new discovery, discrediting other scientists' microbes, Forschung has reached the age of fifty.[7] From the opening of the story, Forschung's life is inseparable from that of the microbes he studies, and the narrator describes both in the same scientific terms. The couple spend their honeymoon searching for new microbes in the Middle East, and, after the appropriate incubation period, they produce two new "bacilli," one bacterial and one human: "the gallant and spirited collaborator brought forth a new microbe, that is to say, a beautiful and robust baby boy, as incubated to the end by the burning sun of Palestine. . . . Needless to say the new offshoot received the name of Max, and the microbe [they had discovered] that of the bacillus *Sandersonni*" (Cajal 1964, 14).[8] The scientists and the microbes share the same names, as did the author, who originally signed the work "Doctor Bacteria."

In Cajal's story, human sexuality proves to be the microbe that the scientist does not see. Forschung has led an ascetic existence and ironically fails to recognize his own vulnerability in reproductive processes over which he imagines he has complete control. When he first meets Emma, he is "inoculated with the terrible toxin of love," an invasion that will be mirrored by his subsequent revenge (Cajal 1964, 12). The very fact of becoming connected to a woman is presented as a violation, an insult that must be avenged. As a man, he will penetrate his wife as he visually penetrates the bacteria's world. From his perspective, however, it is his life that has been penetrated, and this incursion will be his downfall.

The microbial matrimony goes well until Forschung, "working in isolation in his laboratory," encounters a hint that Emma is betraying him with his younger assistant, Heinrich Mosser: two hairs intertwined in a loving embrace on a microscope slide (Cajal 1964 17). Forschung's tragic flaw is his inability to see—and to interpret—living organisms properly. As a human being, Forschung is both a natural and a social creature, possessed of an independent will but connected to his coworkers and to the organisms he studies. The narrator stresses these affinities by describing relationships between people with the language of science. Even the lovers' hypothetical kiss, envisioned by Forschung who perceives everything with the eyes of a bacteriologist, is presented in hygienic terms, the narrator pointing out the danger of establishing contact with a mouth that has not been disinfected.

Forschung's mistakes indicate that gaining control over the invisible requires not just a penetrating gaze but intelligent interpretation and unbiased judgment, both of which the great bacteriologist lacks. He confirms his hypothesis of adultery by rigging a seismographic device to the laboratory couch and, in a hilarious passage, examining the graphic representation of the erotic encounter. Although successful, his attempt to turn biology into writing and thereby gain control over it is laughable, even pathetic.[9] With visual evidence of the formerly invisible affront, Forschung vows revenge that will be equally hard to detect.

Forschung's "secret revenge," a violation of boundaries, reproduces the original crime. In Cajal's story, the aging scientist has been involved in debates with Koch, who claims that there are several tuberculosis bacilli and that the human bacillus cannot produce tuberculosis in other animals.[10] Forschung believes that one single bacillus affects all animals alike. He has been unable to fulfill Koch's third postulate, however, and produce the disease by injecting the microbe into a healthy animal; no human animals volunteered for such experiments. Less scrupulous than Koch, Forschung decides to test his hypothesis by infecting Emma and Mosser with bovine tuberculosis bacillus. The wife and her lover both develop the disease, and Mosser dies, proving Forschung correct.

By arguing for the common susceptibility of higher animals to the same microorganism, Forschung demonstrates the very biological affinities between people and animals that he denies in exacting revenge. His wife is driven by fundamental sexual forces, and, isolating himself in his laboratory, he has neglected her needs. The narrator openly opposes Forschung's stance, calling the secret experiment "vile." No model scientist, Forschung represents the danger in science of "working in isolation" and thus developing illusions about one's own power (Pratt 1995, 123). To see well, the scientists need to acknowledge their ties to other people and to other forms of life and to question their interpretive powers.

Eventually, Forschung and his wife repent their transgressions. Working incessantly, the bacteriologist develops a cure for Emma's tuberculosis, and she returns to him and their microbes. To solve the problem of adultery permanently, however, Forschung seeks a serum that will eliminate the "dangerous beauty" of young women, aging their bodies twenty years without diminishing their mental capacities. He tests his age serum, *senilina*, on a group of syphilitic prostitutes, with highly satisfactory results. In response to government demand, Forschung goes on to produce a modified *senilina, antifreniatina* , which creates true premature senility. Originally administered to criminals, the new serum proves to be a "marvelous sedative of the will" (Cajal 1964, 51). Sociologists recommend that the serum be given to the poor and to natives of Central Africa—to any hungry group, that is, that might rebel against the social order.

Cajal's conclusion mocks the desire for a scientific panacea for all social problems. His irony indicates his disapproval—like Virchow's—of any scheme for social change based on authoritarian mandates rather than individual initiative. Critics have questioned his inclusion of the *senilina-antifreniatina* episode, wondering why Cajal did not end the story with the restoration of Forschung's marriage, but it is a vital part of the narrative (Tzitsikas, 35–36). Forschung's perverse determination to avenge his young wife's infidelity—a breach for which he was partly responsible—mirrors the government's determination to inoculate unruly groups, for both are attempts to deny or kill off "hungry life." Cajal's poverty and his work with bacteria made it clear to him that autonomy did not mean isolation and that hungry people and other organisms were always already a part of the ministries and laboratories built to control them. Forschung's secret offense and secret revenge raise the question, as Virchow did late in his career, of how far the microbe-antiserum paradigm can be carried as a solution to medical and social problems.

Cajal, however, still enjoyed the challenge that invisible microbes presented. The greatest threat of infectious bacteria was that they could enter human beings unobserved; if rendered visible, they could eventually be defeated. Again and again in his preface to Desinfección *doméstica,* Cajal stressed the danger of an enemy that could not be seen. He called microbes "millions of tiny beings, of invisible poisoners" and "the invisible enemy of the human race" (1901, vi, vii). Like Koch, he envisioned a heroic army of health workers analogous to the police who sought hidden criminals, "soldiers destined to shelter us from the formidable gang of poisoning microbes, that lie in wait, traitorously hidden in the invisible" (x). The crux of his argument is that "man can defend himself only against the enemy that he knows" (vii).[11] For Cajal, the enemy to be resisted was not so much the microbes as invisibility itself. Microbes were difficult to see, but with effort and willpower, the scientist could render them visible. His rage against those who dismissed a tangle of individual cell processes as a net becomes more understandable when one reads these aggressive vows to visualize microbes that escaped most people's gaze.

From Cells to Consciousness

For Cajal, the fundamental characteristic of every cell and every human being was its individuality, made possible by the membrane that separated one living unit from the next. Even before he had tried microscopy, the idea of the cell as an independent unit had appealed to him. The great achievement of Turpin, he wrote, had been to see the cell not as a crystal, "but as a living being, with its own autonomy, associated with other beings as tiny as itself" (1904, 147).[12] He had devoured Virchow's descriptions of the cell as "an autonomous living being, the exclusive actor [*protagonista*] in pathological events" (1989, 175). Because of the elaborate arborizations of cells and the contacts between them, that individuality was not always obvious, but in general it held true. "Each element is an absolutely autonomous physiological canton," he wrote about the neurons he observed in the retina of birds (1888, 314).[13] According to Pedro Laín Entralgo, Cajal's idea of the anatomic unity of the cell led him to believe in physiological and psychological independence, but simultaneous analysis of his creative and scientific writing indicates that the notions developed concurrently, feeding and encouraging each other (Laín Entralgo, 288).

The success of microbes, which resembled human cells in so many ways, encouraged Cajal and others to view cells as independent units. Explaining why cut nerves degenerated after part of the cell lost contact with the nucleus, he asserted, "Anything that happen[s] in the unicellular organisms occur[s] in the neuron!" (Loewy, 24). When he discusses nerve cells, his repeated references to microbes convey the notion of independence in a familiar sense, comparing the behavior of the newly identified "individuals" to that of better known autonomous beings.

This similarity between unicellular organisms and the units of their multicellular hosts suggested a phylogenetic affinity. It could be that human cells, which occasionally behaved like amoebae, were the descendants of unicellular ancestors. Although Cajal remained cautious about such speculation, he relied on this resemblance as evidence for the functional independence of neurons and other specialized cells. Leukocytes, white blood cells that roamed freely through the circulatory and lymphatic systems and fought off invaders, intrigued him because they constituted a sort of missing link. In his lost novel, he had taken pains to describe the "epic struggles between leukocytes and parasites" (Cajal 1989, 182). Leukocytes, he wrote, "have conserved, and perhaps perfected, the habit of hunting foreign bodies," and he praised their "vital autonomy" (1904, 195, 151).[14] Leukocytes are especially known for their amoeboid behavior, the ability to move by sending out and withdrawing pseudopods (protuberances of their protoplasm and flexible membranes). In Cajal's writing, "amoeboid" becomes a code word for the autonomy of cells. He compares the progress of a regenerating neuron, for instance, to "the double movement of expansion and retraction of the pseudopods of a leukocyte" (1913, 365).

This ability of cells to move, to respond, and to act independently, observed early in his career in unicellular organisms, would play an essential role in Cajal's conception of consciousness. Ten years after Cajal established the independence of nerve cells, he became interested in a theory of anatomist Matthias Duval's that glial cells (non-conducting cells associated with the nervous system) and perhaps neurons themselves could send out and withdraw processes in an amoeboid fashion (Cajal 1895, 3–14). Intelligent thought appeared to depend on the formation and maintenance of associations between cells, and also upon the level of mental activity. If neurons were truly independent, the analogy to amoebae would provide a mechanism by which they might selectively form new connections based upon their activity.

As Cajal's anatomical studies showed him, the most essential characteristic of neurons in the brain was that their structure was not fixed. If Duval were right, then people could shape their own minds through force of will because the independent cells could change their form according to activities under human control. The "continuous amoeboid behavior" of neurons might account for a great variety of mental phenomena including sleep, dreams, and hypnotism. Duval had proposed that in a sleeping person, neuronal processes were withdrawn "like the pseudopods of an anesthetized leukocyte" (Cajal 1899, 1142). Cajal had reservations about Duval's hypothesis but felt a "great sympathy" for it because it explained mental activity on the level of individual, independent cells (1146).

Cajal's notion of the ideal scientific mind reflects his concept of the cell. In his *Reglas y consejos para la investigación científica* (*Precepts and counsels for scientific investigation*, 1897), Cajal lists "mental independence" and originality as the most essential characteristics of the astute scientist. To become skilled researchers, he proposes, we need to "shape [*forjarnos*] a strong brain, an original mind exclusively ours (1953, 34, 111). The ability to think for oneself, however, does not mean the refusal to listen to others. Just as the independent cell survives not by sealing itself off, but by resisting its environment, the scientist's mind should be semi-permeable, neither wide open nor completely closed. The investigator's self-reliance and resistance to suggestion must never degenerate into rampant egotism and isolation, and Forschung's great weakness is his tendency to work "isolated in his laboratory." Investigators like Forschung may have original thoughts, but they are forever linked to all other human beings. They will think best if they acknowledge these connections.

The issue of connections and associations is one of the most fascinating that arises in Cajal's work. In the last year of his life, he stated that learning "the true relations" of neurons with each other was one of the principal goals of his career. He began his review article, "Conexión general de los elementos nerviosos" (The general connection of the nervous elements, 1889), by stating: "One of the most interesting problems in anatomy is the determination of the way that the cells of the centers are related to one another. . . . Is this connection realized through contiguity, that is to say, through simple contacts between cellular expansions, or rather by means of an anastomosis?" (1924, 479).[15] To what degree are cells connected, he asked in a later review, if a membrane separates them: "Does the naked protoplasm of the cells really touch, or do delimiting membranes exist between the two elements of the synapse?" (1933, 229).[16] Even though the identity of the cell depended on the distinction between inside and outside, the very function and existence of neurons depended on outside influences: on inputs from other cells and from the environment.

Like Mitchell, Cajal conceived of life and mental activity as interactions among autonomous units. Neurons and individuals influenced one another yet retained their identities as distinct beings. At what point, however, does the presence of influence mean the loss of autonomy? The writings of both physician-authors raise the same powerful question: to what extent can outside suggestions infringe on identity?

"The Fabricator of Honor": The Dangers of Suggestion

Cajal's comparisons of unicellular organisms, neurons, and individual human minds encourage related metaphors in which human ideas are transmitted like microbes. Associations between minds always introduced certain risks, for contact brought with it the possibility of unwanted penetration. Throughout his writings, Cajal explores the parallels between cellular and mental autonomy by using bacterial infection as a way to represent the spread of undesirable ideas. Could hidden, infectious thoughts be exposed as easily as hidden, infectious microorganisms?

In *Precepts and Counsels for Scientific Investigation* Cajal confessed that he had suffered from "poetic measles" in his youth, referring to his early romantic ambitions not grounded in any carefully formulated plan of action. To maintain good mental hygiene, he claimed, it was necessary to fend off unhealthy thoughts just as one might "fight" a biological infection. "Let us flee from pessimism," he wrote in the conclusion, "as we would flee from a deadly virus."[17] Cajal, like Mitchell, lets his characters voice his most subversive analogies, and one materialistic intellectual in "The accursed house" proposes that "the idea of the soul is a tenacious parasite . . . The spiritual bacillus . . . enjoys a powerful toxicity" (1964, 139).[18] Cajal even has one character suggest, in a later story, that hungry life took its secret revenge on Hegel for propounding a negative and impracticable philosophy: "Hegel, the prodigious sophist who paralyzed with the toxin of Idea the positive philosophical analysis initiated by Kant, succumbed, poisoned by the *vírgula* bacillus of cholera" (159).[19] Emma's misguided belief in love in the first story, "sickly and dangerous romanticism," is presented as just one more infection that can be fought through willpower and reason (44). Forschung can finally rejoin his wife because he can dismiss her love for Mosser as "a simple effect of suggestion . . . once the hypnotist had disappeared, the enchantment ended" (37).[20] One sees the affinity between infection and suggestion as Cajal compares human passion to both.

Cajal does not compare all ideas to infectious bacteria, only those dangerous suggestions that oppose the voice of reason: philosophical pessimism, religious mysticism, intense emotion, and uncontrolled sexual desire. Like Mitchell, he believes that these irrational impulses can do to the mind what bacteria do to the body. In his first story, Emma—a foreign woman—becomes the focal point in the exchange of unwanted microbes and desires. Forschung's life is penetrated when he "catches" his passion for her. Open to implantations, she is easily infected with a suggestion from Mosser, and Forschung's life degenerates because by establishing a connection with Emma, he has opened himself to everyone to whom she is open. While Cajal posits associations as crucial to human thought, he suggests that connections to a female are risky: they threaten to undermine one's resistance by linking one to a cell whose resistance is considerably weaker. In Cajal's second story, to explain why women yield to hypnotists more easily than men do, the narrator quotes a Madame Necker de Saussure, who states that woman " 'possesses a *self* weaker than that of the man,' a *self* that feels frail and instinctively searches for force of will" (Cajal 1964, 56).[21] To have a weak will is to have a weak sense of identity, and women are generally deficient in both.

Cajal wrote the "Vacation stories" during his years in Valencia when he was most interested in hypnotism. The growing field, enormously popular in the mid-1880s, attracted him because it indicated how external influence might shape one's identity. In one patient, Cajal used hypnotic suggestion to alleviate pain. In an 1889 case study, he described how he hypnotized a mother of five, a "lymphatic-sanguine type," who was terrified of the pains of childbirth. Cajal told the woman that her contractions would be strong but not painful, and the delivery went as he had ordered (Cajal 1924, 447). In this case, the nerves that communicated painful sensations seemed to have been selectively shut down, while those that carried motor impulses had remained active. Even at the cellular level of perception, there appeared to be room for adjustment from the individual mind. An individual actively produced his or her perceptions, and a mind confronted with suggestions could still produce original thoughts.

Several years before he published his article on hypnotism, Cajal toyed with its possibilities in his second "vacation story," "El fabricante de honra-dez" (The fabricator of honor). Like "A secreto agravio, secreto venganza" the tale is ironic and extremely amusing. The main character, Alejandro Mirahonda (either Deep look or Looks deep) caricatures a particular scientific attitude, much as Max von Forschung had parodied modern bacteriologists in the first story. Although Cajal presents Mirahonda as a modern hypnotist, "a disciple of Bernheim and Forel," he describes him in eighteenth-century terms.[22] Mirahonda possesses "nervous batteries of great capacity and tension," eyes that emit "magnetic effluvia," and an "iron and insuperable will" (1964, 55).[23] Mirahonda practices in Villabronca (Rough town), which suffers from an excess of drunken brawls, robberies, and infractions against authority. Why not, he asks himself one day, try to cure moral complaints in his clinic as well as physical ones?

He produces a serum that will remove all desire to sin, eliminating all antisocial tendencies. Most of the townspeople welcome his serum; his opponents are the priest, who believes the plan violates the theological doctrine of free will, and the anarchists, who fear it will reconcile the proletariat and the bourgeoisie. In his defense, Mirahonda asserts Hippolyte Bernheim's view that people are constantly influenced by the formulaic language they encounter in their everyday lives. Associated with veils and texts, language often seems for Cajal to be another "net" restricting individual identity.

Mirahonda calls Villabroncan society "a lukewarm, shaky, and frivolous moral atmosphere formed by blurry and contradictory suggestions from parents, teachers, and friends" (Cajal 1964, 68).[24] He diagnoses in the townspeople the state of consciousness that Mitchell most sought to avoid in his patients, the passive acceptance of any outside thought or impulse in the absence of a strong will. The narrator, who appears to share his view, adds that many people are still terrorized by demons, gods, and miracles, also the products of suggestion. Together, their descriptions present a society at risk, a population of minds susceptible to invasion and external control.

Raised with the notion of free will, argues Mirahonda, people fail to see that all religious and political ideas are imposed: "The most effective helper of the mental orthopedist is the crass ignorance of the common people about the sovereign power of suggestion" (Cajal 1964,70).[25] He proposes that hypnotists might actually do society a favor by "cleaning up the rust of heredity and routine and imposing ideas and feelings that conform to the ends of society . . . reeducating the will" (68–69).[26] Like Forschung, he is simultaneously right and wrong: correct in his diagnosis of vulnerability; mistaken in his plan to correct weakness by imposing his own systematized order.

Mirahonda convinces the Villabroncans to try his "anti-passion vaccine," which proves all too successful. The people are "transformed into automata, into moral machines." Arguments cease, and the political bosses are in danger of having to work for a living. Without vice as reference point, virtue loses its meaning: "in a town of saints, what could honor be worth?" (Cajal 1964, 75, 79).[27] Finally, in response to demand, Mirahonda develops a "passion antitoxin" which works beautifully even though it is tap water, returning the townspeople to their original state. The hypnotist analyzes his results in the prestigious *Zeitschrift für Hypnotismus*, writing that "the possibility of reeducating the people by means of suggestion is a firmly established fact" (85).[28]

In Cajal's fictional context, suggestion has removed the ills essential for social progress. While some imposed thoughts were necessary to keep people in order, the "semisuggestion of authority, religion, and discipline" worked better than that of far-seeing hypnotists because it allowed people to grow by struggling against the evils their society created (Cajal 1964, 89, Tzitsikas, 47). In Cajal's view, as in Virchow's, one does not restore individual control by imposing centralized control; one restores it by encouraging individual development.

As a scientist, Cajal fought vigorously against the suggestive power of authoritative theories to influence his vision. The opening of his textbook *Textura del sistema nervioso del hombre y de los vertebrados* (Histology of the nervous system of humans and other vertebrates, 1899) describes the reticular theory as a hypnotic suggestion, presenting it as a tyrant to be overthrown in order to maintain the individual freedom of the cell and the scientist. Using Mitchell's terminology, Cajal declared that "theories are the despots of science" (1:23). "Once alternative methods with greater resolving power are introduced," he promised, "the preconceived idea is no longer our mistress, tantalizing with whatever she wishes to disclose in our preparations. The strange mirage vanishes and the reigning hypothesis [*la fuerza sugestiva de las hipótesis reinantes*] is toppled from its throne" (1:24). Cajal was hardest on Golgi, whose methodology he knew was sound and who must therefore have been misguided by an attitude or idea. In reality, Cajal asserted, Gerlach and Golgi *saw* independent cellular structures in their preparations, but because of cultural prejudices, "seduced by the presumed necessity of continuous structure, they then *supposed* the existence of an anastomotic net between the dendrites and the axis cylinders" (Laín Entralgo, 310).[29] Cajal viewed the nerve net hypothesis as an easy solution that appealed to weak-willed scientists, writing that "for certain spirits, the reticular theory offers seductions and extraordinary explanatory conveniences" (1933, 217).[30] Something other than the desire to see clearly was motivating their vision.

Cajal's description of the reticular hypothesis as a seductive mistress indicates a contempt that runs deeper than simple scientific disapproval. Depicting the idea as a force that permeates one's mind and clouds one's vision, he hates the nerve net theory as he hates—and fears—authoritative suggestion itself. An investigator could overcome such prejudices, perfecting his or her methods and trusting his or her own vision, but scientific progress demanded a vast network of communications among individuals. The great challenge of neuroanatomy was to listen receptively to others without letting their vision determine what one saw. To young scientists, concerned that their bibliographic searches would open them to suggestion, Cajal replied that one should always keep oneself apprised of other scientists' results. He warned against the "products of self-suggestion that resulted from poor microscopic images," but he knew that science could not be carried on without the exchange of ideas, some of them bad (Loewy, 15). Mitchell had presented social interaction as a key element in the development of willpower, and Cajal agreed. To learn how to resist, one must confront ideas constantly; one must *think*. The resisting will, the semi-permeable membrane that made identity possible, could be maintained only through vigorous mental activity, especially thinking that questioned authority.

"The Accursed House": The Development of Individual Will

Cajal felt that "The accursed house," the third of his "Vacation stories" and the one that most clearly deals with the notion of will, was the best of the five he published. Julián, the protagonist, studied medicine in Spain but emigrated to Mexico to earn enough money to marry his beloved, Inés. As the story opens, he is about to return to Spain from the New World where he has prospered as a doctor and bacteriologist. He has made a fortune but loses it in a shipwreck. His observation of nature saves him from despair, however, and he vows: "Let us follow the example of nature . . . that irresistible ardor of the germ cells to fuse two existences in the burning kiss of conception . . . there are only two serious realities in the world: *to struggle to live, and to live to love*" (Cajal 1964, 99).[31]

The mother country, it turns out, desperately needs such clear-sighted heroes and heroines. A great challenge awaits their rational gaze: a bacterial plague with a foreign source. In Villaencumbrada (Lofty town), Julián discovers an abandoned homestead known to locals as the "accursed house". The original owner, "a heretic or Protestant millionaire"—an Englishman or German from the Antilles—died of an unknown disease, as did two of his children. The subsequent owner, a "rich Indian," built the estate into "an agricultural colony," but soon widespread bacterial infections broke out, and the owner perished along with two of his daughters and much of his livestock (Cajal 1964, 102). A third owner, a cynical freethinker, was bold enough to move into the estate but fled after his child died and he himself fell gravely ill. Inspired by the great red spots that periodically appeared on the house and grounds, "popular superstition had embroidered on that foundation of tragic realities shadowy and ominous legends" (103).[32] Created by colonials in the mother country, the accursed house is a bacterial "colony" established by foreigners, and it awaits a strong-willed native who can purify the site of infection.

Julián, who has already triumphed in Spain's former colonies, is eminently qualified to reconquer the accursed house. The infested estate, in fact, may symbolize Spain itself. The narrator uses the term *reconquista* to describe his mission, the standard word for the eight-hundred-year struggle of the Christians to remove the Islamic invaders from Spain (Cajal 1964, 104). To begin his *reconquista*, Julián sets up a bacteriological laboratory and begins seeking natural causes for the former owners' deaths.

In this story, as in much of late nineteenth-century literature, the old miasma theory meets the new microbial paradigm, for both environment and bacteria have contributed to the "curse." It has arisen through a collaboration of foreign parasites and receptive domestic conditions. Local mosquitoes, infected by malaria parasites introduced by the first foreign owner, have bred in nearby pools and spread the disease. Julián explains that "the focus of infection, purely local, created here, was imported by the English family" (Cajal 1964, 108).[33] Cajal even has him cite a medical reference to support his hypothesis. Typhoid bacteria have been flourishing in the homestead's groundwater, and parasites from cattle that perished in the pasture have been reinfecting those that graze there. This juxtaposition of malaria, typhoid, and anthrax reflects coverage of microorganisms in the medical journals of 1885, which Cajal, still working with bacteria at the time, was no doubt perusing.

Julián refers to the causes of the "curse," collectively, as "a simple conse-quence of the natural conditions of terrain and environment, easy to elimi-nate with a little science and good will" (Cajal 1964, 106).[34] In creating the epidemic, he declares, "neither God, nor the devil have taken part, but the microbe, an invisible demon . . . the microbes of today are the devils of yesterday" (109, 111).[35] As a bacteriologist reclaiming the devil's territory, he acts as a "colonial" missionary.

An inverse colonial, Julián comes from a colony to reconquer the mother country. Retracing the path of those who infected it, he is filled with energy and prepared to instruct the heathen with his trinity of will-power, science, and natural law. The colonies, which provide both these bacterial devils and their exorcist, play a dual role in Cajal's story. On the one hand, they have furnished an environment for Julián to develop his strength of will and to distinguish himself as an individual; on the other, they are the source of the diseases he is fighting (except for typhoid fever, which is endemic to Europe). Julián systematically identifies and defeats the bacteria. As natural stock re-grafted onto itself, he has triumphed over the curse by allowing people to see it for what it really is.

Once Julián has conquered the "curse," the narrative focuses on his woo-ing of Inés, another *reconquista*. As he did with Forschung and Emma, the narrator describes love on the cellular level.[36] By presenting love as physiol-ogy, Cajal reminds readers that everything human has biological as well as social roots, and speaking of love with the language of science creates an irony that reveals the repressed biological ones. The narrator apologizes that he must describe love in terms of cellular activity but explains that "the dictionary of emotion is poorer than that of ideas" (Cajal 1964, 120).[37] In Cajal's fiction, the language of science "colonizes" territory once left to romantic rhetoric. Both Julián's will and his love, rooted in natural impulses, have their basis at the cellular level.

Cajal's rejection of aimless speculation prevented him from assigning complex functions to particular cell groups, but his scientific articles as well as his literature suggest that he, like Mitchell, saw will as having an organic, cellular basis. In his creative writing, the idea emerges in playful metaphors. In "The accursed house," referring to Duval's idea that mental exercise stimulates neurons to form new connections, one intellectual comments to another, "you've remained a bit *spherical*, like an *amoeba* exposed to chloroform that retracts its pseudopods" (Cajal 1964, 134).[38] In his Croonian Lecture of 1894, Cajal expresses a special interest in cell layers where sensory impulses elicit voluntary motor impulses. While he makes no attempt to associate will with any particular region, he is clearly intrigued by the problem of where and how voluntary muscular activity originates.

In conceiving of will as organic, closely related to neuronal activity and personal identity, Cajal concurred with many psychologists besides Mitchell. Théodule Ribot, whose attempts to describe memory, attention, and will as biological phenomena were well-known in the European scientific community, had presented will in terms of physiology in *Diseases of the Will* (1883). Rather than stimulating action, Ribot argued, will was stifling counterproductive impulses, and the ability to focus one's attention was actually a process of inhibition. He viewed will not as desire but as a screening of desire which let a mind maintain its identity and direction.

Like Mitchell and Cajal, Ribot concluded that the breakdown of the will was tied to a breakdown of the sense of self. "In fickle natures," he explained, "the willing ego [*le moi voulant*] is so unstable a compound that . . . the part played by individual character is a minimum, the share of the external circumstances a maximum" (Ribot, 27). Since intelligence, perceptions, and motor activity were intact, the disruption appeared to occur at the level at which perceptions gave rise to actions. As the motor states corresponding to perceptions and desires broke down, so did the boundaries of self. "Which is the real me," asks a desperate patient, "the one who acts or the one who resists?" (85).[39] Mitchell, observing patients at the same time, would have told him he was the self who resisted, and Cajal's stories and scientific writing suggest he would have responded the same way.

Both Cajal and Mitchell were optimists, and both were certain that weak wills could be resurrected, even in women (Pratt 1995, 96). Cajal believed the will operated on a cellular basis because—as is evident in his comparisons of neurons to amoebae and leukocytes—he knew that individual neurons could form new connections. Although no new neurons were produced in the mature brain, its structure was anything but fixed. Ribot had commented that "all organs are developed with exercise," and Cajal made the same argument in his *Precepts and Counsels for Scientific Investigation* (Ribot, 68). Originally, he had entitled the work *Los tónicos de la voluntad* (*Stimulants of the Spirit*, or, more literally, *A Tonic for the Will*). Intelligent thinking, which relies on the formation and maintenance of associations between neurons, could only be achieved through hard work, and the laboratory, with its demands for disciplined action and original thinking, was "an incomparable cure for the straying of the attention and the faintness of the will" (Cajal 1953, 102).[40] Hinting that mental exercise could make the processes of neurons grow and form new connections, he warned that one must develop the habit of hard work early, before "the plasticity of the nerve cells is almost completely suspended" (46). While Cajal's model of the brain traced will and intelligence to cellular activity, like Mitchell, he was no determinist, placing responsibility on the individual for the development and upkeep of his or her own mind. "Each man can be . . . the sculptor of his own brain," he declared (13).[41] A diseased will could cure itself if its bearer changed his or her way of seeing.

"The Corrected Pessimist": Seeing for Oneself

Cajal's fourth story introduces the reader to the scientist's greatest challenge and greatest joy: achieving a truly personal vision of nature. S. Weir Mitchell, describing a character's microscopical studies in *In War Time* (1884), had written that "if our eyes were microscopes and our ears were audiophones, life would be one long misery" (1902, 89). Struck by the same thought a year or two earlier, Cajal explored it in "El pesimista corregido" (The corrected pessimist), his fourth "vacation story." Through the unhappy Juan Fernández, whose eyes acquire the power of microscopes, the reader can see the world as Cajal sees it in his laboratory (Tzitsikas, 56; Benítez, 28). Philosophically provocative, the story raises the same question as Cajal's scientific studies: What is "true" vision? Fernández's microscopic vision is an altered way of seeing made possible only through artificial means, yet the story suggests that "normal" human vision, which fails to see so much, is the vision really based on repression and illusion. Perhaps the finest work in the collection, it is a richly imaginative story. The overwhelming vision of nature just as it is "corrects" Fernández's pessimism and offers to do the same for the reader.

Fernández, a young doctor, has recently lost his mother to a pulmonary infection; his father to tuberculosis, and an academic chair in Madrid to another candidate. He is struggling with typhoid fever and has taken to reading Nietzsche, Schopenhauer, and von Hartmann. Again, the narrator relies on physiology to describe his mental state. Indicating biological potential for improvement, Fernández's brain is "as rich in neuronal *collaterals* as it [is] impregnated with melancholy images" (Cajal 1964, 156). As far as he can see, nature is all pain, all destruction, and people are unfit for the struggles for life in which they must engage. He bemoans the senselessness of nature which, "without distinguishing the genius from the microbe, . . . contents itself in destroying life with life." Why, he asks, did God create microbes, "the enemies of life, the insidious and cruel pathogenic bacteria?" (158–59).[42] Suddenly, a wizard materializes and attempts to comfort Fernández by explaining the positive role that bacteria play in "the economy of nature." The protagonist, however, remains unconvinced. He must see it for himself.

When he awakens, Fernández sees everything magnified a thousand times or more. He is at first unable to associate meaning with the unfamiliar visions, for he "does not see objects as larger, but as more detailed" (Cajal 1964, 172). Fernández's microscopic vision decomposes the world, robbing objects of their unity even as it reveals their component particles. He can see microbes and cinders, "the detritus of life high and low," and in the swirl of particles, all objects lose their forms so that he feels he is "witnessing the dissolution of a world whose elements had regressed to the primordial chaos" (173).[43] The greatest horror of his vision is its destruction of the outlines and the apparent intactness of things, which are now revealed as the illusions of those who do not see sufficiently. He confronts objects transformed into mosaics, all of which look similar. Like cells and minds, they lose their identities when they lose their borders.

So that the reader can appreciate the many illusions society uses to mask biological reality, Cajal sends his protagonist on a walk through Madrid. When Fernández looks at people, he notes that "the differences of lineage, race, and profession had disappeared as if by magic" (Cajal 1964, 177).[44] He cannot tell a beautiful woman from an ugly one. The microbes, which he can now observe, resemble him in their inability to recognize the differences between people, and he is forced to look on as they jump from one unknowing host to the next. Finally, the microscopic vision robs art of its beauty and meaning, and Fernández, wandering through the Prado Museum, notes that "art is less resistant to analysis than is nature" (182).[45] His tour of the city reveals that most boundaries and hence identities are created by society, forcibly imposed on a richer and more complex biological reality.

One would think that this realization might drive the pessimist to suicide, but instead it "corrects" his faulty vision. Even though the new glimpses of reality dissolve the beauty of art and the illusions of society, they reveal the unseen beauty of nature. "In all things there is something beautiful and attractive," he concludes. "It is all a question of placing oneself at an adequate point of view" (Cajal 1964, 186–87).[46] From his new perspective, he can view nature as a whole: what seems like cruelty from the individual viewpoint actually benefits the species. Microbes exist, the wizard explains, to erase imperfections. They perform a "transcendental mission in the economy of nature. . . . Thanks to their capacity to grow in weak and degenerate organisms, they *correct* dissonance, imperfection and incongruence in the superior forms" (167, my italics).[47] Ultimately, what "corrects" the pessimist is the ability to see nature more clearly. Fernández's statement that "the blind were judging the seers," directed toward those who rejected this new vision, suggests Cajal's own frustration with those who had never looked into a microscope. Such people were turning their backs on nature, which must be scrutinized without reservation.

Vision for Cajal was always the most important sense, the one that delivered the most reliable information. "I am," he wrote, "what is called a visual type" (Laín Entralgo, 296). In his autobiography, Cajal traced the development of his special visual sensitivity, noting that even as a schoolboy he had a "decided vocation for painting" (1989, 48). Privileging visual over verbal experience, he decided at an early age that visual images, not verbal descriptions or theories, must form the foundation of knowledge. The medical professors who talked at length about sick and healthy cells without having any notion of what a cell looked like filled him with exasperation. Some even looked down on microscopy, and their resistance to the visual approach only strengthened his conviction that words must be linked to visual images in order to convey meaning.

Cajal's love of drawing preceded his love of histology, and despite the pessimist's discovery that amplified vision reveals the emptiness of art, science and art were one for Cajal, united by his dedication to visual representations (Marañón, 52–58). Cajal's drawings of cells are still admired in the scientific community for their extraordinary clarity and beauty, and they owe their accuracy to Cajal's belief that "a graphic representation of the object observed guarantees the exactness of the observation itself" (Cajal 1953, 159). For Cajal, drawing was a language, an articulation of ideas which allowed thoughts to develop. Cuvier, the great observer of morphology, had commented that "without the art of drawing [*deseño*], natural history and anatomy would have been impossible" (135). By forcing oneself to reproduce exactly what one saw, one gained a new understanding of what one was seeing.

Cajal's story of the corrected pessimist conveys not only the joys and fears of enhanced vision but also an odd sense of guilt about seeing what should remain unseen. God made microbes invisible so that they would not disturb human reason, explains the wizard to Fernández, but at some point reason rebelled and invented the microscope. Cajal's literary and scientific writing conveys this mixture of trepidation and delight, the mixed emotions of a boy peeping under a divine curtain. Under Max von Forschung's gaze, for instance, the microbes "swam and amused themselves prettily, far from presuming that they were the target of determined observation" (Cajal 1964, 20).[48] Cajal's descriptions, like Claude Bernard's, make it clear that the close scrutiny of nature demanded by experimental science involves a certain voyeurism and violation. When he first began studying cadavers with his father, Cajal wrote, his goal was "the defloration of the virginity of the organs," and during the "honeymoon with the microscope," all he did was "examine things superficially [*desflorar asuntos*]" (1989, 142, 252). Aggressively penetrating what might have been left intact, he was reminded how he himself was vulnerable to penetration. He both enjoyed and felt uneasy about his visual power.

At bottom, Cajal's desire to see clearly and to resolve seemingly hopeless tangles into distinct structures is a desire for conquest (Pratt 1993, 5). He called histological explorers "the Columbuses of microscopic anatomy" (Cajal 1904, 145). Cajal's microscopes, cameras, and pencils, like Koch's, became arms in a heroic struggle to expose unknown territory and visualize the invisible. When one considers his political as well as his scientific goals, Cajal's anger against scientists clinging to the reticular theory becomes much more understandable. Refusing to resolve what was difficult to resolve was the same sort of mental laziness, the same rejection of a challenge, he believed, that had cost Spain its colonial empire. For Cajal, the conquest of the unknown could only be achieved if one could maintain a truly independent vision of nature. He exhorts potential scientists to question reigning theories and beliefs and to trust only their own eyes. By providing a "vacation" from the demands of scientific writing, "The corrected pessimist" allows Cajal to explore uninhibitedly the question of who sees reality best: the person who can see biological boundaries, or the person who can see social ones.

Conclusion: Boundaries as a Political Issue

Despite Cajal's calls for clear, straightforward scientific language free from rhetorical flourishes, his scientific and creative writing is alive with metaphors, and he seems highly aware of the role that language plays in constructing scientific knowledge.[49] As a microscopist, he had to construct his own images to describe structures unseen to most readers, and his writing is anything but a simple march of transparent signifiers. Chief among Cajal's metaphorical vehicles is the plant kingdom, and his repeated comparisons of cell processes to trees and branches express his admiration for both. The bird cerebellum, for instance, was "a true tree of life." He admired the "elegance of the arborization" in the elaborate branching of its Purkinje cells and compared the climbing fibers that contacted them to a moss or vine (1888, 308, 311, 312). Trees and plants appealed to Cajal as vehicles not only because of their beauty and sensitivity but also because of their plasticity, their ability to respond to the environment by growing in new directions. In his *Precepts and Counsels for Scientific Investigation*, he compared the brain to a tree because of their common ability to send out new shoots: "The cerebrum [*cerebro*] . . . is a tree whose foliage spreads out and becomes more intricate in pattern with study and meditation" (1953, 147–48). The scientist himself, in fact, resembled a plant because both could grow and were sensitive to "the physical and moral environment" (104). Cajal's plant metaphors even enter his more literal references to contemporary theories when he refers disparagingly to "new shoots of reticularism" (1933, 217). The nervous system, like the dense texts written about it, was a great jungle to be explored.

Cajal's other preferred metaphorical vehicle, war, is related to the first through the theme of conquest. In his writing the scientist becomes a *conquistador* in the primeval forest. This motif can be traced to Cajal's earliest accounts of his active visual imagination; he admitted that when he began drawing, his favorite subjects were "the terrible incidents of war" (1989, 38). Explaining in an article on cholera that administering antiseptic substances internally would probably kill the patient, he wrote that this futile procedure "is the same as if in a battle between two armies, on the pretext of helping the weaker, a third in discord finishes off both the one and the other" (1924, 157).[50] As in Cajal's plant metaphors, the qualities of the vehicle tied the scientist to what he studied. Science itself, not just the living things on which it focused, resembled warfare. In an article challenging the reticular theory, Cajal described the eagerness of many scientists to "measure arms with the champions of antineuronism," and he later wrote that "destruction of these ideal fancies was not the only fruit of victory during this battle" (1907, 123; Loewy, 19). In *Precepts and Counsels for Scientific Investigation*, he described Japanese scientists studying in Berlin as "a formidable army of intellectuals assaulting the laboratories," and he called for similar scholarships for gifted young Spanish scientists to study in foreign countries (1953, 196).

The great creativity of Cajal's writing seems to contradict his call for the elimination of needless rhetoric in scientific writing. His metaphors, though, extend his quest to ground all thinking in visual images, and they always retain a literal dimension.[51] He compares both false hypotheses and intellectuals cut off from society to tumors, for example, suggesting that ideas develop in an organic process and grow best if open communication allows them to work as a part of a "body" of thought (Cajal 1953, 133, 182). R. Salillas, to whom Cajal read his first adventure novel about an imaginary island, wrote that this elusive "island of Cajal" became an anatomical reality when the name was given to an actual structure in the body (1989, 159–61; Benítez 29). A common signifier linked the imaginary to the real.

Cajal's writing, like Virchow's, associates the body with society by discussing both in the same terms. His view of the cell both as an individual and as a unit in a greater being invited such comparisons. In *Elementos de histología normal y de técnica micrográfica*, he reflected that "cells are living individuals associated among themselves to form an organism. . . . The organism is like a town, whose individuals renew themselves many times during the life of the collective." In addition to nutrition and reproduction, every cell had a special function, "its organic profession and its title" (1904, 148, 198, 194).[52] People, like cells, maintained unique identities while participating in a collective life.

As in Virchow's and Mitchell's writing, references to the way the body is "governed" betray the scientist's own political stance. Defending Virchow's cellular pathology as a young medical student, Cajal told a vitalist professor that an infection was "something like a trivial frontier skirmish or a city riot, which the local powers should control automatically, with little or no intervention from the central authorities" (Cajal 1989, 175). In "The accursed house," during the histological love scene, the narrator refers to the brain as "the faithful servant of the community" (Cajal 1964, 122). These descriptions, like Virchow's, suggest Cajal's powerful resistance to authoritarian rule and centralized control. It is particularly significant that as an investigator of the nervous system, he viewed neurons as "representatives" rather than a ruling elite. All cells, as independent individuals, depended on one another but did not need prodding from a central authority to respond to trauma or to grow and change. Although willpower—associated with the brain—drove neurons to form new connections, the real, physical basis of increased mental activity was the cells themselves, cells that gave rise to the will in the first place. Cajal viewed society along the same lines: the government must create an atmosphere in which independent thinking and initiative would be rewarded, but the ultimate responsibility for regeneration lay in the hands of each individual, not in central planning.[53]

A liberal like Virchow, Cajal was an active political writer known for his "notorious leftist tendencies" (Perrín, 193). Like Koch, however, he knew that too much social criticism could undermine his scientific projects. It has been suggested that he restricted the distribution of his "Vacation stories" because he feared their "anti-religious, anti-establishment content" would jeopardize his funding (O'Connor, 100). Since the unpublished seven have been lost, it is difficult to assess this hypothesis, but the opposition of the clergy to Julián's bacteriological investigations in "The accursed house" and the government's desire to administer *antifreniatina* to the poor in "For a secret offense, a secret revenge" certainly suggest tendencies in this direction.

Throughout his life, Cajal supported and defended the Spanish worker. Coming from an impoverished background, Cajal understood from a young age "that repressed hatred . . . which the poor worker feels toward the burger and the professional man" (1989, 27). Despite his scientific success, he was never a wealthy man, and he chose to live in the working-class neighborhood of Cuatro Caminos when he came to Madrid (Lewy Rodríguez, 11). As a scientist, he considered himself a worker and once told his colleagues that he did not want a raise because "without wanting to, I always discern, on every coin I receive, the sweaty, weather-beaten face of the peasant who definitely pays for our academic and scientific luxuries" (21).[54] Cajal responded wrathfully to references to "Spanish laziness," pointing out that while it might be endemic among the upper classes, the workers had never ceased their backbreaking toil. When he did criticize Spanish society, he focused on the snobbery of the nobility who "lived parasitically off the memory of their ancestors" (Perrín, 207). Their belief in innate rather than hard-won superiority was a disease against which Spaniards had to defend themselves.

Cajal's criticism of Spanish society in no way mitigated his patriotism. His fierce desire to rebuild Spain through the renascent will of each Spaniard ties him to the literary Generation of 1898, most of whom were born a decade or two later (Granjel, 229). In 1898 Spain lost its last important colonies to the

United States, causing widespread disillusionment and marking the end of its status as an imperial power. Intellectuals like Pío Baroja, Miguel de Unamuno, and Azorín responded with calls for increased contacts with Northern Europe, innovations in style, and a reconsideration of the qualities that had forged a quintessentially Spanish greatness in the past. For Cajal, as for these other writers, will and regeneration were political as well as physiological issues. Spain was declining, wrote Cajal in his autobiography, because Spaniards had not yet learned to replace religion with patriotism, "the strong and moralizing religion of powerful nations" (Cajal 1989, 233). He listed patriotism as one of the most fundamental requirements for a good scientist, writing that "every discovery credited to foreign countries [is] something like an insult to our flag, shamefully tolerated."[55] Cajal was no xenophobe, expressing great admiration for the German, British, and French cultures; he simply hoped that patriotism would awaken somnolent minds. His quest for a vigorous, regenerating Spain again reflects his vision of the nervous system, in which independent individuals served a free-thinking organism that was infinitely more complex.

Cajal's writings, particularly his metaphorical references to war, suggest that he supported the same sort of new growth in politics that he praised in the mind: the establishment of new contacts, and the conquest—or reconquest—of territory. Cajal wanted to revive the decrepit Spanish colonial empire, and like Koch, he saw scientific investigation as its foundation. In his introduction to the Royal Report on African Tropical Diseases, he wrote—as Koch had—that the ultimate goal of fighting these diseases was to make Africa more accessible to Europeans. Affirming the role of bacteriologists in expanding imperial boundaries, Cajal declared that "only science makes dominion tolerable, and even desirable. . . . It is a wise and prudent policy, in occupying a country, to let the doctor and the naturalist form the vanguard for the administrator and the soldier" (Cajal 1910, 13).[56] The report that followed offered case histories of African natives, including drawings of the bacteria taken from their blood and photographs of their bodies during the illness and of their brains after death. As in Koch's reports, the bodies of the black Africans served to render visible the microbial threats to Europeans.

In the conclusion to "The Natural Man and the Artificial Man," Cajal's final "vacation story", the vigorous hero tells his feeble friend that the loss of the Spanish colonies would not matter if the children of the day could "make an effort to broaden the moral geography of the race with the radiant islands of their intelligence" (Cajal 1964, 286).[57] How does one "broaden the moral geography of a race"? The very language of the appeal posits the regenerative effort in terms of colonialism, for one tends to expand one's boundaries and identity at the expense of other cultures.

In *Culture and Imperialism*, Edward Saíd argues that in the postcolonial era, a new, "dynamic" sense of identity is replacing the static, imperialistic one which viewed the world in terms of "us" and "them." "Partly because of empire," he writes, "all cultures are involved in one another; none is single and pure, all are hybrid, heterogeneous, extraordinarily differentiated, and unmonolithic" (xxv). Cajal's scientific vision of elaborately branched individual cells maintaining their identities while reaching out to their neighbors—a vision affirmed by contemporary neuroscience—can thus retain its validity even though his imperialistic ambitions are worthless. In 1900, to Cajal and Koch, "reaching out" meant conquest. Cajal's own rejection of centralized power, however, suggests another possibility. As long as they are based on changing connections and autonomous units, his analogies between the neuron and the individual, the nervous system and society, remain workable and promise to offer insights about all four. They lose their value only when read "statically," distorted by the conviction that some more worthy individuals must control those who are less worthy and potentially dangerous.

FOUR

Arthur Conan Doyle

An Imperial Immune System

We judge as small what we see from afar or don't know
how to see.   —Santiago Ramón y Cajal

[Holmes] is an amateur of crime, as I am of disease. For
him the villain, for me the microbe. There are my prisons.
Among those gelatine cultivations some of the very worst
offenders in the world are now doing time.
                                          —Arthur Conan Doyle

As European nations incorporated more and more foreign territory into their empires, they opened themselves to new people, new cultures, and new diseases. Koch's and Cajal's scientific writings show how the new science of bacteriology in the 1880s is inseparable not only from the desire to conquer new territory but also from the fear that natives of these lands, in a quest for revenge, would ultimately infiltrate and infect the imperial "nerve centers" (Arata, 623; Brantlinger, 230; Haraway, 223).[1] As the blank spaces on maps rapidly disappeared, the laboratory provided a new realm for conquest in which imperial heroes could unveil, one by one, the microbes that caused infectious diseases. Increasingly, Europeans viewed the maintenance of empires as a defensive rather than an aggressive strategy (Brantlinger, 81). To defend their original borders against invasion, the colonial powers fought at their newer, outermost ones. The very process of expansion, however, left them vulnerable to the new germs, mates, and ideas brought home by their soldiers. The empires needed immune systems.

Sir Arthur Conan Doyle, an enthusiastic supporter of the British Empire, brought to life the fantasy of a national immune system through his character Sherlock Holmes. Trained as a physician from 1876 to 1881, Doyle learned and practiced medicine during the heyday of bacteriology. The British loved Holmes for the same reasons that Doyle admired Koch: he devoted all of his formidable mental powers to identifying and neutralizing living threats to society. In the fall of 1890, Doyle visited the Hygiene Institute in Berlin where Koch's "cure" for tuberculosis was being tested and reported on the "cure" for the *Review of Reviews*. Doyle's description of the German bacteriologist strongly resembles his later ones of his fictional detective: "Somewhere within [those walls] the great master mind is working, which is rapidly bringing under subjection those unruly tribes of deadly micro-organisms which are the last creatures in the organic world to submit to the sway of man . . . [Koch] preserves his whole energy for the all-important mission to which he has devoted himself" (Doyle 1890, 552). For Doyle, bacteriology is an imperialistic battle fought on the home front.

Holmes fights this battle much as Koch does, by exposing tiny aliens who have invaded the imperial city (Rothfield, 140). His calling consists largely of detecting foreign blackmailers, thieves, tyrants, intelligence agents, counterfeiters, women, drugs, and diseases that have worked their way into British society. "You are a benefactor of the race," a grateful client tells him in "The Red-Headed League" (1:251).[2] Holmes serves his "race" by upholding a system that established identity and economic worth through heredity, even as his clients draw their wealth from other races in other lands. In the age of imperialism, it is a losing battle.

Doyle as Doctor: Defending the Empire

Sir Arthur Conan Doyle won his knighthood by using his medical training to serve the British Empire. A large, vigorous man from a family of Irish Catholic intellectuals and artists, Doyle, like Mitchell and Cajal, loved sports and any sort of physically challenging adventure. He went into medicine at his mother's suggestion, primarily as a way to make a living (Carr, 18). Refusing to use his family's Catholic connections to establish himself in private practice, Doyle struggled to survive independently as a young doctor (26). He served as a nominal surgeon on an arctic whaler and then, after taking his degree at the University of Edinburgh in 1881, worked as a fullfledged ship's surgeon on a cargo and passenger liner traveling to the west coast of Africa. This voyage, on which he caught African fever, was nearly eaten by a shark, and survived a fire on board (the cargo was oil), dampened his desire for African exploration (29). After a brief partnership with a friend who proved to be a charlatan, he lived in poverty as he set himself up in private practice, performing medical exams for a life insurance company and treating a grocer's fits in exchange for butter and tea (37). Doyle survived as a general practitioner, writing his first Holmes stories between consultations, but, like Koch, he retained his longing to travel.

His trip to Berlin in November 1890 to investigate Koch's cure resulted more from this desire to explore the frontiers of medicine than from any special interest in tuberculosis (Carr, 61). Although Doyle never met Koch or entered the laboratory where the cure was being prepared, he did examine many of the patients being treated with it, and the character sketch of Koch that he created provides a competent and vivid picture of the experiments underway in Berlin (Brock, 208). In 1891, after the traveling to Vienna to study eye surgery, Doyle decided to abandon medicine and devote all of his time to writing.

Doyle, however, would work as a physician one more time. In early 1900, believing that the Boer War "was a righteous war and well worth sacrifices," he attempted to enlist. Rejected as a soldier because he was forty-one, he signed on as a doctor and took command of a hospital (Carr, 124–25). The chief enemy Doyle faced in South Africa was not the irate Dutch farmers but local disease. In an intelligent strategic move, the Boers had immediately seized the Bloemfontein waterworks, waging a kind of biological warfare, since the British troops were then forced to drink unpurified water. Five thousand died of enteric fever in Doyle's hospital during the months of April and May 1900 (129–30). In *The War in South Africa: Its Cause and Conduct* (1902), Doyle defended British troops against charges of rape, farm-burning, and the herding of Boer women and children into disease-ridden camps. He claimed that the British camps, constructed to care for women and children, were not infested with typhus due to poor sanitary conditions. Instead, he blamed the whooping cough, measles, and chicken pox the children had contracted on their mothers because they failed to air their tents and sponge their children properly, and because they preferred home remedies to the official ones offered by the British army (156–57). He received his knighthood for his medical service and for his effort to publish a true account of the war.

The fight against bacteria, the most pressing medical issue of the day, played a central role in Doyle's medical experiences from 1876 to 1900, creating a perspective that is evident in all of the Holmes stories (Ginzburg, 87).[3] In 1892, Doyle revealed that he had based Holmes on his professor of clinical surgery at the University of Edinburgh, Dr. Joseph Bell (Liebow, 125). Selected as Bell's out-patient clerk because of the copious notes he was always making, Doyle had extensive opportunity to observe the master at work. Bell awed students with his ability to determine a patient's profession, origin, and ailment through close observation and deduction. Like Holmes, he could infer how a patient had reached his clinic by looking at the mud on the man's boots, and he urged students to "use your ears, use your brain, your bump of perception, and use your powers of deduction" (132). Doyle wrote to Bell in June 1892: "It is most certainly to you that I owe Sherlock Holmes. . . . Round the center of deduction and inference and observation which I have heard you inculcate, I have tried to build up a man who pushed the thing as far as it would go" (172).

Like his student Doyle, Bell closely followed developments in bacteriological research. According to Bell, "The greatest stride that has been made of late years in preventive and diagnostic medicine consists in the recognition and differentiation by bacteriological research of those minute organisms that disseminate cholera and fever, tubercle and anthrax" (J. Bell, xvii). Holmes's keen eye for details developed out of the eye of the diagnostician and bacteriologist, and the affinity is evident throughout his cases.

Seeing Small Threats

Doyle, who once wanted to become an eye specialist, resembles the neurobiologist Cajal in his fantasy of enhanced, voyeuristic vision. In "A Case of Identity," written not long after Doyle's visit to Berlin, Holmes expresses to Watson a desire to "fly out of that window hand in hand, hover over this great city, gently remove the roofs, and peep in at the queer things which are going on" (1:251). Able to scrutinize every cranny of the imperial capital, Holmes comes closer to living out this fantasy than did most doctors. He owes this accessibility to his capacity to see in new ways, to find what he seeks because, like Koch, he knows what to look for.

Aware of the qualities that had allowed Koch to succeed, Doyle wrote that the tuberculosis bacillus had "harassed mankind from the dawn of time, and yet has become visible to him only during the last eight years" (Doyle 1890, 552). Explaining his strategy as a scientist, Koch confessed that he had invested the greatest effort in developing staining, photographic, and plate culture techniques that had allowed him to detect, identify, and isolate bacteria. "Once appropriate methods had been found," he wrote, "these discoveries fell into our laps like ripe fruit" (Carter, xvii). Holmes is not quite so successful but essentially follows the same strategy. Watson observes in "The Adventure of the Veiled Lodger" that "sometimes he had with much effort to pick the fruit; sometimes it fell easily into his lap" (2:624). To harvest their fruit, both the detective and the bacteriologist rely on their special vision, a vision enhanced by prior deductions about what they should be seeing.

Again and again, Holmes tells Watson that to be a good detective, he must learn how to see. Having discovered the tell-tale wax vesta in "Silver Blaze," the detective confesses, "it was invisible . . . I only saw it because I was looking for it" (1:466). When Holmes's initial scrutiny fails, he must persist, for the threats he hunts will undermine his society if undetected. Like diseases, they become considerably less frightening when identified. When Holmes warns the governess in "The Copper Beeches" of potential danger and she asks him, shocked, "Danger? What danger do you foresee?" he tells her, "it would cease to be a danger if we could define it" (1:436–37). Only the invisible is truly threatening.

Doyle's military experience, as well as his medical training, inspired him to create a hero with penetrating vision. Observing a mock battle at Salisbury in 1898, a worried Doyle asked the staff officer, "suppose, in a real battle, the enemy took cover and we didn't?" (Carr, 109). When they went into battle with the Boers, whose pride did not prevent them from digging trenches and crouching behind rocks, the British troops were slaughtered by invisible guns. Doyle personally witnessed the ravages an unseen enemy could wreak when he traveled to the front while on leave. In 1900, British army commanders finally admitted that concealment provided a major tactical advantage, and they specified that in future fighting, guns must be hidden and the infantry must dig trenches (133–34). After 1910, when war with Germany seemed inevitable, Doyle continued to warn his government about attacks by stealth. He focused particularly on the threat of submarines that might destroy the key to Britain's imperial power, its navy. Fearing a blockade by small, invisible crafts, he campaigned for the construction of a channel tunnel (226–28).

In the 1880s, because of their minuscule size and deadly effects, bacteria became a metaphor through which one could articulate fears about all invisible enemies, military, political, or economic. Smallness itself became menacing. In his 1892 introduction to *A Study in Scarlet*, Bell—Holmes's model— wrote: "The importance of the infinitely little is incalculable. Poison a well at Mecca with the cholera bacillus, and the holy water which the pilgrims carry off in their bottles will infect a continent, and the rags of the victims of the plague will terrify every seaport in Christendom" (J. Bell, xvii). By mentioning contaminated water supplies and unwary pilgrims, Bell invokes Koch's discoveries about cholera in India eight years earlier. In this genocidal fantasy, he envisions infection in the Islamic Holy City, disseminated by Muslims, a bungled attempt at germ warfare in which the biological weapon returns to infect Christians. The sharp-eyed surgeon saw only too well that knowledge of bacteria dissolved any illusions of national insulation.

Holmes retains his model's respect for the small and apparently trivial, telling his client in "A Case of Identity," "It has long been an axiom of mine that the little things are infinitely the most important" (1:257). Since smallness confers invisibility, or at least increased freedom of movement due to lack of conspicuousness, it also means power.

Doyle reveals the danger of allowing "small" people to operate unchecked in *The Sign of Four*, in which Holmes makes the famous statement "Man's real greatness lies in his perception of his own smallness" (1:153). In this story, the anger of "small" people who have been overlooked—both British and foreign—threatens to corrode the empire (Farrell, 43). The villain, Jonathan Small, is the black sheep in a family of "small farmers." Seeing no possibility for success in British society, he travels to India to seek his fortune. After losing a leg to a crocodile, Small works as an overseer, reporting "idlers" among native workers on a plantation. While holding the Agra fort during the Mutiny, which he describes as "two hundred thousand black devils let loose," Small enters into a pact with three Sikhs to share the jewels they will steal from a miserly rajah (1:187).[4] They tell him: "We only ask you to do that which your countrymen come to this land for. We ask you to be rich" (1:190).

The subversive element in Doyle's tale, the second of Holmes's adventures, develops through Small's identification with the natives, who see themselves as rightfully retaking wealth that has been usurped from them by the rajah (Farrell, 44).[5] Racial and class resentments, however, mingle in a complex fashion; while Small feels rejected by his own society, he retains its belief that his whiteness makes him superior to Indians, privileged or unprivileged. He insists he has earned the jewels by being "bullied by every cursed black-faced policeman who loved to take it out of a white man" (Doyle 1986, 1:185). Besides plotting with three Sikhs, whom he never betrays, Small wins the loyalty of an Andaman islander, Tonga, who murders his enemies with a blowgun and is a member of one of "the smallest race on earth." Seeking traces of Major Sholto's killer, Holmes spies footprints "scarce half the size of those of an ordinary man," and Watson whispers in horror, "Holmes, a child has done this horrid thing" (1:139). The Augustinian view of the child as marked by sin and violence in the absence of parental control underlies the imperialistic drive, the "parent" fancying he or she imposes civilized order on people who would otherwise destroy themselves through their own passions (Farrell, 42). Working with Tonga, Small "acts out the wrath of an excluded child . . . Fleeing abroad, exploited along with the native 'children' there, they are forced to resort to violence to reclaim their rightful place at home" (43–44). One of the desperadoes is "small" for genetic reasons; the other, for economic. Together, they will try to circumvent the borders and laws of the empire that has deprived them of power.

Thanks to Holmes, however, Small never succeeds in reentering British society as a respectable citizen. Instead, respectability remains with the descendants of Major Sholto and Captain Morstan, Small's jailers in India after the mutiny. The two officers steal his treasure after trying to convince him, unsuccessfully, to betray the Sikhs: "What have three black fellows to do with our agreement?" (1:200). Morstan's lovely daughter, who brings the case to Holmes and whom Watson marries in the conclusion, comes across as a wronged woman, the individual with the "right" to the loot. To whom, one wonders, does the treasure belong? The rajah steals it from his people; Small and the Sikhs steal it from the rajah; Morstan and Sholto steal it from Small and the Sikhs; and Small and Tonga steal it from Sholto's estate. In the end Small scatters it over the bottom of the Thames, the thoroughfare of the empire, telling Holmes that "no living man has any right to it, unless it is three men who are in the Andaman convict-barracks and myself . . . I have acted all through for them as much as for myself" (1:185). The story thus acts out the complex but essentially irreversible movement of wealth under the British Empire: from the "small" people into the Thames.

Holmes can track down Small and his tiny cohort only because he forms his own collaboration with "small" people: the Baker Street Irregulars, "a dozen dirty and ragged little street Arabs" who "invade" his house and, for a nominal fee, act as his intelligence agents (1:160). Holmes can detect and defeat the "small" because he knows them intimately and can enlist them for his own purposes. Like Small, he despises his little associates, but he respects their power to move freely because of their relative invisibility. Small had called Tonga "a little bloodthirsty imp"; Holmes calls the boys' leader, Wiggins, "my dirty little lieutenant" (1:203, 158). Written while Doyle was still practicing medicine, *The Sign of Four* shows not only a preoccupation with "man's own smallness" but also a preoccupation with smallness in general, its powers and its dangers.

In Doyle's 1890 description of Robert Koch, the *Review of Reviews* included a cartoon of the bacteriologist depicting him as St. George. Mounted

Robert Koch as the new St. George, vanquishing the tuberculosis bacillus. This drawing originally appeared in the humorous German journal, *Ulk*, and was reproduced by the *Review of Reviews* as an illustration for Arthur Conan Doyle's article on Koch.

on a steed labeled "investigation," Koch brandishes a microscope at a threatening (but diminutive) serpent labeled "tuberculosis bacillus." The German artist conceived of Koch's microscopical vision as the deadliest weapon of the imperial knight. The drawing had originally appeared in the humorous Berlin journal *Ulk,* and the editors of the British journal felt that it was appropriate for their own readers as well.

Like the German bacteriologist and the physician-author Doyle, Holmes is an imperial knight who serves his empire through his enhanced vision. As such, he voices and legitimates its ideology. "What is the use of having powers, Doctor, when one has no field upon which to exert them?" he asks Watson seconds before Mary Morstan knocks at the door to present the case of the Agra treasure (1:113). Watson, horrified by Holmes's cocaine use, tells him he risks "the loss of those great powers," implying that he does his society a disservice by failing to maintain his mind and body (1:108). When describing Koch as a country doctor, Doyle uses the same words. Perhaps recalling his own frustrating early days as a physician, Doyle calls Koch "strong and vigorous, with all his great powers striving for an outlet . . . he was a man of too strong a character to allow himself to be warped by the position in which he found himself" (Doyle 1890, 552–54). Doyle, a "Liberal Imperialist" like Cajal, presented the minds of his fictional hero and Germany's scientific one as imperial resources that should be used to defend their respective realms against prospective invasions (Carr, 137). The Holmes stories represent a genre that Patrick Brantlinger has called "Imperial Gothic," characterized by a fear of "individual regression or going native; an invasion of civilization by the forces of barbarism or demonism; and the diminution of opportunities for adventure and heroism in the modern world" (Brantlinger, 230). In other words, Doyle's tales betray a fear of smallness.

The Imperial Body

Frequently in Holmes's adventures, one encounters images of England as the detective's clients and readers would like to see it, and this dream-image of the peaceful domestic circle contrasts with the nefarious one of imperialistic intrigue and conflict (Brantlinger, 12). *The Sign of Four,* for instance, pits Mary Morstan against Small and Tonga as owners of the Agra treasure, and a mere glance suffices for Doyle's British readers to decide who has the more legitimate claim. Inspired by the warmth and brightness of Miss Morstan's home, Watson thinks, "it was soothing to catch even that passing glimpse of a tranquil English home in the midst of the wild, dark business which had absorbed us" (1:146). Both Holmes's clients and the narrator refer to England as a refuge where law and order reign in an otherwise chaotic and crime-ridden world. The very existence of Holmes, however, reveals that these statements are fictions, for a realm of perfect law and order would have no need for the detective and his formidable intelligence network. Instead, these idealized images represent the longing that gave rise to Holmes in the first place: the desire to be safe, with one's imperial loot, on one's own turf.

Doyle represents this imperial capital in organic terms. The empire perpetuates itself through its vigorous young males, and fears about threats to its hegemony are consequently expressed as anxieties about corporeal damage or exhaustion. The body of the empire is best represented by Watson himself, middle-aged, overweight, and troubled by the Jezail bullet he has carried in his leg since the Afghan campaign. It is a body in decline, under siege, a body with a dubious capacity to reproduce and renew itself.

As the country's greatest hope, Holmes's own body and mind become the focus of imperial fears about exhausted resources just as they convey fantasies about limitless ones. Doyle compares Holmes to an intelligence network, and it comes as no surprise that both the fears and the fantasies settle on his nervous system. As Doyle describes him, Holmes "loved to lie in the very center of five millions of people, with his filaments stretching out and running through them, responsive to every little rumor and suspicion of unsolved crime" (1:579). This exquisitely sensitive network, however, has a limited capacity. Just before he encounters Moriarty in "The Final Problem," Holmes remarks to Watson, "I have been using myself up rather too freely" (1:643). At the same time, however, Holmes fulfills a desire for a man with "inexhaustible stores of nervous energy upon which to draw" (1:737). For long periods, he can maintain his remarkable mental activity without even taking nourishment, which makes him an ideal, if demonic, servant of his empire.

Both Holmes and his brother Mycroft are agents of the British Empire, providing an all-seeing, all-knowing team to protect the country's interests. The crucial military issue of the era, the political stories imply, is the maintenance of superior naval power, particularly over the up-and-coming Germans, and Mycroft calls in Sherlock when the plans for a new submarine disappear. A "dense yellow fog" provides the setting for the story ("The Bruce Partington Plans"), murky air which can hide anyone or anything and reflects the paranoia implicit in the plot. Holmes asks his brother for "a complete list of all foreign spies or international agents known to be in England," spies whose existence everyone acknowledges, including Doyle's readers (2:368). Both brothers become resources available to detect these spies. Holmes explains to Watson that his brother "*is* the British government. . . . He has the tidiest and most orderly brain, with the greatest capacity for storing facts, of any man living . . . The conclusions of every department are passed to him, and he is the central exchange, the clearing-house, which makes out the balance. All other men are specialists, but his specialism is omniscience" (2:360). Doyle's description of Mycroft presents his mind as an imperial control center, a nucleus in its communications network.

Mycroft Holmes's mind, in which "everything is pigeon-holed and can be handed out in an instant," is mirrored in "His Last Bow" by the desk of German spies, who store their documents in their own embassy: "Each pigeon-hole had its label, and his eyes as he glanced along them read . . . 'Harbor-defenses,' 'Aeroplanes,' . . . 'Egypt,' . . . 'The Channel,' and a score of others. Each compartment was bristling with papers and plans" (2:445). Pitting Holmes against the German agent Von Bork, Doyle warns his readers about German armament. Holmes outwits Von Bork by posing as an Irish American; the German accepts him as an informant because "our most pan-Germanic Junker is a suckling dove in his feelings toward England as compared with a real bitter Irish-American" (2:446). "Passing," once again, because of his perfect ability to impersonate the empire's enemies, Holmes wins Von Bork's confidence and tells him: "England is not ready . . . even our special war tax of fifty million . . . has not roused these people from their slumbers" (2:444). The German agent says of his servant Martha, who has been quietly knitting throughout their conversation, "she might almost personify Britannia with her complete self-absorption and general air of comfortable somnolence" (2:447). His comparison of the empire to a drowsy old woman expresses imperial anxieties once again in terms of physical weakness, and Doyle's story both indulges and alleviates fears of degeneration. Holmes defends Britannia with his superior mind and his ability to impersonate the enemy when the enemy infiltrates the empire's nerve center, but even Holmes cannot protect the imperial body single-handedly.

Doyle's stories abound with threats to this national body. British literature of the 1890s often conflates biological and political threats, and Doyle, a doctor who had fought in South Africa, allows the two to merge in Holmes's adventures (Arata, 630). When foreign germs and poisons are manipulated by vengeful malefactors in his fiction, the biological dangers are not a metaphor for political threats; they *are* political threats.

Doyle reportedly "begged" Joe Bell for plots, and "Dr. Bell suggested in 1892 that Holmes pit himself against a germ-murderer, and hinted at knowledge of one such case" (Liebow, 178). The idea led to "The Adventure of the Dying Detective," in which a panic-stricken Watson encounters the great man's mind and body apparently disintegrating under the force of a tropical disease. Holmes's long-suffering landlady tells Watson, "he has been working at a case . . . in an alley near the river, and he has brought this illness back with him" (2:386). Holmes himself calls the illness "a coolie disease from Sumatra," explaining that "there are many problems of disease, many strange pathological possibilities, in the East, dear Watson" (2:388). Holmes states that his disease must be Eastern in origin because he has recently been working with Chinese sailors, investigating the death of a man from the same disease because he found it "very surprising that he should have contracted an out-of-the-way Asiatic disease in the heart of London" (2:395–96). Sending for Culverton Smith, a Sumatra planter and an independent bacteriological researcher who has studied the disease, Holmes reveals that Smith, through bacteriological warfare, had murdered the first man for revenge and then attempted to murder Holmes when he discovered it.

In *The Sign of Four*, the Agra treasure is housed in an exotic box fastened with a Buddha hasp. Watson reports, "under this I thrust the end of the poker and twisted it outward as a lever," thus reenacting the imperial rape of a feminized East (1:183). Smith's murder weapon, a biting "box" suggesting phallic womanhood, avenges this rape.[6] The planter has rigged a small, attractive ivory box so that a "sharp spring like a viper's tooth emerges as you open it," drawing blood and infecting the curious Englishman with the foreign bacteria (2:399). S. Weir Mitchell, in "The Poison of the Rattlesnake" (1868), had written, "that deadly head will return upon you with a swiftness which seems as though you had touched some releasing spring in a quick machinery" (454). While Doyle compares a technological mechanism for delivering poison to a biological one; and Mitchell, a biological to a technical one, both physician authors express anxiety about how easily a person's protective boundaries may be pierced. Both betray a common horror of penetration, rooted in the masculine fear of becoming a sexual object. In Doyle's description, an alienated imperialist has created a device that mimics a foreign snake and delivers a foreign poison—a hideous collaboration that allows England's colonies to bite back, and the box's phallic bite and deadly microbes now threaten the imperialists on their home ground. Doyle's representation of Smith's biological warfare expresses his readers' simultaneous guilt and fear over colonial activities, a fear that their colonial "children" will someday violate and infect them as they have infected their colonies (Arata, 623). How sharper than a serpent's tooth is an ungrateful child.

Holmes, of course, renders both the box and its designer powerless by revealing its mechanism; the "dying detective" has merely feigned the symptoms of the disease with makeup in order to entrap Smith. Although the plot is
far-fetched, Doyle's story diagnoses his readers' fears with a clinical accuracy.
What, wondered the British, were people bringing home from the colonies?

In "The Adventure of the Blanched Soldier" (1927), an "illustrious family"
sequesters its son when he contracts a foreign disease. The case, narrated by
Holmes, is set "in January, 1903, just after the conclusion of the Boer War"
(2:486). James Dodd, "a big, fresh, sunburned, upstanding Briton," seeks
Holmes's help, fearing that his military "mate" is being held against his will
(2:486). Dodd remarks that young Godfrey was "easily influenced by those
around him," leaving him and his family dangerously open to outside forces
(2:491). Such unmanly penetrability proved to be his undoing. Sure enough,
when Dodd glimpses Godfrey while staying overnight at his house—a "ghastly
face glimmering as white as cheese in the darkness"—the young heir seems to
be possessed by an insidious foreign force: "something slinking, something
furtive, something guilty—something very unlike the frank, manly lad that I
had known" (2:492). The young man's disease plays on the readers' fears in
many senses. The "slinking and furtive" invader, which suggests both the
Boers' military tactics and an evil, feminized foreign presence, threatens to
undermine the empire's manhood by slipping into this young heir of one of its
prominent families. Having once penetrated him, it will convert him into a
replica of itself, a deceitful, effeminate alien operating in a British male body.
Godfrey has not "caught" a foreign disease; the disease has caught him.

Holmes suspects either crime, madness, or serious illness and sets about
eliminating the alternatives, one by one. The young soldier, it turns out, had
been wounded and lost in the darkness after a skirmish. By chance, he had
stumbled into a building where he spent the night, only to be told, "you are in
far greater danger here than ever you were on the battlefield. You are in the
Leper Hospital, and you have slept in a leper's bed" (2:500). Here, once
again, Doyle presents the Boers' military tactics, South Africa's bacteria, and
much murkier notions of invasive, exotic forces as parallel, perhaps analogous
threats. The disease Godfrey has caught "in bed" suggests fears of venereal
diseases spread by foreign and lower-class women, which likewise endan-
gered the procreative manhood of the upper classes. As often happens in
Doyle's stories, however, good fortune saves the scion of this noble family. A
physician determines that the disease is not leprosy but pseudoleprosy, and
hope is restored in this particular case, while fears of infection remain on the
broader social level.

Not only microbes were making their way to England from the tropics. In "The Adventure of the Devil's Foot," Holmes reveals that a mysterious "curse" killing the members of a Cornish family is actually devil's-foot poison, a secret drug known only to medicine men in West Africa. Like Culverton Smith's box, the drug is being manipulated by an angry Englishman who has spent time in the tropics and is seeking revenge. Furthermore, it is a weapon that could threaten the empire if wielded by the natives who developed it. In Africa, medicine men use the drug to control their tribesmen, for "it stimulates those brain centers which control the emotion of fear" (2:439–40). The poisoner points out that the devil's-foot root is unknown in the European pharmacological literature and that it is obvious "how powerless European science would be to detect it" (2:440).

Even more frightening than devil's-foot root is an "elixir of life" which has made its way to England from Prague. Derived from a climbing monkey of the Himalayas, the drug reduces a respected professor to a creeping, crawling degenerate in "The Adventure of the Creeping Man." The story implies that the price of enhanced biological vigor—so highly coveted by the empire—is a sharp drop on the evolutionary scale, which the professor enacts by creeping about his estate at night and trying to bite his own dog. After the man's grateful son tells him, "Thanks to you, Mr. Holmes, it is very clear that we have traced the evil to its source," Holmes, in a rare moment, directly expresses public fears of degeneration: "When one tries to rise above Nature one is liable to fall below it. . . . There is danger there—a very real danger to humanity. Consider, Watson, that the material, the sensual, the worldly would all prolong their worthless lives . . . It would be the survival of the least fit. What sort of cesspool may not our poor world become?" (2:605). Holmes worries that poisons like the one he has detected will create an inverted natural selection process through which the strongest men, the empire's greatest resource, will be winnowed out as a result of their curiosity and mental vigor.

Despite Doyle's Manichean representation of England and its foreign threats, the empire appears inseparable from its criminals, its poisons, and its diseases, metaphors for the anger of its oppressed. Moriarty, who is supposedly to evil what Holmes is to good, resembles him remarkably as the center of a communications net. Moriarty "sits motionless, like a spider in the center of its web, but that web has a thousand radiations, and he knows well every quiver of each of them" (1:645). The image of Moriarty, who uses his web to sense every movement of victims he might eat, expresses anxiety about enemies within England who use the empire's own intelligence and power structures to entrap "respectable" citizens. The strikingly similar description of Holmes, who appears more vital because the filaments of his web are processes of his own body, conveys a wish for an omnipotent intelligence system that operates incessantly, safeguarding citizens with bad consciences against the revenge of those they have wronged. Both networks, the good and the evil, reflect the actual network of the British Empire, whose quivering filaments betrayed the anger of victims throughout the world. The hero, his archrival, and their creator all speak the language of the economic system that gave birth to them.

Dr. Van Helsing in Bram Stoker's *Dracula* (1897) views the bloodsucking Eastern marauder as an "unavoidable consequence of any invasion" (Arata, 627). Conquest means the breaching of borders, and the resulting traffic will move in more than one direction. Doyle, well aware that conquering new lands meant exposing oneself to infection, referred to "enteric fever, that curse of our Indian possessions" on the very first page of the first Holmes story. The very existence and functioning of the empire opened the imperial body to foreign diseases, foreign anger, and foreign revenge because it opened so many new possibilities for "communication."

Unwanted Relations

The opening of *A Study in Scarlet*, Holmes's first story, reveals that the detective's worst fears have already been realized: London is a gathering place for germs and has been for some time. Watson, as narrator, describes the city as "that great cesspool into which all the loungers and idlers of the Empire are irresistibly drained" (1:4). In the noisome capital, the heart of the empire's communications system, the offal of the old world mingles with the refuse of the new, and the city becomes a breeding ground where ferment spreads rapidly among the disgruntled foreigners and natives. The city is most frightening because of the innumerable connections it establishes between people, making the communication of deadly diseases and seditious ideas inevitable yet difficult to trace.

Holmes, however, loves London. He loves London because he *is* London, and Doyle describes the city and the detective's intelligence in the same terms. On the way to Sholto's house in *The Sign of Four*, Watson observes "the monster tentacles which the giant city was throwing out into the country" (1:122). Like its protector and its greatest fiend, London is a web, a living network forever extending its processes and its connections. Holmes revels in the city's limitless possibilities for communication, watching with pleasure "the ever-changing kaleidoscope of life as it ebbs and flows through Fleet

Street and the Strand" (1:581). Watson calls the story of "The Blue Carbuncle", in which a precious gem is concealed in a goose, "one of those whimsical little incidents which will happen when you have four million human beings all jostling each other within the space of a few square miles" (1:328). By creating unwanted connections among its millions, the city itself invites the mischief Holmes must investigate.

One detects the structure of London not only in Doyle's descriptions of Holmes himself but also in his descriptions of Holmes's epistemology. "So all life is a great chain," he tells Watson in *A Study in Scarlet*, "the nature of which is known whenever we are shown a single link of it" (1:14). Holmes's job is to uncover hidden connections, to follow the scarlet thread and reconstruct the logic of a crime until "the whole thing is a chain of logical sequences without a break or flaw" (1:102). Holmes's process of detection thus resembles the task of the bacteriologist, since both trace links between people, one to follow malicious intentions, the other to follow a microbe. The creation of an empire has brought the jungle to London, so that it becomes possible to hunt big—or small—game in the imperial city. When Holmes miraculously reappears after Doyle's campaign in Africa, Watson remarks in his first new adventure, "I knew not what wild beast we were about to hunt down in the dark jungle of criminal London" (1:671). Holmes, who loves to hunt, thrives in the environment he is so aptly suited to police, an ever-growing web with limitless connections.

Few people in British society, however, liked these relations as much as Holmes did. The traditional concept of identity, rooted in heredity and advocated by Doyle's mother ("a fearsome stickler for genealogy"), had featured carefully controlled family "connections" (Carr, 7). Placing great value on privacy, the British respected individual boundaries, so that the many new possibilities for connections created by imperial expansion quickly became a threat. The frustrated goose merchant in "The Blue Carbuncle," a link in a chain of buyers and sellers, expresses this popular desire to disengage himself from the people who flank him: "When I pay good money for a good article there should be an end of the business!" (1:339). To prosper, he must maintain these connections economically, but he refuses to maintain them socially. Holmes thus serves a society that simultaneously wants and does not want relations, and he serves it by "doggedly" bringing them to light. He demands not that his illustrious clients face punishment, but that they admit the truth about their "connections," for connections hidden or denied present the greatest danger of infection.

Most of these new bonds were economic, binding the elite to shady colonial characters who made their new wealth possible. Marriage, itself an economic institution, ranked first as a creator of such bonds, and in the Holmes stories it is one of the primary means by which the colonies permeate noble families. Although Holmes's clients surround their estates with stone walls and raise their drawbridges at night, they marry foreign women. It is significant that almost every such case concerns a British man with a foreign wife and not the reverse, the female becoming associated with the insidious germs penetrating the society. It was men who left England, seeking prosperity in the colonies, and it was men who brought emasculating diseases back with them, microbes that threatened the economy the colonies fed.

In "The Adventure of the Noble Bachelor," an article warns that American women are out-competing British ones, entering noble families in distressing numbers: "There will soon be a call for protection in the marriage market, for the present free-trade principle appears to tell heavily against our home product. One by one the management of the noble houses of Great Britain is passing into the hands of our fair cousins from across the Atlantic" (1:391). When British noblemen fail to scrutinize their foreign mates sufficiently, they find themselves connected to the evils of their wives' past. Holmes's client in "The Adventure of the Dancing Men," who eventually dies for his mistake, tells the detective, "You'll think it very mad, Mr. Holmes, that a man of a good old family should marry a wife in this fashion, knowing nothing of her past or of her people" (1:706). The wife, an American who was once betrothed to a gangster, tells Holmes, "I have had some very disagreeable associations in my life, . . . I wish to forget all about them" (1:706). The repressed inevitably returns, crossing oceans on the ever-improving steamers to seek its revenge in England. One client tells Watson, "of all ghosts the ghosts of our old loves are the worst" (1:514). Holmes unmasks these ghosts, sometimes too late to save his clients.

As a "private" consulting detective, Holmes solves the crimes of England's most illustrious families because their reputations and their identities, as traditionally constructed, depend on the suppression of unwanted connections. In a society where the communications network is burgeoning, Holmes's clients fight a losing battle to distinguish the public from the private.

If the Holmes stories are any indication, England's first families have a great deal to hide, although the stories may merely reflect the wishful thinking of middle-class readers.[7] Like the author, Watson loves and reveres these families and sees it as his duty to protect them even as he hints about their sins; the awe with which Doyle regarded the nobility manifests itself in Watson's descriptions. In "The Adventure of the Beryl Coronet," the nobleman who offers the coronet as collateral for a £50,000 loan bears "a name which is a household word all over the earth—one of the highest, noblest, most exalted names in England" (1:410). Even Holmes, with his voyeuristic tendencies, claims he is unwilling to invade a client's life without good reason: "We have no excuse for an intrusion upon his privacy until we have some reason to think that there is a guilty reason for it" (2:344). Maintaining the discretion that keeps him in business, Holmes upholds a cultural rule that the wealthier and "older" the family, the more tightly its borders must be maintained. As in Mitchell's model of the mind, these boundaries maintain identity because of what they hold in as much as what they keep out.

In "The Adventure of the Priory School," Holmes is brought in by a school master to assist "one of the greatest subjects of the crown," a duke who owns 250,000 acres and has served as Lord of the Admiralty and Chief Secretary of State (1:746). The duke's son has disappeared from school, along with his German master, under mysterious circumstances. The client finds it difficult to talk to Holmes because "to his intensely aristocratic nature this discussion of his intimate family affairs with a stranger was most abhorrent" (1:753). At first, the culprit appears to be a fired coachman seeking revenge, but Holmes discovers that the father knows very well who is responsible for the kidnapping. The duke is being manipulated by an earlier illegitimate son who "deeply resented those social laws" which precluded his inheriting his father's estate and "hated [the] young legitimate heir from the first with a persistent hatred" (1:770, 769). The angry natural son has joined forces with the angry servant to sequester the socially sanctioned heir and will restore him only if the duke recognizes him as principal heir in his will. Although the client is an accessory to murder, Holmes views the respected aristocrat as a victim and helps him to solve the problem quietly, once he has reproached him for his bad judgment. The duke sends his natural son to Australia, a temporary solution to a larger social problem. As a dumping ground for the empire's unwanted people, this colony breeds many of the threats with which Holmes must deal. In the end, he resigns himself to silence, stating that "having secured the future, we can afford to be more lenient with the past" (1:771). Holmes has been able to "secure the future" (to rescue the legitimate heir) only by revealing the past, without which he could never have diagnosed the problem. Although he declines to bring the duke to justice, he makes any further denial of the past impossible, a denial which had put the future at risk.

This duke who has condoned the kidnapping of his own son, tormented by the fruit of an illicit love affair and the rage of a servant unfairly dismissed, is typical of Holmes's clients. As part of an imperial immune system, the detective rarely engages foreign particles working in isolation. The greatest threats to the empire, Doyle's stories suggest, come not from without, but from within, particularly when native outcasts ally themselves with foreign invaders as Small did with Tonga. Foremost among these potential enemies are those of the lower classes. Holmes, whose elitism ensures that he is at least half serious, tells one client, "Sorry to see that you've had the British workman in the house. He's a token of evil" (1:563). Servants present a great danger, since as impoverished people who know one's household secrets, they can easily become the agents of an enemy: "there are no better instruments than discharged servants with a grievance" (2:313). When reading Holmes's adventures, one concludes that above all, one must take care whom one allows into one's house.

Suitors constitute a great risk because of their ability to win the confidence and affections of the more impressionable members of the household. A jealous husband who eventually killed his wife and cut off her ears tells Holmes that "For a month [her seducer] was in and out of my house, and never once did it cross my mind that harm might come of his soft, tricky ways" (2:338). Evil could enter a household through its wayward sons, but its daughters, the weakest links in family armor, constituted a threat because of their susceptibility to both foreign and native-grown scoundrels. With their tendency toward weak wills, as Mitchell had suggested, they were the point of least resistance. In "The Adventure of the Beryl Coronet," the frantic banker holding the crown suspects it has been damaged by his "wayward" son, who has introduced the confidence man Sir George Burnwell into his household. Holmes, however, quickly uncovers the real culprit. It is the banker's angelic niece. She has tried to steal the coronet and elope with Burnwell (whose knighthood suggests that he has also conned the Queen) after "he bent her to his will" (1:425). The threat to the empire that emerges here, one audacious enough to make off with the imperial jewels, is homegrown.

In "The Adventure of the Illustrious Client," Doyle uses modern science's discourse on this vulnerability just as Cajal did in his "Vacation stories."[8] The client, whose name is a "household word in society," begs Holmes to save his daughter, "a lovely, innocent girl," who is determined to marry a scoundrel (2:463, 465). This time the confidence man looks foreign, though it is unclear what sort of blood he may carry: "His face was swarthy, almost Oriental, with large, dark, languorous eyes which might easily hold an irresistible fascination for women" (2:480). The clever interloper has specifically told the girl that everyone will slander him and has influenced her through hypnotic suggestion to believe only him. Holmes and Watson try, unsuccessfully, to enlighten her as to the nature of her fiancé, and the seducer is bold enough to explain to them why she has ignored their warnings: "You have heard of post-hypnotic suggestion, Mr. Holmes? . . . a man of personality can use hypnotism without any vulgar passes or tomfoolery" (2:469–70). The seducer is finally stopped not by Holmes or Watson but by an infuriated ex-lover who hurls acid in his magnetic face. The disturbing tale reveals that illustrious clients can never fully control the forces that enter their houses because they can never fully control the minds of their women and children, which can be "infected" by any of the unsavory characters lurking in the heart of the empire.

In 1888, Doyle wanted to write a book "dedicated to all the bad boys of the Empire, by one who sympathizes with them" (Carr, 56). Almost every Holmes story fulfills this wish. The economic structure of the empire appears to have corrupted many potentially upstanding citizens, who then, like Kurtz in Joseph Conrad's "Heart of Darkness," threaten the system that produced them by playing its game too well.

Professor Moriarty epitomizes these cells that have turned against the imperial body. A "man of good birth and excellent education" who once held a mathematics chair at a respected university, he has become "the Napoleon of Crime" (1:645). Moriarty terrifies his society because he has apparently *chosen* crime. Given every opportunity available to the empire's most privileged citizens, he has decided to direct all of his mental powers against it. Holmes calls his mind "the organizer of every deviltry, the controlling brain of the underworld, a brain which might have made or marred the destiny of nations" (2:150). It is Moriarty's free choice of evil over good, even more than his formidable intelligence, that makes him Holmes's and the empire's greatest enemy. As a controlling element in the empire's immune system, Holmes will always vanquish its "native" criminals first, for the destruction of England's own worst products will frequently neutralize foreign interlopers simultaneously. They cannot operate without the weak and/or traitorous Britons who help them infiltrate the imperial nerve center.

Here again the strategy of Doyle's detective reflects Robert Koch's discoveries in the laboratory and the clinic. Observing the patients treated with Koch's tuberculosis "cure," Doyle comprehended immediately that the treatment—which proved to be a tremendous disappointment—functioned not by killing the bacillus directly but by killing and expelling the damaged tissue in which the bacillus grew. When it did work, Koch's fluid succeeded because it left the bacillus no foothold in the body it was attacking. "Koch has never claimed that his fluid kills the tubercle bacillus," wrote Doyle. "On the contrary, it has no effect on it, but destroys *the low form of tissue in the meshes of which the bacilli lie* . . . it will only be in very exceptional cases that the bacilli are all expelled." He concludes that "it continually removes the traces of the enemy, but it still leaves him deep in the invaded country" (Doyle 1890, 556, my italics). When he returned home, Doyle made sure that his own fantasy cure would do Koch one better, targeting both diseased tissue and foreign invaders. Holmes's priorities and strategies reflect their creator's medical knowledge.

Masking and Unmasking

As an imperial leukocyte, Holmes succeeds so often in reaching his target because he moves freely throughout the imperial body. Although he scorns most servants, workers, and country bumpkins, Holmes can always assume their identities, win their confidence, and enlist them for his cause, making him the perfect imperial agent. He states proudly that "my ramifications stretch out into many sections of society," and his connections with the empire's lowest elements surely provided the greatest assurance to its most powerful (1:863). For intelligence purposes, Holmes will work with anyone, from the notorious blackmailer Milverton to the "street Arab" Irregulars who "scamper away downstairs like so many rats" (1:41). He can uncover evil because of his intimacy with it.

Nothing has delighted Doyle's readers more than Holmes's ability to disguise himself, his uncanny talent for assuming any face and any voice. He loves masking himself to unmask his opponent. In *The Sign of Four*, when his disguise of an aged sailor fools Watson and Athelny Jones, Jones exclaims, "You would have made an actor and a rare one." Holmes explains that "a good many of the criminal classes begin to know me . . . so I can only go on the war-path under some simple disguise like this" (1:170). Despite the wealth and social status of many of the criminals Holmes has uncovered, for him, the "criminal classes" are the poor; and he usually disguises himself to penetrate the lower end of the social scale, as a cabdriver, a workman, or a beggar.

Praising Koch before the Colonial Society in 1898, Medical Privy Councilor Gerhardt called him "the one who unveiled the secret life of the anthrax bacillus."[9] Both Koch and Holmes epitomize the experimental scientist described by Bernard, a man who "forces nature to unveil herself by attacking her with all manner of questions." As a doctor, Doyle knew all too well the lesson that Cajal illustrated in the "Accursed House": terrifying supernatural threats lose their potency when revealed as natural ones. The first short story Doyle ever published, in fact, described "a Kaffir superstition about a demon with glowing eyes: which eyes, when faced by the hero's, turned out to be diamonds in rock-salt" (Carr, 27). Holmes unmasks innumerable "curses," reinforcing the empire's confidence that its science and technology could overcome demonic threats it associated with the people it was colonizing. "The Cornish Horror," for instance, is actually the African devil's-foot root; the Sussex vampire is a desperate mother trying to suck poison out of her son's neck; the "curse" of the Sussex coast is a jellyfish; and the hell-hound of the Baskervilles is really a large dog covered with phosphorous.

Like Koch and Cajal, Holmes is a national hero because he renders the invisible visible. "Unveiling" is precisely what he does to the criminals he tracks down, sometimes literally, as he peels off their false faces and disguises. Holmes's unmasking of the beggar in "The Man with the Twisted Lip" indicates that any subversion of the social system through which identity is established may qualify as a crime that requires exposure. The beggar's crime, rather than panhandling, is his denial of the work ethic and of Victorian notions of respectability. A man of "excellent education," an actor and a reporter in his youth, he had once disguised himself as a beggar to write an investigative report and discovered that he could earn much more through panhandling than through journalism: "You can imagine how hard it was to settle down to arduous work at two pounds a week when I knew that I could earn as much in a day by smearing my face with a little paint, laying my cap on the ground, and sitting still. . . . As I grew richer I grew more ambitious, took a house in the country, and eventually married, without anyone having a suspicion as to my real occupation" (1:326). Holmes's unmasking of the impostor—who is using a disguise the detective often resorts to himself—is literal, violent, and total. As he roughly wipes the face of the sleeping man, "the man's face peeled off under the sponge like the bark from a tree" (1:324).

Lawrence Rothfield, who associates Holmes's techniques with new developments in medicine, describes his unmasking procedure as "an invasion of privacy by the private eye," a "humiliation ritual" (Rothfield, 139). Koch's vision of every individual as a potential hiding place for deadly bacteria encouraged societies to scrutinize every person for the sake of the group, so that people became "objects of knowledge to be identified" (132). Holmes's unveiling alleviates not merely the hygienic but also the social and economic fears of middle-class Victorians. If anyone could mimic the signs of bourgeois respectability, suggesting that such respectability depended on appearance alone, then bourgeois respectability would lose its meaning.

Holmes, that is, exposes counterfeit people who have infiltrated the social body as free signifiers. By imitating people of actual "worth" and convincing people they signify something of value, the impostors threaten to disrupt the accepted pairings of signifier and signified that make the society work. As Rothfield puts it, Holmes "identifies in order to exclude, and by excluding he shores up a concept of personal identity and a social order that already exists" (Rothfield, 140–41). In *The Sign of Four,* for instance, the detection and punishment of Jonathan Small, a "bad" representative of the empire, "justif[ies] 'legitimate' imperialism and 'respectable' new money" (Farrell, 35). Holmes's unmasking fulfills the desires of the upper and middle classes to see their society as a private club, a closed system that one may enter only by birth or through "connections" they carefully control. To preserve the structure of his society, he must uncover all those who are "passing" as respectable citizens (Rothfield, 140; Arata, 638).

Holmes's most astonishing feat of unmasking occurs in "The Yellow Face," one of the few cases in which his chain of deductions proves faulty. A "reserved, self-contained man . . . more likely to hide his wounds than to expose them" comes to Holmes for help when his wife begins asking him for her money and making mysterious trips to a nearby cottage (1:481). The wife, an Englishwoman, had lived in the American South until her former husband and child had died of yellow fever. The frightened man, who has spotted an "unnatural and inhuman" white face in the cottage window, asks Holmes, "What link could there be between that creature and my wife?" (1:483, 486). Holmes suspects blackmail, and together they enter the cottage where they confront the specter face to face: "Holmes, with a laugh, passed his hand behind the child's ear, a mask peeled off from her countenance, and there was a little coal-black negress, with all her white teeth flashing in amusement at our amazed faces" (1:491).

The mother, afraid of "gossip about there being a black child in the neighborhood," has personally masked her own daughter (1:493). She explains that her first husband was black and that the interracial marriage led to an intensification of blackness: "I cut myself off from my race in order to wed him . . . It was our misfortune that our only child took after his people rather than mine. It is often so in such matches, and little Lucy is darker far than ever her father was" (1:492).[10] After the unmasking, it is unclear what will become of the black child. Holmes's client, who needs to think for a full ten minutes before speaking, says only that he is a better man than his wife takes him for, and Holmes is concerned only with his own misjudgment of the case. His assessment of blackmail, however, is not far off the mark, since the mother is motivated chiefly by fear that her husband and society will discover her past "sin." By placing a white mask on the child's black face, she repeats the action of all those respectable citizens trying to suppress the traces of their colonial wealth and "connections."

Counterfeiters and Blackmailers: The Empire and Its Crimes

Certain crimes predominate in Holmes's cases. Although his foes kidnap and murder (they never rape), steal, and kill, most often they attempt to get something for nothing, using special knowledge to subvert the economic system. Doyle's stories express the anxieties of the day, and foremost among these are fears that traditional sign systems that confer meaning are breaking down. British society abounded with "masked" characters. A hundred years previously, a noble name had supposedly guaranteed both a pedigree and wealth from "respectable" sources. By 1890, despite Holmes's valiant efforts, heraldic signifiers were becoming detached from the genealogies and the funds that they promised. If present at all, wealth might be new and earned by questionable means. In Doyle's stories, the crimes of the empire's malefactors reflect the empire's own economic structure. What is imperialism, after all, but getting something for nothing?

Counterfeiters present a formidable challenge to the British Empire, since when worthless bank notes perfectly mimic those of real economic value, the entire system by which worth is represented falls into disrepute. Anxiety about counterfeit money, of course, reflects a deeper anxiety about counterfeit people: the foreigners, criminals, anarchists, and scoundrels who populate the Holmes stories. Successfully passing themselves off as gentlefolk in the British countryside, such individuals may bear respectable names but carry neither the genetic nor the economic value that those names should guarantee. To a certain degree, all of Holmes's foes are counterfeiters, those who are so literally serving as a synecdoche for the rest.

In "The Adventure of the Engineer's Thumb," German counterfeiters kidnap a hydraulic engineer and force him to maintain their press. "Who were these German people," he wonders, "and what were they doing living in this strange, out-of-the-way place?" (1:378–79). The Germans, readers learn, have been "turning out half-crowns by the thousand" (1:386). Holmes uncovers their operation only after they have fled; they lose their press and their engineer but escape to begin afresh in a new location.

The American Pinkerton agent McMurdo who infiltrates a "union" of murderers in *The Valley of Fear* gains entry to the secret brotherhood partly because his alleged profession of counterfeiter—which he calls "shoving the queer"—promises to be useful to them (2:235). Products of an expert counterfeiter, McMurdo's name, history, and good will are all fabricated, as is his British identity as the gentleman Douglas. While he exposes their criminal operations, McMurdo is ultimately unable to escape the avenging brotherhood. In England, he falls victim to Moriarty's agents whom the brotherhood has contracted out to kill him. A mirror image of the ruling authorities, the criminal ones are even less tolerant of falsification.

. In "The Adventure of the Three Garridebs," another American, the gangster "Killer" Evans, seeks the notorious counterfeiter Prescott's printing press. To remove an eccentric old collector from the apartment where it is concealed, he concocts an elaborate scheme about a millionaire named Garrideb seeking eponymous heirs. Cornered by Holmes, Evans compares the empire's sign system to that of a master artist, boasting that, had he succeeded in restarting Prescott's press, not even Holmes could have distinguished the meaningless from the meaningful notes: "No living man could tell a Prescott from a Bank of England, and if I hadn't put him out he would have flooded London with them" (2:563). Holmes saves his empire from inflation but more importantly from a loss of confidence in its symbols.

It is no coincidence that the counterfeiters in the Holmes stories are Germans and Americans. Doyle greatly admired Americans and saw them as an energized and revitalized offshoot of the Anglo-Saxon race, transformed by the environmental challenges, increased social mobility, and the general wildness of their society. Economically and morally exhausted in contrast to what Doyle viewed as a more "vigorous" Anglo-Saxon country, England relied upon Africa and Asia for its resources and wealth. Prescott and "Killer" Evans, like the German counterfeiters, have come to England to disseminate their false signifiers because they feel a natural affinity for its counterfeit society. In a rising power like Germany or the United States, the stories suggest, social position is still linked to achievement. There is no need to mimic traditional class signs to win status, and counterfeiters have no place there.[11]

Blackmail, the most common crime in the Holmes stories, is intimately related to counterfeiting because it threatens the "names" of the empire's great families. Holmes at first leaves Sir Henry Baskerville in Watson's hands because, he explains, "at the present instant one of the most revered names in England is being besmirched by a blackmailer, and only I can stop a disastrous scandal" (2:41). Such a calling makes Holmes a busy man, because he serves an empire in which almost all of the prominent citizens have something to hide. The imperial gentleman, as one old servant aptly puts it, has "sold his soul to the devil in exchange for money and expects his creditor to come up and claim his own" (2:313).

Typical of such gentlemen is James Armitage in "The Gloria Scott." Armitage is the father of Holmes's only college friend. Transported to Australia in 1855 for embezzling to pay gambling debts, Armitage participated in a mutiny and then, with his friend Evans, unearthed his fortune in the Australian gold fields: "Evans and I changed our names and made our way to the diggings, where, among the crowds who were gathered from all nations, we had no difficulty in losing our former identities . . . We prospered, we traveled, we came back as rich colonials to England, and we bought country estates. For more than twenty years we have led peaceful and useful lives, and we hoped that our past was forever buried (1:526). Blackmailed by a sailor from the transport ship, Armitage comes to Holmes in desperation. The case, in the end, resolves itself. Holmes suspects that the man's partner Evans has killed the sailor and left the country, and, seeing that Armitage has owned up to his past, the detective leaves his client free to enjoy the rest of his respectable life.

The Moriarty of blackmailers, Charles Augustus Milverton, is a man with whom Holmes periodically collaborates to obtain information. Described as "the worst man in London," Milverton presents a constant threat to the empire's most illustrious families. Employing the same "foreign" vehicle that S. Weir Mitchell had used to represent threatening *internal* forces, Holmes compares this "king of all the blackmailers" to a gigantic, evil snake who "will squeeze and squeeze until he has drained [his victims] dry" (1:792). Doyle's image involves a foreign snake, most likely the boa constrictor, but simultaneously it suggests a bleeding process—which is not the snake's objective—with an intelligent design. More indicative of the empire's own actions, Doyle's description of Milverton illustrates what Stephen Arata has called "imperial ideology mirrored back as a kind of monstrosity" (Arata, 634). A foreign snake is doing to the British what the British are doing to foreign countries.

Collecting compromising documents from "treacherous valets or maids" and "genteel ruffians, who have gained the confidence and affection of trusting women," Milverton enriches himself by threatening noble families with ruin (1:792). He always succeeds, explains Holmes, because he never attacks an innocent person, ensuring his invulnerability. Quite possibly, there are no innocent people in the society in which he operates.

Engaged by a desperate woman when Milverton threatens to reveal imprudent letters to her illustrious fiancé, Holmes first confronts Milverton unsuccessfully and then resolves to burgle his house. The detective, with his own sense of justice, finds the burglary "morally justifiable, though technically criminal" (1:797). He takes great pleasure in cracking Milverton's safe, "this green and gold monster, the dragon which held in its maw the reputations of many fair ladies" (1:800). While Holmes and Watson hide, one of Milverton's female victims enters and fatally shoots the blackmailer; then, with the body beside him, Holmes coolly unloads the safe and burns all of the letters it contains. Holmes gives Watson to understand "that it was no affair of ours, that justice had overtaken a villain," and he tells inspector Lestrade, "I think there are certain crimes which the law cannot touch, and which therefore, to some extent, justify private revenge" (1:804, 805). His own goal, his personal uncovering of the "scarlet thread" of the case, does not require that he bring the guilty to justice.

Holmes's values prove convenient to his wealthy employers, many of whom are criminals themselves. He carries his own sense of justice, one that does not require official punishment for upper-class offenders, and Doyle supports this notion of "natural" resolutions by ensuring that poetic justice resolves a case when Holmes fails to call in the police. The respectable criminals uncovered by Holmes sometimes try to justify their actions, like robber barons, by pleading their philanthropy and their high hopes for the future. In "The Boscombe Valley Mystery," for instance, Turner kills his blackmailer McCarthy when the man demands his daughter's hand in marriage in exchange for silence about Turner's former career as a highway robber in the Australian bush. He explains, "I set myself to do a little good with my money, to make up for the way in which I had earned it" (1:287). Holmes does ask that Turner, who is likely to die of diabetes within a month, sign a confession so that no innocent man can be convicted for the murder, but he promises only to use it "at the last extremity," if it is "absolutely needed" (1:287). Watson concludes the tale of blackmail optimistically, writing that "there is every prospect that the son and daughter may come to live happily together in ignorance of the black cloud which rests upon their past" (1:289).

Apparently, if Holmes and Watson revealed to the public all of the crimes they discovered, they would endanger the ideology they seek to uphold. Holmes tells Watson that "once or twice in my career I feel that I have done more real harm by my discovery of the criminal than ever he had done by his crime . . . I had rather play tricks with the law of England than with my own conscience" (1:895–96). This startling confession recalls Lessing's revelation that he cared more for the search after truth than for truth itself, and it suggests that the empire's legal system no longer fulfills its citizens' desires for justice in a new social order (Nietzsche 1872, 95). Doyle's readers want to be pardoned for their theft and murder in the colonies, and, simultaneously, they want to see themselves as living in a land of law and order. Holmes exists because of this unstable relationship between their ideal notion of British justice and their new notion of imperial justice, in which a crime in the colonies is not a crime at home and one can safeguard the dirty secrets of one's imperial wealth. A believer in "private" justice, Holmes acts as an intermediary between the traditional and the modern, the ideal and the actual law, insisting only that his clients "face up" to the truth.

Conclusion: The Face in the Window

The pale face that so frightens Holmes's client in "The Yellow Face" recurs, in many forms, throughout his adventures. As the imperial hero struggles to unmask foreigners and expel the corrupted tissue around them, his employers are repeatedly terrorized by disembodied faces that stare at them, either suspended outside their own windows or appearing briefly in the buildings they pass by. Originally, Doyle had entitled his story "The Livid Face," the adjective implying anger as well as whiteness, and his shift to "yellow" is at first puzzling, since the face is not yellow at all but a "livid, chalky white" (1:483). "Yellow," however, suggests anger in a jaundiced and choleric sense, and it resonates with the yellow fever of which the black husband conveniently died. It also links the black child to England's Asian colonial subjects, who are occasionally referred to as "black." The "livid yellow face" staring down at Holmes's client can thus be read as a dream symbol, a condensation of all of England's colonials, their diseases, and their anger. It appears inexplicably in a cottage in the English countryside, stares out at the inhabitants, and will not go away.

In *The Sign of Four*, Major Sholto dies of terror, just as he is about to tell his sons the location of the Agra treasure, when he spies a face looking in out of the darkness: "We could see the whitening of the nose where it was pressed against the glass. It was a bearded, hairy face with wild cruel eyes and an expression of concentrated malevolence" (1:128). The description suggests the faces and emotions of Small and Tonga, who have returned to avenge the theft of their treasure. Here, the face in the window is that of the victim/thief stalking the thief/victim, who, well aware of the source of his wealth, projects his own sense of evil onto the stalker (Arata, 623; Brantlinger, 81; Farrell, 34). It is not they who are threatening their colonials; it is their colonials, represented by their "small" invaders, who are threatening them.

The face in the window reflects the psychology of imperial doublethink, as the invaders and the thieves, determined to see themselves as virtuous in their own land, project onto their windowpanes their repressed fears of avengers who will invade the empire's heartland. In "The Adventure of Wisteria Lodge," a frightened man believes he has seen "the devil" looking in at him through a window: the face "wasn't black, nor was it white, nor any color that I know, but a kind of queer shade like clay with a splash of milk in it. . . . And the look of it—the great staring goggle eyes, and the line of white teeth like a hungry beast" (2:306). The man has actually seen a mulatto cook, a practitioner of voodoo, the servant of a bloodthirsty Central American dictator who has concealed himself in the British countryside. The violent tropics and the British domestic sphere are not as far apart as they appear to be.

When Holmes asks Miss Burnet in "The Adventure of Wisteria Lodge," "How can an English lady join in such a murderous affair?" she replies, "What does the law of England care for the rivers of blood shed years ago in San Pedro, or for the shipload of treasure which this man has stolen? To you they are like crimes committed in some other planet" (2:317). Although in this case the crimes that have been committed are not the direct results of British imperialism, the face reminds Doyle's readers that the blood spilling they associate with the tropics is never far from home. Her reply encourages readers to "look into" British colonial practices which may likewise be criminal.

These disembodied faces abound in the Holmes stories not merely because the British fear an invasion of small, angry creatures, but because they fear for their own identity. Bodies in the imperial age exist as fragments, and Holmes's refusal to respect "the body's integrity as a living totality" reflects both cultural and medical changes (Rothfield, 135). While it multiplied the possibilities for connections between people, the imperial communications net with its monster tentacles dissolved the traditional hierarchy that had conferred upon the elite a feeling of personal wholeness. Watching the London pedestrians pass by lighted shop windows, Watson describes the "endless procession of faces which flitted across these narrow bars of light . . . Like all humankind, they flitted from the gloom into the light and so back into the gloom once more" (Doyle 1986, 1:120–21). The anonymous citizens of London, like their invaders, appear as disembodied faces, lacking identities and histories. Holmes's genius bears an uneasy relationship to his society's denial, since the very industrialization and imperialism that made it prosper destroyed the "closed" sense of self to which its citizens so desperately clung. If one conceives of one's identity in terms of borders, new connections can only undermine it.

FIVE

Arthur Schnitzler

The Open Self

You know so many people?   —Arthur Schnitzler

In his descriptions of microbes, Santiago Ramón y Cajal had revealed how effortlessly the boundaries between people can be crossed. Miraculously endowed with microscopic vision, his pessimistic character is horrified to see the arbitrariness of social boundaries and the meaninglessness of social differences in the light of biological sameness:

I refer to the open-hearted and essentially egalitarian nature of the microbe. For pathogenic bacteria, men and animals, rich and poor, represent mere fields to cultivate and lodgings as advantageous as they are desirable. One had to see how a woman of apparent noble lineage unconsciously breathed in the flu bacillus just expelled from the chest of a ragged and brazen tramp. As he descended from a luxurious coach and at the moment he was about to penetrate the government ministry, one could see an arrogant and haughty ex-minister breathe in, with enjoyment, the tuberculosis bacillus vented moments before by the ulcerated lung of a furious anarchist. . . . What a desolating spectacle! In the face of the invisible enemies everywhere, the most absolute indolence, indifference, and defenselessness were the only weapons (Cajal 1964, 179–80).[1]

Scientists like Cajal, who observed bacteria during the 1880s, were themselves the wizards who offered Europeans a new "microscopic vision," and Cajal's pessimist might well represent any educated man of his time. Everywhere, he sees unwanted affinities: there could be no doubt that Koch's and Pasteur's microbes crossed all socially constructed borders between individuals. The question, of course, was how to react to these affinities. One could dig in, making every effort to maintain the boundaries on which identity was based, or one could seek a new concept of selfhood that did not rely on borders. Just as colonialism called for a rethinking of national identity, germ theory demanded a new notion of the self, one that would take these new, unwanted affinities into account.

As the nineteenth century drew to a close, younger authors interested in psychological notions of selfhood began to show the consequences of basing personal identity on divisions that did not actually exist. Since the impermeability of the self to microbes and suggestions was pure fiction, definitions of individuality must allow for a certain openness to the environment. Creative writers thus faced the same question that had challenged Cajal in his quest to understand the nervous system: how "open" could an individual be to outside influences without losing his or her autonomy?

Because of his simultaneous interests in infectious diseases, hypnotism, and identity, physician-author Arthur Schnitzler is a figure whose works illustrate particularly well the late nineteenth-century tension between the desire for boundaries and the consciousness of openness. His early works, "Der Empfindsame" (The sensitive one, 1895), "Lieutenant Gustl" (1900), and *Reigen* (1900) explore the destruction that can result from belief in barriers and paranoia about penetration, and they begin to develop a new concept of individuality that takes this openness into account.

Hypnotism: Invasion of the Self?

Throughout much of the nineteenth century, hypnotism was dismissed as an offshoot of eighteenth-century magnetism and was not respected by the European medical community as a legitimate therapeutic practice. Many doctors, however—like J. K. Mitchell—experimented with it anyway, and it became central to their views of health and pathology. Like Mitchell, Cajal, and Doyle, Schnitzler was taught germ theory and hypnotism when he was trained as a physician, but he responded to them very differently. Studying medicine in the culture of fin-de-siècle Vienna, he took this evidence of human permeability not as a challenge demanding a counterattack but as an invitation to revise strained notions of human identity.

While human responsiveness to suggestion had been known and used for centuries in the medical community, it became scientifically respectable only during the peak years of germ theory. The timing of this shift could represent a mere coincidence, but it is more likely that the willingness to analyze suggestibility answered new cultural needs. In February 1882, neurologist

Jean Martin Charcot (1835–93) gave a lecture to the French Academy of Sciences entitled "On the Various Nervous States Determined by Hypnotization in Hysterics," reintroducing hypnotism to mainstream medical discourse. Even Charcot, however, the leading European neurologist of the era, could not have made hypnosis reputable and fashionable if physicians like J. K. Mitchell had not been practicing it for some time and if it had not been receiving coverage in the popular press (Ellenberger, 750–51). Hypnotism came into vogue in the years of Koch's and Pasteur's key discoveries because it provided a medium through which scientists and other writers could explore social and psychological definitions of selfhood and articulate their fears about permeable borders.

Hypnosis, according to Charcot, represented a physiological process and a pathological state, an induced neurosis that might actually damage a normal subject (Ellenberger, 89–93; Sulloway, 42–49). A group of physicians at Nancy challenged his association of hypnosis with hysteria, however, claiming instead that all people could be hypnotized. Led by Hippolyte Bernheim (1840–1919), the Nancy group promoted the much more subversive hypothesis that all people were open to suggestion all of the time.

Bernheim had earned his reputation as a physician studying typhoid fever and tuberculosis; Charcot, in contrast, had earned his through achievements in geriatrics and neurology (Ellenberger, 87). In his first textbook on hypnotism, published in 1886, Bernheim repeatedly stresses the affinity of hypnosis to mental states accepted as normal, such as ordinary sleep. "To prove that the very great majority of subjects are susceptible to suggestion is to eliminate the idea of a neurosis," he argues. "For, as we all have nervous tissues, and as it is a property of such tissues to be impressionable, we should all be hysterical" (Bernheim 1957, viii). August Forel, who visited Bernheim's clinic in 1887, agreed that "every mentally healthy person is more or less hypnotizable" (Forel, 58). Bernheim estimated that at least 80 percent of people could be hypnotized; Forel, at least 90 percent. The remainder had succeeded in imposing on their own minds the auto-suggestion that they could not be hypnotized (57, 60). Ultimately, Bernheim believed that all people are open to suggestion because the human nervous system and the human mind by their very nature are open to new ideas and impressions. Human capacity for belief (*crédivité*) formed the basis not only for psychic life but also for most social and cultural interactions.

The conflict over people's openness to suggestion created considerable public debate about the effects of social practices and interactions on individual personality. Bernheim opens his second textbook on hypnotism with a historical review of medical and religious practices, attributing their success to people's receptiveness to suggestion. Like Cajal and Schnitzler, who read and admired his works, Bernheim believes that suggestion plays a central role in everyday life: "Lawyers, preachers, professors, orators, merchants, charlatans, seducers, politicians, all use suggestion," he writes (Bernheim 1980, 19). Forel again backs Bernheim's claim, writing that all people are "intuitively credulous" and that "unconsciously and hypoconsciously we believe in things which do not exist or exist only in part" (Forel, 57). Bernheim discovered that hypnosis worked best in people long resigned to obedience, such as soldiers and aging workers. He had greater difficulty giving hypnotic orders to members of the wealthier classes (Ellenberger, 87). When critics accused him of reducing all medical treatment to suggestion, Bernheim replied: "I have not said that everything is suggestion, but rather that suggestion is in everything" (Bernheim 1980, 46). By hypnotizing his patients, Bernheim merely hoped to use human *crédivité* for therapeutic purposes.

When one considers Bernheim's early work with typhoid fever and the enormous attention being paid to infectious bacteria in the mid-1880s, it is particularly interesting to see how his wording reflects the premises of germ theory. When he discusses the interaction of incoming suggestions with the brain, he writes that "ideas can be insinuated into the brain, embodied ... in an inert medication" (Bernheim 1980, 40). Bernheim defined suggestion as "the act by which an idea is introduced into the brain and accepted by it," and he described the brain as an "entryway to the psychic centers" (18, 21). Hypnotists were merely observing the "port of entry" and the "port of exit" (22). Bernheim's phrasing suggests a self surrounded by biological, ideological, and perhaps sexual threats and recalls S. Weir Mitchell's concept of the individual defined by his or her resistance to dangerous influences.

Ordinarily barriers of reason protect people from insidious suggestions, but sleep and hypnosis lower these barriers. "Susceptibility to suggestion exists in the waking condition," writes Bernheim, "but it is then either neutralized or restrained by the faculties of reason, attention, and judgment." In the sleep of hypnotism, however, "impressions are accepted without verification" (Bernheim 1957, x). In highly suggestible people, who responded to extraneous ideas without the need for hypnosis, Bernheim believed that "each idea, confidently introduced into their brain, is accepted, since they do not know how to protect themselves against it" (1980, 108). Both Bernheim and Forel pointed out the ease with which subjects under hypnosis played out designated roles. Forel noted that hypnotized people could *jouer au naturel* and were always more convincing than real swindlers. It appeared to these scientists that human minds were designed to take up suggestions and play roles in response to them according to behavior previously observed. By its very nature, the human nervous system was open to incoming commands.

It is particularly interesting that Forel, who proposed that neurons were intact and independent a year before Cajal provided the definitive anatomical evidence, concurred with Cajal in preferring Bernheim's theory of hypnosis to Charcot's. Like cell theory and germ theory, Bernheim's theory of universal suggestibility demanded belief in a personal "membrane." While this boundary was permeable, it could still resist unwanted intrusions, according to the energy one was willing and able to invest.

Those who opposed hypnotism in the 1880s presented it as a dehumanizing process in which the subject was reduced to a mere automaton in the hands of the hypnotist. To them, it represented an invasion of the self and an undermining of free will, permitting a hideous promiscuity in which any unscrupulous person with the necessary skills could penetrate and impregnate minds with any idea he or she desired to implant. Theodor Meynert, who taught Freud and Schnitzler neuroanatomy, wrote that under hypnosis "a human being is reduced to a creature without will or reason, and his nervous and mental degeneration is only hastened by it" (Sulloway, 42). Meynert was convinced that hypnosis had a sexual basis and that when the cortex yielded control, all kinds of erotic impulses were released, potentially harming or humiliating the patient. Mental barriers preserved human dignity and identity not just by screening out foreign suggestions but also by holding back internal impulses. Their breaching would thus be doubly horrifying, and in describing this breakdown, scientists revealed the sexual basis of their anxieties. To be entered, whether physically or mentally, was to be "unmanned."

To a certain extent, these fears about invasion and penetration were justified. Bernheim, Forel, and Schnitzler all had their hypnotized patients enact imaginary crimes, and Bernheim, to test for anesthesia, pricked his with needles. Bernheim, however, repeatedly stressed that no one could be hypnotized against his or her will: "Anyone who does not want to be hypnotized, and who knows that he need not be influenced if he does not wish to be, successfully resists every trial." He then qualified this statement, however, admitting that unwilling subjects could yield if they were convinced—by means of suggestion—that they were in the hands of a superior power: "No one can be hypnotized unless he has the idea that he is going to be" (Bernheim 1957, viii–ix).

Forel generally supported Bernheim's claim that the hypnotized subject was no automaton, writing that "the blind, automatic obedience of the hypnotized is never complete; suggestion always has its limits, which are some-times wider and sometimes narrower and may vary considerably in the same individual" (Forel, 100). Rather than taking away the subject's ability to resist, Forel maintained, the hypnotist takes away the subject's *belief* that he or she can resist. He describes the encounter between the two minds as a struggle for power with a strong sexual resonance: "suggestion means a sort of tourna-ment between the dynamisms of two brains; one gains mastery over the other up to a certain point, but only under the condition that it deals skillfully and delicately with the other, that it stimulates and uses its inclinations skillfully and, above all things, that it does not make its dealings go against the grain [*daß es dasselbe nicht widerhaarig macht*]" (102–3). In his comparison, the sub-ject hypnotized (who is skillfully stimulated, not hardened against the other) assumes the female role. Disturbingly, all people could find themselves in this role at any time. Not as convinced as Bernheim of the limits of the hypnotist's power, Forel confessed that the idea that no one could be hypnotized against his or her will might actually be wishful thinking. It was based on "the psychologically erroneous assumption that the freedom of the human will is essential" (59). No hypnotist could overcome a subject who was actively resisting, but anyone could be taken by surprise.

Supposedly, "strong-willed" patients could not be manipulated by un-wanted suggestions. Most physicians in the 1880s conceived of the will as Mitchell and Cajal did: as a force intimately related to personal identity and as a defense mechanism against pernicious suggestions from without. Bernheim had his doubts. "An evil thought can steal into the imagination without control and that thought tends to become an action," he wrote. "Up to what point can we resist this tendency?" (Bernheim 1980, 102). It was this open-ness to influence or "infection" from the environment that most fascinated Bernheim, and he studied its variation from person to person. When describ-ing cases of highly suggestible individuals, Bernheim occasionally sounds like Mitchell or Cajal, associating extreme sensitivity to suggestion with weakness of moral sensibility, weakness of will, and even weakness of identity. The three are closely linked through their common tendency to question and resist infectious ideas.

Bernheim's and Forel's theories of suggestibility could be used to support the model of the self as a fortress under siege offered by both Mitchell and Cajal. The most essential principle of Bernheim's theory, however, the open-ness of all minds to suggestions, is an invitation to incorporate extrinsic ideas into a notion of selfhood. For some writers, people were no longer forming their identities in opposition to these extrinsic suggestions; they were creating identities in relation to them. A new view of selfhood was developing concurrently with the new concepts of the mind and the cells that composed it.

Schnitzler as Physician: Openness to Ideas,
Openness to Disease

In recent years, consideration of Arthur Schnitzler's role as a physician has led to new insights about his literary works and his observations of Viennese society (Alexander, Alter, Couch, Schlein). Because of Schnitzler's interests in hypnosis and hysteria, studies have concentrated on his psychological theories and their relationship to Sigmund Freud's (Hausner, Nehring, Urban, Thomé).[2] Schnitzler, however, must also be recognized as a laryngologist and a physician in his own right. An analysis of his somatic interests, especially one attending to contemporaneous medical debates surrounding infectious diseases, also promises to enrich readings of Schnitzler's literature. Both his scientific writing and his fiction show how the social environment can be an "epidemic" to susceptible minds.

As a physician and author, Schnitzler knew the Viennese and their diseases intimately. Like Mitchell, he was the son of an influential physician; his father, Johann Schnitzler (1835–93) helped to establish the field of laryngology in Vienna and to develop its technology (Lesky, 365–79). One of the "pioneers of electrocauterization," he was the first in Vienna to use hypnosis to treat laryngeal disorders and was a first-hand observer of Koch's "cure" for tuberculosis in the 1890s in Berlin (376–77).

Arthur Schnitzler studied medicine in the 1880s, receiving his M.D. in 1885 and opening his practice in 1893. He continued to see patients into the 1920s and never ceased practicing medicine completely. Like S. Weir and J. K. Mitchell, Schnitzler and his father collaborated in many ways (Nehring, 184). In the late 1880s and early 1890s they ran the *Internationale Klinische Rundschau*, a respected medical journal in which Schnitzler reviewed texts by Mitchell, Bernheim, Forel, Charcot, Meynert, Fournier, and other leading psychologists and physicians of the day. Even in the absence of a busy practice and his father's broad-reaching interests, Schnitzler's work as a reviewer would have kept him extremely well informed on contemporary medical developments.

Arthur Schnitzler's interest soon turned to a distinctive and growing field: to clinical treatments using hypnosis. In an 1889 review of Bernheim's textbook, he described the polarized opinions on the use of hypnotic suggestion as therapy, some calling it "one of the most *valuable therapeutic achievements* of our century"; others denouncing it as "something *degrading to mankind*"

(Schnitzler 1988b, 210).[3] Schnitzler, who was decidedly pro-hypnosis, pointed out that what critics regarded as subversive invasions of the psyche actually occur routinely and that suggestion is the normal course of life: "Pedagogy is suggestion, great men were really practicing suggestion. Religious institutions have practiced suggestion, and entire peoples were their subjects. The automatic tyranny that the great spirit exerts over the smaller ones is suggestion, and when we resolve to get up at five in the morning and not to oversleep, we have carried out an autosuggestion (179).[4] "If suggestion was degrading, then so was life in human society.

One aspect of hypnosis particularly appealed to Schnitzler: its theatrical dimensions. He enjoyed watching his hypnotized patients play out roles he specified, and once, to test his powers as a hypnotist, he even arranged a mock murder attempt against himself (Urban, 136). In his medical practice, Schnitzler used hypnotic suggestion to restore the voices of his patients; unfortunately, the cure was rarely permanent, and the patients often returned mute several days or weeks later. So strong was Schnitzler's faith in hypnosis, however, that he proposed in an original article ("On Functional Aphonia and Its Treatment with Hypnosis and Suggestion," 1889) that it might be used to treat the more general neurotic conditions responsible for loss of voice: "I tend to think that with hypnotic suggestion, I have a means at hand to influence favorably certain general neurotic conditions, of which aphonia can be a symptom" (Schnitzler 1988b, 209).[5] Schnitzler also believed in the special "magnetic" relationship between the physician and the patient he or she hypnotized; this explained why other doctors were unable to restore the voices of a given doctor's patients by applying similar treatments (206).

Both Bernheim and Freud (whose German translation of Bernheim Schnitzler was reviewing) defended hypnosis against those concerned about this intimacy by pointing out its limits. Freud responded to the free will argument that had bothered many, asserting that limited interference with a troubled individual's mind was justified because could it cure the patient. "Can one really forget that the suppression of the independence of the patient through hypnotic suggestion is always only partial," he wrote, "that it is directed against the symptoms of disease?" (Urban, 141). In his textbook, Bernheim pointed out the parallels between hypnosis and acting, and he explained that hypnosis could never put anything into the patient that was not already there: "Each person plays his roles with the characteristics that he possesses, with the capacities at his disposal" (Schnitzler 1988b, 213).[6] Schnitzler, in his review, even proposed that hypnosis did not actually reveal the unconscious, just the theatrical roles that the patient wanted to play (Thomé, 77).

For Schnitzler, hypnosis as a medical treatment merely intensified the suggestion and role-playing already occurring in everyday life. The psyche had no real barriers to suggestion and was in its essence an open system.

As with Bernheim, Schnitzler's medical reading and clinical experience confronted him not simply with the prospect of psychological openness but also with the far more dangerous prospect of an individual's vulnerability to infection. The years 1885–1914, during which psychoanalytic theory was developed, also marked an age of "obsessive propaganda" in which European physicians and governments waged campaigns against infectious diseases, especially syphilis (Corbin 1990, 263).

The French physician Alfred Fournier, another scholar reviewed by Schnitzler, was the reformer largely responsible for this crusade. Fournier stressed the dangers of hereditary syphilis and the disease's ability to break up marriages, decrease the population, and create degeneration among the bourgeoisie (Corbin 1990, 262–64). He also pointed out what he saw as the paternal origin of the disease: poor women "poisoned" rich men, who then infected their own women, thus destroying an entire family line (Quétel, 169). In a solution reflecting bourgeois attitudes, Fournier believed that the disease could best be combated through the surveillance of prostitutes and through education, which he hoped would eliminate extramarital sex and return mankind to a "golden age of innocence" (Corbin 1990, 266).

Among the texts that Schnitzler reviewed for the *Internationale klinische Rundschau* between 1887 and 1894 were four books on syphilis that addressed the issues of transmission (both contagious and hereditary), prevention, and the all-important question of whether syphilis had a microorganism. In 1892, he reviewed Ernest Finger's translation of Fournier's *On the Heredity of Syphilis*. Schnitzler called heredity "one of the most important questions in the field of syphilis, which touches closely not only on medical but also on social interests" (Schnitzler 1988b, 268).[7] Revealing his knowledge of the literature, Schnitzler complained that Finger had taken great liberties with the translation, replacing Fournier's views with his own, particularly on the questions of whether sperm could transmit an infection and whether an uninfected mother could catch syphilis from an infected fetus. The central issues of the book, Schnitzler stressed, were (1) that "in general, Lues must be treated much more carefully and for a much longer time than it commonly is," and (2) that those infected must defer marriage, considering the frightening statistics on the death of syphilitic children (269). Overall, he concluded, the text "can be most warmly recommended for the ongoing study of all doctors" (270).[8] Five years before he wrote *Reigen*, which depicts a circle of sexual partners, Schnitzler knew and praised Fournier's studies on syphilis as well as the most eminent local work on the topic.

As a physician dealing with this disease, Schnitzler was also aware of the rush to find a syphilis microbe. In the late nineteenth century, syphilis was treatable with mercury but had no cure. Although its means of transmission was common knowledge, the disease remained mysterious because it did not yet have its "own" microorganism. While there had been claims of a syphilis germ as early as 1837, attempts to isolate a microbe in the 1870s and 1880s had led only to frustration (Quétel, 140). In his review of Heinrich Fülles' *Über Mikroorganismen bei Syphilis* in 1887, Schnitzler expressed skepticism for Fülles' certainty that a syphilis microbe would eventually be found and warned against identifying a product of the disease as its cause. He also pointed out the essential role of the microscope in such investigations. Without a microbe, syphilis was an invisible and thus terrifying disease, one that remained invisible in the years that Schnitzler wrote and began to distribute his forbidden play *Reigen*. The elusive microorganism, a very small spirochete, was identified only in 1905 and could be observed with ease only in 1906 when the ultramicroscope came into use (Quétel, 140–41). The conception of Schnitzler's early literary works thus coincides with the peak of concerns about syphilis, both in the medical community and in popular culture.

Schnitzler's reviews convey not only the contemporary anxiety about the individual's vulnerability to the disease but also concern about the general public's health. Fully conscious of the disease's destructiveness, Schnitzler was most critical of these contemporary texts on syphilis when they tried to deny that direct sexual contact spread the disease. At the close of one review, he stated firmly: "Above all it remains clear that Lues not only 'prefers' . . . but 'most likes' to be acquired through extramarital sexual intercourse" (Schnitzler 1988b, 249–50).[9] Syphilis was thriving in Schnitzler's Vienna, and it was thriving because of interpersonal connections whose existence no one wanted to admit. Disease violated the sacred bonds of matrimony because people violated them, and the disease could be treated only if people admitted their exposure to the germ. It is no wonder, then, that discussions of the disease converge with discussions of hypnotic suggestion and social structure, and that Schnitzler would "discuss" infection and suggestion in his fiction.

"The Sensitive One": Counterproductive Borders

Much of Schnitzler's early fiction deals with the tragic and sometimes violent interplay between outside forces and the sensitive self in the making.

Often cited to show Schnitzler's use of his clinical experience, his story "The Sensitive One" does far more than incorporate theories about the treatment of aphonia (Alexander, 9–11). Describing a young man who died of *Empfindsamkeit* (sensitivity), this early work raises questions about identity that Schnitzler would explore in much greater depth over the next five years. In a Viennese coffee house, a young man reads his friends a letter addressed to a man who has shot himself, and they try to comprehend what provoked his suicide. A sort of case history, the tale unfolds as a gradual explanation of his initial puzzling diagnosis, "he died of sensitivity" (255).

"The sensitive one" does contain extensive references to clinical techniques used by Schnitzler and his father, who treated many of the most famous singers of the day. In Schnitzler's story, the letter is from the young man's lover, a singer, who was being groomed as a performer of national stature when she suddenly lost her voice. "I have been painted, electrified, cauterized, massaged—massaged over my entire body because of two little vocal cords that won't close properly" she has written (Schnitzler 1961, 257).[10] None of the twenty-three doctors she has visited have succeeded in restoring her voice, and all, in their own ways, have suggested that the aphonia may have another, psychological cause. Schnitzler delights in studying the formulas, euphemisms and clichés of Viennese language, which manage to convey ideas despite their detachment from their intended meanings. The singer describes:

Some had already said, ah, my dear young woman, you are a little nervous, it would be good for you to marry; and others expressed themselves with tremendous caution and spoke of a drastic change of lifestyle; and some were extremely cunning and said, my dear young woman, haven't you ever been in love: . . . And still others were fresh and said, 'You know what you need?'(258)[11]

Finally she asks the twenty-fourth doctor, the bluntest of the lot, "What should I take?" ("*Was soll ich nehmen?*"), and he answers, "A lover." She does so immediately, selecting the unfortunate "sensitive one" at random out of a number of passers-by, and her voice is restored. She then leaves him and resumes her career, while he kills himself after reading her letter and learning how he was used.

Like Cajal, Schnitzler presents the reader with the latest theories and techniques available to solve complex physiological and psychological problems. Both Schnitzler and his father had used electricity to treat singers having difficulty with their voices. Bernheim had written that this technique was ineffective in itself but was sometimes beneficial because of the

suggestions it created. Schnitzler had proposed in his own article on aphonia that sexual satisfaction might cure the condition in some cases.[12] Also
like Cajal, Schnitzler incorporates such theories into his fiction in a highly
ironic, playful fashion. Subtitled "eine Burleske," "The sensitive one" is a
burlesque not merely of social mores but of the Viennese medical community's belief in its own techniques. While the humorous and ironic framework
frees Cajal and Schnitzler to explore the implications of controversial new
medical ideas, it simultaneously encourages readers to doubt new therapies
even as the physician-authors hint at their marvelous possibilities. The solution is too easy, and despite the suicide, "The sensitive one" is extremely
amusing.

The reader, who becomes one of the coffee house circle, shares the friends'
disbelief that this brief exploitation—which should have been no more than
the material for a good *Kaffeehaus* joke—could have driven the young man to
suicide. Here the young man who reads the letter acts as psychologist and
steps in to offer an explanation. "Just think," he tells us, "to believe, that one is
idolized by a young girl, and to discover, that she had—*taken you in*. After
receiving this letter, he must have seemed really disgusting and monstrous to
himself" (Schnitzler 1961, 261, my italics).[13] The friends agree that this kind
of disillusionment can destroy a person "when one is too sensitive [*wenn man
zu Empfindsam ist*]" (261). Through their interpretation, Schnitzler offers
Mitchell's view that hypersensitivity is the quintessential pathological condition. It is just one, however, of several possible readings.

In accounting for the man's violent death, Schnitzler's story plays with the
words *nehmen* (to take) and *einnehmen* (to take in). The young woman, advised
to "take" a lover, has "taken him in" in several senses. On a literal level, the
words suggest capture and engulfment, perhaps absorption by a leukocyte.
While this expression suggests that he penetrates her, as an infectious particle,
the opposite is the case: it is he who has lowered his barriers; he who is the
passive party. To a Viennese man of 1895, cast as the one who "takes," this
collapsing and confusion of borders would be horrifying for its social as well
as its biological consequences. "*Sich selber unheimlich vorkommen* (to seem
monstrous or unfamiliar to oneself)" indicates self-alienation, a collapse of his
identity that occurs when his personal boundaries give way and he is "taken
in." The man's "sensitivity" is rooted not in the weakness of his borders, but in
his need to conceive of identity in terms of borders, so that it is lost when they
fall. If his concept of self had permitted him to take in and be taken in, he
might have survived the insult.

"Lieutenant Gustl": Killing Intruders

Schnitzler's short story "Lieutenant Gustl," famous for its early stream-of-consciousness narrative structure, offers a direct look at a psyche that is equally sensitive. With an aggressive personality that is the antithesis of his predecessor's self-destructive one, Gustl responds to environmental intrusions with violence. A young and insecure soldier, Gustl lives for the pleasures of his coffee house, his mistress, and his status as a young officer. He bases his identity purely upon his honor, on the way that he is seen by other people, and his very thoughts are a jumble of social formulas supplied to him by his society. Even though Vienna has created his identity, however, he conceives of it in opposition to the people and language around him and feels obliged to defend it against all intrusions, which he perceives as threats. He demonstrates his control over his identity by killing the people who question its validity.

"Lieutenant Gustl" takes place in the course of a single night. As it opens, the young soldier is scheduled to fight a duel the next day over a trivial insult and has gone to hear an oratorio, to which a friend happened to give him a ticket. While jostling to get his coat, he is shoved by a baker, who becomes disgusted with the young soldier's aggressive and childish challenges, calls Gustl a fool, and threatens to break his sword. Uncertain how to reply, Gustl allows the incident to pass unavenged and then spends the night in anguish, wandering through the Prater and deciding when and how to commit suicide now that his honor has been lost. Having been so violated, his "sword" effectively broken by the Baker's speech-act, he sees murder and suicide as his only alternatives. His excessive sensitivity about the piercing of his honor betrays his lack of substance as an individual. In reality he has nothing to defend, for his identity consists of a border alone.

Gustl is a ridiculous figure, and despite its existential quality, Schnitzler's story is extremely funny.[14] Because Gustl narrates, or rather thinks the story, the reader perceives his self-doubts as experienced by his own mind. Clearly Schnitzler hoped that the narrative structure, highly unusual in 1900, would enhance readers' awareness of the issues at stake: how could an individual conceive of his or her identity so that criticisms and disappointments would not destroy it?

Both halves of Schnitzler's story begin with Gustl's desire to look at his watch. While he reacts aggressively toward the world around him, he needs constant reinforcement from the outside to convince him that his actions are appropriate for the time and the place, and watches and clocks provide answers to his constant questions about what he should do. At dawn, having resolved to kill himself and spying the clock at the railroad station, he wonders whether he should commit suicide at seven o'clock Vienna time or railroad time (Schnitzler 1994, 271). Gustl rarely trusts his own perceptions, expressing them as questions and continuously looking about him for confirmation. About the oratorio, which bores him, he thinks, "perhaps this one's very beautiful, and I'm just in the wrong mood" (251). Without awareness of definite rules to follow, Gustl has no confidence in his own ability to read and to judge. Later, in the park, he thinks to himself, "Perhaps I was momentarily demented, and it's all not true" (261–62). His memory of the baker's voice, which he can still hear, reminds him that the incident did occur, but his final conclusion that "nobody knows about it, and nothing's happened," indicates that other people's perceptions, not his own, tell him about reality (278).

Gustl's thoughts and behavior raise issues discussed in the 1880s hypnotism debates when Schnitzler was a medical student. Certainly, as a case history, the soldier illustrates Forel's doubts about the power of free will. Gustl is a creature of habit, and the humor of the story arises from the way that mundane details permeate powerful resolutions regarding life and death. At the railroad station at dawn, wondering exactly when to commit suicide, Gustl thinks, "they're the last street cleaners I'll ever see." He then discovers that he is hungry. Having resolved to kill himself at seven or eight, he finds that his legs have carried him to his coffee house and, out of habit, he goes in for breakfast and picks up a newspaper. Forel had speculated that the will was at the mercy of human emotions; here it seems subordinate even to frequently repeated movements.

Gustl's sentences often begin with "*ich muß*" (I must) or "*ich darf*" (I am permitted) rather than "*ich will*" (I want to), as though someone or something were dictating his behavior to him. His resolutions to die, for instance, are expressed as "*ich muß mich umbringen*" (I must commit suicide) and "*sterben muß ich*" (I must die) (Schnitzler 1994, 261, 268). Only late in the story does "*ich muß*" evolve into "*ich will,*" and then only momentarily, experimentally: "Am I so quiet because I still imagine that I don't have to? . . . I do have to! I must! No, I will!" (274). Gustl's tendency to respond to suggestions from his environment may represent a quality ingrained in soldiers as Bernheim discovered, but it is also one of people in general. Gustl has succeeded until now in Viennese society by playing the roles it has offered him.

There is a crisis and a story to tell when Gustl encounters the baker because the baker, in his anger, turns both on Gustl and on the system in which Gustl can thrive. As a result, predefined behavior fails, and—faced with lines not in the script—Gustl finds he has nothing to say. The men's impotent questions at the crucial moment, "What's he saying? Did he say that to me? What did you say? Exactly what did you mean by that?" indicate a failure of communication (Schnitzler 1994, 256–57). Gustl can respond as long as the baker limits himself to standard reproaches like "just have a little patience" (*nur ein bissel Geduld*). But when the baker seizes his sword, the symbol of Gustl's power in every sense, calls him a "*dummer Bub*" and threatens to draw and break it if Gustl makes a scene, the soldier is paralyzed, unable to defend himself verbally. Rather than acting freely, Gustl appears to be watching himself play a role: "Is he really talking to me? How shall I answer him?" (257). Gustl's encounter suggests that there may be no self apart from the roles that one plays and the social formulas that one repeats.

When he addresses himself in the story, Gustl tends to parrot bourgeois wisdom, advice that he has internalized but not integrated into a coherent personal philosophy. His statements, "I ought to go to concerts more often" and "I ought to go to the Prater more often at night" are laughable not only in light of his boredom at the oratorio and his misery in the park, but also in their resemblance to each other. Just before entering the coffee house, he tells himself, "Yes, Gustl! Don't put off till tomorrow what you can do today"; he is referring not to suicide but to the half-planned seduction of a young girl who has lately caught his attention (Schnitzler 1994, 276). He tells himself that "death is no child's play," but the context repeatedly indicates that it is (260). Existential questions of life and death have no existence outside of the habits and formulas of Gustl's society because they can be thought of in no other terms. He experiences them only as his culture speaks them.

What Gustl never questions is that what people call him is what he *is*. Because his identity depends on the way people speak to him and of him, maintaining his reputation is more important than remaining alive: "honor lost—everything lost!" (Schnitzler 1994, 262). The reason he must fight a duel, he recollects with difficulty, is that a socialist insulted his title and his calling. The quarrel began because he did not like the way the man pronounced his rank:

"Lieutenant"—just the way in which he said "Lieutenant" was annoying [*unverschämt*]. . . . "Lieutenant, you'll admit, won't you, that not all your friends have gone into military service for the sole purpose of defending our Fatherland!" What nerve! [*So eine Frechheit!*] How dare anyone say a thing like that to an officer! I wish I could remember exactly how I answered him—Oh yes, something about "fools rushing in where angels fear to tread" [*Leuten, die sich in Dinge dreinmengen, von denen sie nicht verstehen*] (255).

Here he has successfully—if he survives the duel—responded to a threat with a formulaic but hardly relevant reply. He notes with satisfaction that "the colonel said I did exactly the right thing," but he wonders to himself, "How did I ever get into conversation [*mich in Gespräch einlassen*] with a Socialist?" (254).

Because of Gustl's need to crush all forces that penetrate his self-perceived barriers, the problem is not the challenge but the very existence of the conversation. Relying on arbitrary boundaries and mechanical, prepro-grammed defenses, Gustl's self-concept fails with every unexpected interaction. After the encounter with the baker, filled with fear and rage, Gustl resolves, "I must kill him on the spot, wherever I happen to meet him! . . . Great heavens, he knows me—knows who I am!" (Schnitzler 1994, 258). What most frightens Gustl about the confrontation is the prospect that he has somehow been penetrated, his inner self—or lack thereof—becoming known and discovered. He has been raped, and he feels the shame and rage of one who has been violated. When he awakens in the Prater after having fallen asleep, murder and suicide have merged in his semiconscious mind as analo-gous actions despite his subsequent attempts to distinguish them: "Three o'clock, and I'm to have my duel at four.—No, not a duel—a suicide! It has nothing to do with a duel; I must shoot myself because a baker called me a fathead" (269). Because his sense of self depends on borders alone, such a breach of security has ruined it, and he must either kill the intruder or kill himself. By insulting him, the baker has robbed him of his identity, something he can retain only as long as people choose to let him retain it. Any challenge punctures the borders and allows it to become infected, to go bad.

Ironically, when Gustl stumbles into his coffee house, he learns that the baker died of a stroke during the night. He thinks joyously, "he's dead, and I can keep on living [*ich darf leben*], and everything belongs to me again!" (Schnitzler 1994, 278). Gustl's heavy use of *ich muß* and *ich darf* suggests that he is playing out his life as he must, as he is permitted. Schnitzler's character brings to life Bernheim's belief that the normal mind (and Gustl is utterly, distressingly normal) responds constantly to the suggestions of society, inter-nalizing ideas and behavioral patterns. Gustl also illustrates Forel's concept of a will overcome by suggestions, emotions, and unconscious urges, a will that may not even exist at all. Like "The sensitive one," "Lieutenant Gustl" illus-trates the violence that results when individuals deny their natural openness and attempt to define themselves with inflexible, illusory boundaries, bound-aries on which they stake their lives.

Reigen *: Connections, Their Formation and Their Consequences*

Reigen was conceived and performed during what Alain Corbin has called "the golden age of venereal peril" (Corbin 1981, 148). In 1896–97, when Schnitzler wrote the play, bacteriologists were actively seeking the microbe responsible for syphilis. While they still could not identify the germ, they knew it was transmitted along paths exactly like the one Schnitzler depicted spanning Viennese social levels. As the former and future hosts of bacteria, all people were linked in chains of which they wanted no part. *Reigen* thus documents this age's shaky medical knowledge as well as its aesthetic and social values, and it can be read in parallel with Eugène Brieux's *Les Avariés* (Damaged goods, 1901) and Henrik Ibsen's *Ghosts* (1881). While all three explore connections spanning the greater social hierarchy, the medical dimension of their social critique cannot be overlooked. One reviewer, commenting on a performance in Washington DC in 1955, called *Reigen* "the Viennese doctor's worldly treatise on venereal disease" (Schneider, 82).

No literary work has expressed the anxiety about illicit connections better than *Reigen*. It depicts relationships established for biological reasons but denied for social ones. Schnitzler's play privileges the viewer with magnified vision like that of Cajal's pessimist, a voyeurism in which the audience observes ten couples prepare for and recover from sex, although the sexual act itself is never seen or referred to directly. Like a frustrated microbiologist seeking an elusive germ, the viewer perceives much more than the characters passing it along and yet still not enough, since the crucial element of each encounter remains invisible. Each new couple shares one person with the previous one, so that the ten individuals involved constitute a chain without their knowledge or consent. Since the same prostitute appears in the first and last scenes, the chain closes into a circle, which Ludwig Marcuse has associated with the Nietzchian Eternal Return (Marcuse, 51).

In a metaphorical sense, the perspective of the viewer in this circulatory system is the perspective of the microbe, moving from couple to couple. The protagonist of the play, the only "character" to appear in every episode, is the *Gedankenstriche* (series of dashes) that cuts across the middle of each scene, causing the dialogue to "fade out" and then reemerge (Marcuse, 51). The reader or viewer must decide for him- or herself what these *Gedankenstriche* represent, providing his or her own images of sexuality. Consequently, rather than representing the sexual act itself, the *Gedankenstriche* represent all the fears and desires associated with sexuality in the reader's mind. In early-twentieth-century audiences and readers, the fear of venereal disease would have been foremost among these associations. Often interpreted as the de-humanizing depiction of universal drives, *Reigen* can also be read as a story of infection, a violation of illusory personal and social boundaries.

In *Reigen*, disease has the origin that the public would have expected. Although theoretically the bacteria have no preference and bonds established between characters should allow for an exchange of parasites in either direction, Schnitzler initially focuses—like Cajal—on the movement of microbes from the poor to the rich, expressing the particular fear of the upper classes.[15] Schnitzler's open system of circulation is set in motion when an aggressive prostitute accosts a rather passive soldier. This opening scene immediately ties the play to contemporaneous concerns about syphilis because, since the sixteenth century, regulators had been especially concerned about the relationship between prostitutes and the military (Quétel, 228). The origin of Schnitzler's circle—if a circle can have an origin—also reflects Alfred Fournier's view that "it is syphilis in the depths of society which produces syphilis higher up" (227). As Thomas Mann would in *Death in Venice*, however, Schnitzler complicates his representation of infection by incorporating an alternative view: he locates the sexual encounter at the edge of a river, long identified in miasma theory as an origin of sickness.

Particularly striking in the scene is the prostitute's motivation, a desperate desire that seems to go beyond her need to make a living. Ironically, when she initiates the deadly chain, she uses her consciousness of imminent death as an argument to make a sexual connection. To the uninterested soldier, she exclaims: "Come on, stay with me. Who knows if we'll still be around tomorrow?" (Schnitzler 1994, 56). This initial motivation, a desire to defy death through an action that can bring death, will drive the circulatory movement throughout the play. Sexuality both affirms and threatens life, and Schnitzler's characters, simply because of their will to live, become the apparatus in a system of compulsory circulation, acting as the temporary hosts of microbes, words, and desires.[16]

The initial encounter also activates a system of conflicting wishes focused on personal identity, one that treats sexual energy as a biological infection rather than a sign of individuality. With the "action" motivated by universal drives and the dialog conducted largely in clichés, Schnitzler's characters suffer from a lack of personal uniqueness. Identifying his characters only by their social roles (the whore, the soldier, the maid, etc.), Schnitzler encourages his audience from the outset to view them as social types rather than unique individuals. Because making connections threatens one's identity and because uncontrollable drives lead characters to make connections anyway, there are simultaneous, conflicting urges to know and not to know one's partners.

This instability of identity expresses itself strongly in the characters' fumbling and joking over one another's names. Repeatedly, the desire to know names arises only after the sexual connection has been made. The prostitute, for instance, after her brief interlude with the soldier, suddenly wants to know who he is:

> *Whore*: Tell me, soldier—what's your name?
> *Soldier*: What's my name got to do with you?
> *Whore*: Mine's—Leocadia.
> *Soldier*: Ha! That's a new one! (Schnitzler 1994, 57)

Her name, reflecting a romantic fad in Vienna, epitomizes all of the clichés that will "make the rounds" in Schnitzler's play, along with the microbe. Selected for its uniqueness and literary resonance, it has become laughable in its new mundane context.[17] The name, like the encounter, is meaningless; microbes do not need to know their hosts' names, and biology mocks the social devices through which difference is established.

In the next episode, the soldier is the aggressor, seeming to have "caught" Leocadia's desire as he pursues a young housemaid. With the maid, he returns to his usual diet of working-class girls, and he hits her name on his second guess:

> *Soldier*: What's your name? Kathi?
> *Parlor Maid*: You've got a Kathi on your mind.
> *Soldier*: I know. I've got it: Marie. (Schnitzler 1994, 57)

For the soldier, Marie has no individual identity, and he prefers that she remain indistinguishable from his many past conquests. "A Kathi" may refer to an actual woman, to his most recent lover, or to a generic rival, any working-class girl in Vienna. The indefinite pronoun and the common name are almost equally nonspecific.

Often in *Reigen*, the question arises as to whether characters who do not recall or even know each other's names should call each other "*du*" or "*Sie*." "Can I call you . . . Marie?" the soldier asks the maid, and she protests, "We haven't known each other very long" (Schnitzler 1994, 58).[18] Expressing a frustration that will recur in almost every scene, she complains that she can barely perceive her prospective lover in the darkness: "I can't see your face at all" (59). The unfulfilled wish to see and know one's partner, however, never prevents the formation of a sexual connection, since biological urges override social needs. After their sexual union, which is best described as a rape, the maid calls the soldier "*du,*" a linguistic substitute for true personal knowledge. It is a sign of a social connection that does not live up to its biological one.

Calling both people and things by their names is a challenge in *Reigen*, for the words are no better defined than the identities of the characters. Schnitzler's Viennese court each other with phrases that lose meaning with repetition, much like the characters' sexual adventures. The play depicts words that move like spirochetes from person to person and scene to scene, taking their course independent of the characters (Delius, 110). In their encounters, the lovers either speak in fragments or recycle clichés like "It is only now that I know what happiness is" (Schnitzler 1994, 68). The first word in the play, *komm,* recurs in almost every dialogue, usually as an aggressive invitation to sex but sometimes almost as an incantation, "*komm, komm, komm,*" spoken more for its sound than its meaning. In the end, the question of meaning becomes as irrelevant to language as it is to disease: apparently sexuality, a drive toward oneness, is incompatible with significance. This explains Schnitzler's use of the *Gedankenstriche* which replace the sexual act yet can be tied to no particular concept. As each dialogue gathers momentum, accelerating toward the inevitable series of dashes, language disintegrates; the actual point of the encounter, it seems, is something not expressible in language at all.

This inability to articulate desire comes through particularly clearly in the scene between the maid, Marie, and her young master, in which the viewer first enters a respectable bourgeois household. The middle-class young man, motivated mainly by boredom, brings on the encounter by repeatedly calling the maid. Both he and the girl are playing roles: he uses a series of pretexts to bring her close to him; she protests, yet primps before she enters. It is a Freudian *fort-da* game,[19] an exchange that can be transacted only through a series of lies. The deeper truth can barely surface into social space because of its biological roots.

As the viewer encounters higher and higher social levels, these falsehoods grow more articulate, but they only make it more apparent that social difference masks biological sameness ineffectively. In Schnitzler's chain, the ultimate compliment to a lover—telling him or her that he or she is "different"—is also the ultimate lie. When the middle-class young man attempts to flatter a bourgeois wife in this way ("you aren't like the other young women"), he receives the wonderfully ironic reply, "How do you know?" (Schnitzler 1994,

69–70). He desperately wants a connection with an *"anständiger Frau"* (a respectable woman), and his desire unsuccessfully conflates social and biological motives.

Here he is the more innocent figure, simply because he is not as skilled at deceit. Although the young wife feigns confusion at the outset, she suddenly changes roles after their sexual activity, revealing a pragmatism that can have come only from experience. It is she who warns of the possible consequences of their actions. "Everything takes its revenge," she tells her lover, and as she hurriedly dresses, she adds, "This can cost us both our necks!" (Schnitzler 1994, 69, 74). The admonition that extramarital relations can kill strongly suggests a consciousness of disease—knowledge that biology can destroy what society tries to define as immune and impenetrable. The young man's hollow words of triumph at the close of the fourth encounter assume even greater ironic force if one thinks of all that may have been transmitted in the episode: "Well, now I'm having an affair [*ein Verhältnis*] with a respectable woman!" (75).

The central dialogue between this "respectable" wife and her husband provides a point of symmetry in *Reigen*. Socially, the brief residence with the bourgeois couple marks the high point in the viewer's and the spirochete's progress. It also marks the highest degree of hypocrisy depicted in the play, as the husband, who will be seducing a young working girl in the next scene, lectures his wife, fresh from her interlude with the young man, on the ugliness of extramarital sex. When the bourgeois husband orders his wife not to maintain any friendship with an adulterous woman, his wording indicates not only a fear of infection but also a fear of social revenge:

> *Husband*: It frequently happens that women who don't enjoy the best
> reputation seek the company of respectable women, partly for contrast
> and partly out of a certain—how shall I put it?—out of a certain nostalgia for virtue (79).

It is the husband, who wields more social influence than any other character in the play, who becomes the mouthpiece for concerns like Fournier's, conflating social and biological fears.

Such discourse pervaded the fin-de-siècle vocabulary, and the husband's admonitory speech closely resembles that of the powerful father-in-law in Eugène Brieux's *Les Avariés*, written only a few years later. Denouncing his son-in law, whom he believes has violated his house and daughter by infecting them with a disease from the streets, Brieux's character says:

He has, as it were, thrust her into contact with the streetwalker with whose vice he is stained, and created between her and that common thing [cette femme de tout le monde] a bond of blood [je ne sais quelle mystérieuse parenté] to poison herself and her child. Thanks to him, this abject creature, this prostitute, lives our life, makes one of our family, sits down with us at table. (238–39)

What most deeply offends him is that because of the disease, a permanent bond has been established between the "poisoner" and his daughter and grandchild. Their susceptibility to the disease suggests that they are no different from the prostitute whom he reads as its source.[20]

By penetrating "common" women, such men allowed themselves and their families to be penetrated, a condition as terrifying as it was intolerable. "Nostalgia for virtue," as Schnitzler's patriarch puts it, projects onto the women he has seduced his own longing for an uninfected, unconnected state in which the boundaries of his mind and body were secure. Simultaneously, it suggests a fear that those who have lost their virtue plan to avenge themselves by destroying the virtue of those who still possess it. The husband's fear for his wife, who might be infected by the idea of adultery, reveals a fear that, ultimately, his family line is at risk (Corbin 1981, 147).

Schnitzler's work as a physician and a medical writer gave him special access to such discussions of social and domestic health. As his review of Fournier's book shows, debates were continuing in the late 1890s about whether syphilis acquired by a man could be passed to his wife and child, and whether an infected fetus could transmit the disease to an "innocent" mother. The idea of congenital syphilis, transmitted by an infected middle-class mother to her fetus through the placenta, was even more repugnant, since men preferred to think of the bourgeois wife as above reproach (Quétel, 165–66).

Schnitzler's character, who clearly sees his wife as capable of adultery, is either more cynical than Fournier, or he is projecting his own guilt onto her. Because he knows he cannot be faithful physically, the effort to protect his line must be carried out verbally and psychologically. So great is the husband's desire to distinguish his wife from women in general circulation that he refuses to call them by the same name. She is a Frau, a "wife," a woman with social standing; the others are Geschöpfe, "creatures," who are defined biologically. Of course, attempting to distinguish biologically identical beings by attaching social labels is a futile task. The husband's comment late in the dialogue expresses a sad fact with which any contemporary doctor would have agreed: "I have the feeling that all these women die young" (Schnitzler 1994, 80).

That the husband can have such thoughts and yet go on to seduce a young girl in the next scene indicates the triumph of natural over cultural urges. The characters in *Reigen* embody S. Weir Mitchell's worst nightmare, an entire society of people controlled by the "despotism" of instinctive drives. Whatever motivates them operates independently of any personal judgment, and they form connections in spite of themselves. In this amusing episode, the issue of past sexual connections (*Beziehungen*) becomes key. The husband and a *süße Mädel* (sweet young thing) are dining in a well-outfitted *chambre separée* in a fashionable restaurant. Several comments by each character, initiated by the husband's question "Have you ever been in a private dining room before?" suggest that each has enjoyed a number of such meals in the past (Schnitzler 1994, 83). For the man, the thought of the girl's past *Beziehungen* is disturbing, even disgusting. To maintain the pleasure of the present moment, he must maintain the illusion of its uniqueness, but history and memory continually break though, keeping him from savoring the present experience. After kissing the girl, he tells her, "You remind me of someone" (86). If sexual pleasure depends on the uniqueness of a bond with an individual, there can be no fulfillment, since the identity of a person depends so much upon his or her history, and hence upon his or her past *Beziehungen*.

Again, the biological and social desires of each character work against each other. The husband's first words after the *Gedankenstriche* are: "Who knows what sort of person she really is—God in heaven! . . . So quickly . . . Wasn't very careful of me . . . " (Schnitzler 1994, 87). With the satisfaction of his sexual appetite, his fear of infection has overcome his need to delude himself about the relationship's uniqueness, and he begins interrogating her about her past lovers. He seems suddenly to remember that anyone can be a carrier of disease.

Appropriately, it is this hypocritical bourgeois patriarch who makes it clearest how words and phrases, like diseases, circulate freely in Viennese society. Although they are not always transmitted directly from couple to couple, their recurrence in the dialogues suggests that they have been acquired unknowingly in analogous encounters. Just after the young man boasts of his relationship with an "*anständiger Frau*," the woman's husband refers to her as "*anständig*" while warning about insidious fallen women. He calls adulterous women "*Geschöpfe*," and, sure enough, two dialogues later, the writer addresses the *süße Mädel* as "*du süßes Geschöpf*." She, like her description, has been passed on to a new lover.

Usually the characters are conscious that they are spreading a word plague, and this nervousness about used language evokes a biologically-based anxiety about used mouths:

Husband: (*kisses her violently*) Your lips taste of whipped cream.

Little Miss: Oh, they're sweet by nature.

Husband: Many men have told you that, have they?

Little Miss: Many men! The ideas you get!

Husband: Be honest with me. How many men have kissed these lips?

　(Schnitzler 1994, 83)

Despite his actions, the husband seems aware that the connection he has made and does not want to maintain may cost him dearly. His concluding line, "*die Rechnung!*" (the check!) has an ominous ring (90). The presence of disease means that sex, like a meal, must always be paid for in the end.

These same anxieties about history and identity, and even the same questions, recur when the *süße Mädel* talks with her next lover, a writer. Like the two dialogues with the "respectable woman," the two with the *Mädel* uncover the ironies, the fears, and the clichés of Schnitzler's society through their relationship to each other. The *Mädel* says they should not go out for a walk together because some acquaintance might see them, and the writer responds, irritated: "You know so many people?" ("*Hast du denn gar so viel Bekannte?*" 90). He, like her bourgeois lover, is concerned about the number of men she has "known." A slip from her leads him to ask—using the exact words that the husband used in the previous scene—"Have you ever been to a private dining room (chambre separée)?" and she answers, "As a matter of fact I have" (93). Because the past is so uncertain, and because one would often prefer not to know the past, one never knows exactly whom one is with.

As they reintroduce phrases that have arisen in the early dialogues, this encounter and the two that follow continue to emphasize the instability of names and identities, but on a much more sophisticated and ironic level. Like Schnitzler's patients under hypnosis, the characters play out numerous roles, to the extent that their "real" identities are indeterminate. The *süße Mädel* has been under the impression that the writer was a doctor, but he now presents himself as a playwright and composer, again showing the irrelevance of these social identities in an essentially biological encounter. After joking about her knowledge of *chambres séparées*, he exclaims "It's gotten dark in here. I can't make out your features," and she chides "Well, take care you don't mix me up with another girl" (Schnitzler 1994, 93). Soon thereafter, the question of names arises:

Poet: Tell me, doesn't it interest you at all to know my last name [*wie ich mit dem Zunamen heiß*]?

Little Miss: Oh, yes—what is it [*wie heißt du*]?

Poet: I'd better not tell you my name. I'll tell you what I call myself [*Ich werd dir lieber nicht sagen, wie ich heiß, sondern wie ich mich nenne*]. (94)

The writer, who creates characters for a living, associates *nennen* (naming) with these temporary roles that one assumes consciously, and *heißen* (calling) with some deeper sort of identity. As in the earlier dialogues, it is just after Schnitzler's *Gedankenstriche* that the characters want to discuss names, as if to cover biological "knowledge" with social:

Poet: That was bliss supernatural . . . I call myself [*ich nenne mich*] . . .

Little Miss: Robert, oh Robert!

Poet: I call myself [*nenne mich*] Biebitz.

Little Miss: Why do you call yourself [*nennst du dich*] Biebitz?

Poet: Biebitz isn't my name, it's what I call myself [*Ich heiße nicht Biebitz, ich nenne mich so*]. (95)

While the characters talk too much about names, true identity remains unspoken, and social pretense does no good. The simple *Mädel* has never heard of Biebitz, a supposed playwright for the Viennese theater, so that the writer's assumption of this role has been wasted. He confesses in the end: "I'm not Biebitz, Biebitz is a friend of mine" (Schnitzler 1994, 97). The audience is left feeling that there is no way (or, in a sexual sense, need) to distinguish him from the roles that he plays.

When the writer encounters an actress—a professional role-player—in the subsequent episode, the game goes too far even for him, and he begs her to "call me simply by my name" ("*mich einfach so zu nennen, wie ich heiße*") (Schnitzler 1994, 103). The ironic exchange of formulaic praise reaches a climax in this dialogue between two expert manipulators of language. The writer had exclaimed to the *süße Mädel*: "If only you had an inkling of what you mean to me"; to the actress, he says, "You have no idea what you mean to me" (94, 98). Having just heard the formula in the previous scene, the audience can only laugh as it resurfaces. While the recurrence of the phrase subverts any attempt on the characters' part to supply the meaning to which it refers, the audience has quite a good idea of just how much they mean to each other. The new scene, like each new lover, fails in its claim to uniqueness. Each is a mere host, an opportunity for the growth of parasites.

Eventually, language turns to noise and back to biology. The sounds of crickets and frogs interrupt the poet's and the actress's discussion of their feelings for one another, recalling Flaubert's agricultural fair in *Madame Bovary*. This animal language, just as meaningful as the human interchange that preceded it, defies interpretation:

> *Actress*: How about the chirping? Are they still chirping?
> *Poet*: All the time. Can't you hear?
> *Actress*: I can hear. But that's frogs, my child.
> *Poet*: You're wrong: frogs croak.
> *Actress*: Certainly, they croak.
> *Poet*: But not here, my dear child. This is chirping. (Schnitzler 1994, 103)

The actress calls the writer "my cricket" and "my frog," incorporating the language of her environment into her consciousness just as the characters have been doing all along, but now pointing to a biological source.

The final dialogues, those between the actress and a young count and the count with the original prostitute, return to the issue of personal identity, or the lack thereof. After complaining about his inability to see in the darkness, the count tells the actress that people will never be able to distinguish themselves from others: "People are the same everywhere" (Schnitzler 1994, 106). Again in semi-darkness, watching Leocadia sleep in the final encounter, he muses, "If one didn't know what she is . . ." (112). Socially, the characters never know what or who their lovers are, nor will the audience ever know. Identity, based on unknown encounters in the past and untrustworthy statements in the present, is fluid and uncertain. In Schnitzler's system, all individuals are open to one another, and there is no *chambre séparée*.

As Austrians and Germans became aware of *Reigen*, they treated the drama itself as an infectious disease. Schnitzler wrote the play during 1896–97 while in a mood of "deep melancholy" (Schinnerer, 840). Suspecting the reaction it would cause, he resisted authorizing a production; he published a limited edition for his friends in 1900 and a more widely circulated one in 1903. Both the book and the production were banned in Germany in 1904, but numerous unauthorized performances, many of poor quality, were staged in Hungary, Russia, and the United States (Schneider, 75–76). Finally, in 1920, Schnitzler gave permission for a production in Berlin which he personally supervised (Schinnerer, 846). Word spread quickly that a filthy play was about to appear, and during 1921, numerous groups came forward to protest in the name of Christianity and moral hygiene. From the beginning, hostile views of *Reigen* stressed the religion of its author, referring to the play as "*jüdische Schweinerei*" (Jewish filth) (851). On 22 February 1921, when a cry of "*Schweinerei*" interrupted the performance, "one rebel stood up and cried:

this is a robbery of our freedom. The freedom to poison the air is what should be robbed from people!" (Marcuse, 53).[21] The evening ended in a near-riot as hostile members of the audience hurled stink-bombs to protest the play that "poisoned the air."

From November 5 to 18, 1921, a trial was held to determine to what extent *Reigen* was injuring public morals in Berlin. The plaintiffs, a great array of "*Anstoßnehmer*" (the offended), were not regular theater-goers; most had not read or seen the play. Many protested the subversion of German morals by a Jewish author, and Ludwig Marcuse views the trial as a harbinger of the Third Reich. A phalanx of professors and intellectuals emerged to defend Schnitzler's play, but—as in the trial of *Madame Bovary*—they invoked the author's moral uprightness and desire for reform rather than challenging the proceedings (Marcuse, 41). In the end, the verdict was favorable; Schnitzler was judged as having an artistic rather than a pornographic aim. Ironically, those who condemned *Reigen* took for granted the very penetrability that had "offended" so many in the play: his drama could infect the social body because people were open to suggestion.

Conclusion: Meaningless Boundaries

Both as a writer and a healer, Schnitzler posited a concept of selfhood that was open to biological and social interaction. His experience with medicine, he believed, helped him "to understand the problem of human conduct" (Segar, 117). Certainly his knowledge of germ theory influenced his views of the natural and cultural components of identity, for as *Reigen* suggests, a disease that knows no social boundaries calls attention to the arbitrariness of those that exist. Throughout his career, he opposed basing knowledge or identity on any sort of arbitrary divisions, such as social roles or names.[22]

Schnitzler believed the human mind existed in a state of *Kernlosigkeit* (lacking a core) a fragmented, plural condition brought about by unresolved tensions between opposing drives.[23] For him, mental pathology arose from an unresolved conflict between a biological group identity and an artificial, socially-generated sense of self. Given the divided structure of human consciousness, he wondered, could anyone ever identify personal "reasons" for one's actions?

Central to Schnitzler's literary and scientific writing are the problems of selfhood and free will, and his case studies and medical reviews repeatedly question where one individual will ends and the next one begins. He mistrusted the Freudian tendency to look to the unconscious for the causes of mental phenomena and doubted whether psychiatrists ever truly gained access to the unconscious. He preferred the term *Mittelbewußtsein* (intermediate consciousness) as a name for mental activity which was not fully conscious but which was visible to skilled investigators. For Schnitzler, there was a "systematic interconnection [*Zusammenhang*] of freedom, responsibility, and '*Mittelbewußtsein*,'" and he hoped that psychiatry would eventually examine people's ethical drives. (Thomé, 79). Although Schnitzler did not articulate these ideas on psychology until much later, his medical writing makes it clear that the problem of personal identity, rooted in the individual's relation to society, occupied him even in the 1880s.

The mixture of biological and social concerns inherent in Schnitzler's works emerges frequently in late nineteenth-century writing. In literature, syphilis had long been depicted as an instrument of revenge. It is the bourgeois baby who threatens to infect the wet nurse in Brieux's *Les Avariés*, but in the doctor's warning that the nurse may avenge herself, anxiety about disease merges with long-standing fears of revenge for social inequity: "for them the bourgeois is always something of an enemy, and they are ferocious when they can take revenge on him for their inferiority" (1938, 53)[24] In the final scene, the doctor describes a prostitute who, finding herself infected, tries to infect as many men as she can, out of sheer rage. He proclaims: "this victim, transformed into a pestilence, is a symbol of the evil created by us and which falls back upon us" (1938, 101)[25] Like the tropical diseases depicted in Doyle's stories, syphilis became associated with the anger of the oppressed, anger which the guilty and fearful bourgeoisie projected onto it. The prostitute, like Doyle's colonials, threatens to return and infect her oppressors. Schnitzler is not as inclined to myth or to melodrama, and he is even less likely to think in terms of blame or origins for infectious diseases. In *Reigen*, whatever is transmitted is transmitted in a circle, so that there is no true source, no true origin.

As *Reigen* suggests, Schnitzler objects to the absurdity as well as the injustice of social laws that cast the *süße Mädel* and the middle-class wife as *Geschöpf* and *Frau*, respectively, when the two are forever joined through their common partner, their sexuality, and their language. Yet neither, as indicated by his psychological writings, did Schnitzler regard the individual as wholly determined by hereditary and unconscious drives, despite his insistence that we recognize the role of biology in shaping behavior. Free will came into play as one struggled with the many elements of personality, hereditary and social, over which one had no control. Reviewing Krafft-Ebing's *Psychopathia Sexualis* in 1890, Schnitzler concluded: "we can never be completely sure about the contradictions in the laws that nature on the one hand and society on the other demand. To feel individually means to try to reconcile these contradictions after a fashion" (Urban, 148) Unique personal identity was possible, within limits. It relied on the way that one reconciled inborn drives and social restrictions, according to one's ethical impulses.

To writers like Mitchell and Cajal, the characters of *Reigen* would lack wills and identities because they compulsively play roles, recycle phrases, and act only in response to universal drives. Schnitzler's medical writings, however, indicate that he did not view biology as a dehumanizing force. Role-playing, the transmission of phrases and diseases, and the inability to see, to know, and to name, did not threaten identity; they *were* identity, an identity achieved as a temporary equilibrium between social and biological demands. People lived in the roles that they created for themselves, in minds subject to language pandemics and bodies subject to microbes. Schnitzler's own consciousness of infectious diseases shaped the way he conceived of the individual: a mind and a body without barriers, forever open to suggestion in a system of free circulation.

SIX

Thomas Mann

The Tigers of Wrath and the Origin of Cholera

There are many problems of disease, many strange
pathological possibilities, in the East, dear Watson.
—Arthur Conan Doyle

The Castilians have a proverb, that in Valencia the earth is
water and the men women; and the description is at least
equally applicable to the vast plain of the lower Ganges.
—Thomas Babington Macaulay

In 1890, when Arthur Conan Doyle visited the wards where Robert Koch's
"cure" for tuberculosis was being tested, he observed, under a microscope,
the bacteria that caused cholera. Describing Koch's comma bacilli for British
readers, he wrote: "In one year they would claim more victims from the
human race than all the tigers who have ever trod a jungle" (Doyle 1890,
552). In Koch's 1884 paper identifying the comma bacillus as the cause of
cholera, the bacteriologist had pinpointed the Ganges delta as the "Heimat"
(homeland) of cholera. He described its landscape in a strikingly visual and
literary fashion, specifically mentioning tigers: "Luxuriant [*üppige*] vegetation and abundant animal life have arisen in this uninhabited area. This area is
shunned by humans, not only because of floods and tigers, but principally
because of the pernicious fever that befalls everyone who remains there even
for a short time" (Koch 1987, 166).[1] Twenty-seven years later, envisioning
the origin of Venice's unmentionable disease, Thomas Mann's fictional Gustav Aschenbach also imagines a tiger:

His desire acquired vision. . . . He saw, saw a landscape, a tropical swamp [*ein tropisches Sumpfgebiet*] under a vaporous sky, moist, luxuriant, and monstrous, a sort of primitive wilderness of islands, morasses, and alluvial estuaries; . . . saw the eyes of a lurking [*kauernden*] tiger sparkle between the gnarled stems of a bamboo thicket; and felt his heart pound with horror and mysterious desire.[2] (*DV,* 5)

It is highly unlikely that Mann took the image directly from Koch or Doyle or ever saw their articles. More probably, the coincidence of imperialism with germ theory and European fantasies about Asia invited writers of many nations to make the same comparison.[3] Koch's vision, like Aschenbach's, expresses simultaneous fear and longing. By, associating the origin of the cholera with the tiger, Koch, Doyle, and Mann project onto their landscapes the same European fears of reverse colonization and of the revenge of repressed desires.[4] The discourse of disease in Mann's novella echoes the plurality of opinions, medical and nationalistic, voiced in late nineteenth- and early-twentieth-century German society.

Unlike Mitchell, Cajal, Doyle, and Schnitzler, Thomas Mann never studied medicine and did not come from a medical family. Largely self-taught, he never formally studied science beyond the high-school level, and he learned of Koch's discoveries not as a physician but as a reader and an artist. In his fiction, however, Mann explores the same anxieties about the violation of borders and the use of boundaries to construct identity, and he expresses these concerns in a similar way. Koch, who wrote no fiction, and Mann, who wrote no serious scientific essays, use the same metaphor because the culture of European imperialism offered its language and mythology to artists and scientists alike. The tiger in their writing is a violent beast that waits to attack, studying its prey, representative both of their own imperial conquest and of their own violent and erotic drives. Europeans preferred to localize these forces outside of their imperial boundaries.

Even as Mann mythologizes disease in *Death in Venice*, encouraging us to read Aschenbach's demise in terms of classical sources, his representation also incorporates much more modern attitudes toward sickness and its causes. His choice of the tiger as symbol does more than associate the cholera with Dionysus; it ties his depiction of the disease all the more closely to the fears and the imagery created by germ theory and colonialism. Mann's story draws its greatness from the way that his symbols "interweave" the mythological and medical levels of meaning. Represented through common images like the tiger, they are always intimately related.[5] By reading Mann's story in the context of early-twentieth-century beliefs about disease, one can see the interdependence of myth and science not only in the work of an "unscientific" writer, but in contemporaneous medical writing as well. As Koch's paper reveals, "interweaving" was not unique to literary texts, and scientists as well as creative writers employed images that drew upon and reinforced a mythology of disease.

While Mann's tale of penetration and dissolution shares the discourse of scientific texts, its terrible irony challenges cultural assumptions about the usefulness of "membranes." The bacteria in *Death in Venice* may be foreign—if one accepts that a bacillus can have a homeland—but the colonial meaning attributed to them emerges as a European projection. With the words "desire projected itself visually," Mann introduces a psychological landscape drawn after this image of foreign countries and their bacteria. The Ganges delta, which neither Aschenbach nor Mann nor Koch has actually seen, becomes the image for the "horror and mysterious desire" that originate in the German mind.[6] When criticized late in life for his nationalist stance during the First World War, Mann replied that his "apology for the Prussian attitude" could only be "judged psychologically" in terms of *Death in Venice*, "in which the Prussian ethos attacked by diseases from the rest of the world suffers a fall of the most ironic tragedy" (Lehnert, 55). While Mann's text does associate "luxuriance" and disease with the East, it also presents the corruption and decay projected onto Africa and Asia as *"heimisch"* (familiar, indigenous) to Europe, to the "Prussian ethos." Hamburg, like Venice and Calcutta, is open to cholera, and Aschenbach's journey to Venice is a merging of like with like.

What One Needs, One Must Have: Foreign and Immanent Disease

Mann's biography confirms his ongoing concern with disease and psychology, and his experiences point to a conflict between bacterial and miasmatic theories of disease as an underpinning to his novella. In a letter to Carl Maria Weber in 1920, Mann refers to "the *naturalistic* attitude of my generation, which . . . [has] forced me to see the 'case' as *also* pathological and to allow this motif [*climacteric*] to interweave iridescently [*changieren*] with the symbolic theme" (*DV,* 203).[7] Critics have long observed that Mann's story of disease creates its effects both on realistic and on mythological levels. Besides recreating the invasion of Europe by a foreign god, *Death in Venice* describes the literal, physical action of a real pathology. Mann, from his own experience, knew all too well what bacteria could do. In 1890 his father had died of blood poisoning following an operation to remove bladder stones. The operation was performed in the family ballroom, so sanitary conditions could not have been stringent, and the death confirmed Koch's view that disease resulted from external organisms' penetration of a healthy body (Heilbut, 54).

Mann's preparatory notes for *Death in Venice* reveal a genuine interest in bacteria, their spread, and their action in the body. He specifically mentions the comma bacillus and describes in detail the symptoms of the disease. In autopsy reports, for instance, he writes that microscopic examination of the intestines of cholera victims uncovers "numerous bacteria, among them the specific causative organisms [*Erreger*]."(Mann 1983, 109)[8] Particularly intrigued by the dissemination of cholera, Mann stresses the roles of human contact and of water, fruits, and vegetables in spreading the disease. The bacteria move from one person to another, he notes, either by direct contact or through contaminated water, so those who distribute food present a particular danger: "If there is a vegetable salesman or a milk saleswoman among those taken ill then comma bacilli can infect the wares" (*DV,* 87). Late summer, when the water temperature is highest, creates the most favorable conditions for an outbreak of cholera, "good for the bacilli" (87). He preserves these details in the plan of the story.

In *Death in Venice*, Mann stresses one of the most disturbing findings of bacteriology, the discovery that disease-causing agents are alive. He uses terms like "the terrible vibroid bacteria" and "causative organisms," which can be found in the press and in medical journals, but he also anthropomorphizes the comma bacillus, inviting readers to interpret it as a self-willed, avenging force: "It almost seemed as though the pestilence had been reinvigorated, as if the tenacity and fecundity of its microscopic agitators [*Erreger*] had been redoubled" (*DV,* 54). Mann's choice of overripe strawberries as the vehicle through which the disease penetrates Aschenbach again reveals his determination to make the story work both on realistic and mythological levels. While the "blackening corpse" of "a woman who sold vegetables" makes the infection plausible based on contemporary scientific findings, the "overripe and soft" fruit, suggesting an eroticism past its prime, implies that Aschenbach dies as much from his own fermenting libido as from a foreign disease (54, 60).

Since the mid-1880s, Europeans with colonial holdings had begun to realize that the Orient and its microbes were closer and closer to home. The German government promoted Koch's scientific achievements as evidence of their national superiority in science, and his discoveries at home and abroad received great attention in the press. Frequently, Mann's versions of Koch's theories provide ironic echoes of these contemporaneous newspaper accounts. He need not have gone to scientific journals to have learned the latest developments in bacteriology or to have encountered the tiger metaphor associated with them.

Koch's triumphant mission of 1884 provided scientific "proof" for the long-standing legend that cholera was native to India. The fact that outside of India, cholera epidemics never arose spontaneously indicated that "cholera is caused by a specific organism indigenous to India" (*welcher seine Heimat in Indien hat*) (Koch 1987, 165). Popular accounts of his achievement, as well as his own rich and literary description of the Ganges delta, suggest that he confirmed an accepted belief about the origin of disease. When cholera reached Hamburg in August 1892, Dr. Blasius wrote in the *Berliner neuesten Nachrichten:* "How cholera was born in its Indian Fatherland, will never be revealed. It is certain, however, that among us the disease is spread only by infection, and never arises on its own" (27 August 1892).[9]

Diseases from the East were spread by people in the West, and the West could not stop the offensive. In his notes for *Death in Venice*, Mann wrote that cholera was "*heimisch*" to the Ganges delta, although since 1817 it had exhibited a "conspicuous tendency toward dispersion and migration" (*DV*, 83). He carefully records the pace of the major nineteenth-century cholera epidemics, tracing the *Seuchenzug* (the path of the disease) and its ravages in 1817–23, 1826–38, 1846–59, and 1865–75, the fourth wave distinguishing itself with "the rapidity with which it reached Europe from Asia" (83–84).

When Mann declares that cholera is native to East India, however, he does so both with scientific authority and with a certain irony. In August 1892, a cholera outbreak in Hamburg revealed the disease to be a very German phenomenon despite official assurances. The national press provided widespread coverage, offering a great variety of preventive measures, and it is impossible that the seventeen-year-old Mann, then finishing school in nearby Lübeck, could have failed to hear of the outbreak. "One must take care of raw fruits and vegetables, which often, unfortunately, are eaten when still unripe," warned the *Leipziger Zeitung* (26 August 1892).[10] The *Kleiner Journal* compared the canals of Hamburg to the canals of Venice: "The *Fleete* in Hamburg are worse than the canals in Venice, and Venice, too, is a preferred city of pestilences and all diseases" (30 August 1892).[11] When Mann juxtaposes *home* with foreign lands in his story, he is echoing an analogy that had been made decades earlier.

The first serious outbreak since Koch had identified the bacillus eight years previously, the Hamburg epidemic claimed seventeen thousand victims, about half of whom died over the course of two months. In this case, it is very possible that Mann read Koch's reports, for the Prussian authorities had sent the bacteriologist to investigate as the primary expert in the field. Koch found in Hamburg, as he had in India, that water carried the bacilli. Altona, downstream of Hamburg on the Elbe but with a filtered water supply, had almost no cases of cholera (Brock, 229–31; Genschorek, 124). In his notes for the novel, Mann recorded, "in Hamburg *30 percent of the population fell ill* because (in contrast to Altona, where well-filtered water is used) in Hamburg, unfiltered water was directed into the city" (*DV,* 85–86). Although the story takes place in Italy, the point of departure remains Germany, with its need for public health measures.

Thus even while planning *Death in Venice,* Mann clearly bore in mind the central tenets of bacteriology concerning both the nature and the transmission of the disease. Because one individual could infect an entire city, society now began claiming the right to examine all individuals for its own protection (LaTour, 36). Reactions to the Hamburg epidemic in 1892 articulate this new sense of connectedness and individual responsibility. Berlin's *Vossiche Zeitung* warned that "the isolated person, the individual, should become aware that he is one member surrounded by a great community, whose care and duty it must be to protect his health. Formerly, when one attributed cholera to dormant, intangible causes in the air or ground, one could not speak of the responsibility of the individual in the sense or to the extent that one does now" (25 October 1892).[12] Mann takes a special interest in the issue of individual immunity and in the possibility of a healthy carrier, noting that "these individuals are, however, just as dangerous for the spread of the disease as the severely ill, perhaps even more so because the pathogenic agents are spread [*verschleppt*] by them unchecked" (*DV,* 85). In particular, Mann seizes upon an issue that bacteriologists were criticized for underrating: the role of individual disposition in the development of a disease.[13] Perhaps not all Germans were equally susceptible to diseases from the East.

In 1911, Mann's readers may have been considerably less sure of their safety than leading scientists were. From the 1880s onward, germ theory posited all people as potential victims and carriers of disease, but the miasmatic theory persisted among scientists and remained very popular in the press. This more traditional view presented disease as an environmentally induced phenomenon with the consequence that a person, as well as a place, could provide the ideal "environment" for disease.

Certain that soil factors, climate, and individual disposition controlled the development of cholera, the hygienist Pettenkofer had long exasperated colleagues who argued that bacteria alone could create disease in a healthy individual. After a scientific meeting in 1885, he declared that "they've cooked [*geKocht*] me for five days, but I still haven't softened" (Genschorek, 121). Pettenkofer created a sensation in the fall of 1892 by using himself as an experimental animal to prove his hypothesis. His experiment took place in Munich, where Mann's family was living at the time, and it received vast attention in the press. On 7 October 1892, Pettenkofer consumed a culture of comma bacillus following a breakfast of hot chocolate and two soft-boiled eggs, as described by the *Neues Tageblatt* of Stuttgart (23 November 1892). The seventy-four-year-old scientist suffered only a mild case of diarrhea. Pettenkofer's graduate student Emmerich, however, who washed down the culture with three and a half liters of beer, almost died of cholera (*Schlesische Zeitung* 18 November 1892). All over Germany, Pettenkofer's triumph was big news. Despite Koch's status as a national hero, many took Pettenkofer's side, tying disease to locality and personality type rather than to the bacteria alone.

It is very likely that Mann knew of Pettenkofer's daring experiment and, like other Germans, had thought about the questions it reopened. The *Berliner Tageblatt* proposed that the bacteria were like trees that could grow only in certain kinds of soil. Pettenkofer himself concluded that "the bacilli are thus . . . the cause [*Ursache*] of the disease, without constituting the disease itself or the essence [*Wesen*] of the disease" (19 November 1892).[14] What was, indeed, "the essence of the disease," and what was its relation to national soil? Along with Mann's references to bacilli, a reader hears Pettenkofer's challenging voice in *Death in Venice* as the mocking street singer asks Aschenbach, "A disease? What sort of disease? Is the sirocco a disease? Do you suppose our police force is a disease?" (*DV,* 51).

In *Death in Venice*, as at contemporaneous scientific conferences, bacteriological and miasmatic explanations of disease coexist and engage one another in dialogue. It is significant that both Aschenbach and his Italian hosts think more like Pettenkofer than like Koch; it is the narrator, prompted by the truth-telling Englishman, who finally describes the disease with the modern scientific discourse of bacteriology. Only late in the fifth chapter does Mann incorporate his notes on cholera, after clinging, through most of the story, to an older, more popular notion of disease and of Germany's relation to it.

The "medicinally sweet smell that put in mind thoughts of misery and wounds and ominous cleanliness" ties the disease to foul odors, as hygienists had in the eighteenth century, and the stench of carbolic acid from the street singer's clothing recalls measures of disinfection thirty years out of date (*DV,* 44).[15] Aschenbach perceives that "the evil emanations from the canals hindered his breathing" and fears "the noxious extra of the lagoon and its fever-inducing vapors" (29–30). Like the Italians, he associates disease with the sirocco, a hot wind that blows from Africa to Europe. Finding, however, that for the second time the city is making him sick, he differs from his hosts in linking the disease with Venice itself: "He breathed the atmosphere of the city, this slightly stagnant smell of sea and of swamp [*Sumpf*] from which he had felt so strongly compelled to flee, breathed it now deeply, in tenderly painful draughts" (31–32). Mann's notes, like the text of the story, reveal an intentional juxtaposition of Venice with the Ganges delta when he describes the Asian landscape as "a luxuriantly [*üppig*] overgrown, *very unhealthy swamp and island labyrinth*" (88). Mann compromises between miasma and germ theory by equating Venice, a *Sumpf* that is a portal to Europe, with the Ganges delta, the *Sumpf* of Aschenbach's original vision. The discourse of miasma theory competes with that of modern medicine in explaining the disease, but neither one alone can account for its essence as Mann presents it. Underlying the dialogue about what causes disease is a more profound discord about what Germany and the Germans are.

No one, neither Pettenkofer nor Mann nor the German public, would relinquish the idea that some individuals provided more fertile ground for disease than others. In depicting the *Wesen* of the disease, Mann relied upon an older, romantic idea of individual disposition when he cast Aschenbach as disease victim. He was not alone in this move. After warning its readers to avoid raw fruits and vegetables, the *Leipziger Zeitung* had added with irony worthy of Mann, "the old saying, taken literally, is as valid as ever: what one needs, one must have" (26 August 1892).[16]

In Mann's notes for the novella, a list of words suggests an intense struggle to describe the relationship between Aschenbach, or perhaps Venice itself, and the cholera: "*Gemäßheit* (appropriateness), *Angemessen* (suitable), *Gehörig* (belonging to), *Gefällig* (pleasing)" (Mann 1983, 115). While city officials struggle to conceal the cholera, Mann seeks to present it as appropriate, "pleasing" to Aschenbach and to the nominally European city—not because of its foreignness but because of its familiarity. The aging artist, who for half a century has carefully controlled his passion in order to create, feels a natural affinity for the city hiding the disease, a disease that it denies and yet which seems to be an integral part of it. Aschenbach's whole life, Mann suggests, has been a progression toward this humiliating passion and pathology, toward this very "appropriate" death in Venice.

As part of a generation schooled in miasma theory, Aschenbach feels his affinity for the disease. Mann's extensive use of the term *Leidenschaft* (passion or suffering) evokes both passion and disease, associating the cholera both with Aschenbach's personality and with the East from the outset. Three times Aschenbach observes that Tadzio, a Pole, is sickly and suspects that he may not live long. The "satisfaction" (*Genugtuung*) that Aschenbach feels at this prospect reminds the reader of his sympathy with the disease as someone who shares the boy's Eastern roots [*Elsaghe*]. The term recurs when Aschenbach learns of the epidemic: he now feels "satisfaction" (*Genugtuung*) with "the loosening of the social fabric." Mann depicts a strengthening bond between the artist's mind and the diseased city, rather than with his own German ground: "Thus Aschenbach felt a dark satisfaction [*Zufriedenheit*] over the official cover-up of events in the dirty alleys of Venice. This heinous secret belonging to the city fused and became one with his own innermost secret, which he was likewise intent upon keeping" (*DV,* 45). Aschenbach's own consciousness of his *Mitwisserschaft* (guilty knowledge) and *Mitschuld* (guilty complicity) intoxicates him like wine, softening his resistance and leaving him open to invasion (56).

While Aschenbach is related both to Venice and to its disease, he retains his personal boundaries through most of the story. Mann's descriptions present his transformation as a process of penetration and dissolution as foreign forces permeate him to mingle with their counterparts within. Aschenbach thinks like Mitchell: the protective "membranes" he has so desperately struggled to maintain are as crucial for what they hold in as for what they screen out. The foreign microbes, foreign boy, and foreign city that penetrate his borders all reflect the desires those borders have been holding back.

More than any other writer, Mann conveys the sexual terrors that underlie preoccupations with "membranes." Aschenbach's subjectivity, as he has constructed it, has focused almost entirely on these boundaries. Like a cell, he has been able to exist because of what his membrane retains and excludes. As his membrane loses its ability to "resist death," his most terrible realization is that the cell metaphor does not work: identity based on exclusion can end only in chaos as the "hungry life" one has rejected overwhelms one's defenses. While Aschenbach's demise inspires the pity and fear of a classical tragedy, his ridiculous pursuit of Tadzio is also extremely funny. His "invasion" is above all a humiliation, as the great classical writer becomes the object of internal forces he once mastered. On the plain of the lower Ganges, men become women.

Aschenbach's adventure represents the penetration of one world by another, simultaneously an infection, a kind of colonialism, and a sexual act. The process begins in Aschenbach with "a sudden, strange expansion of his inner space" following his encounter with the red-haired stranger and introducing his initial vision (*DV,* 5). In the second chapter, Mann's narrator reinforces this notion of a closed self that must inevitably open with the analogy of the clenched fist and the reference to St. Sebastian, the pierced martyr, as symbolic of Aschenbach's works. After the encounter with the rogue gondolier, the narrator remarks that the experiences of the "lonely, quiet person," like Aschenbach, are "more penetrating [*eindringlicher*]" than those of extroverts, again suggesting a predisposition toward being pierced (20). His love of the sea and his "affinity for the undivided, the immeasurable, the eternal, the void" provide the greatest possible contrast to the "rigorous self-possession" of his ancestors and betray the tremendous energy he has had to exert to maintain the boundaries of his own being (26, 47). In Venice, Aschenbach is discovering the futility and the inappropriateness of this expenditure. As Mann concludes the third chapter with his delight over his failed escape, the traveler's gesture is one of invitation, the closed fist now replaced by the open hand: he makes "a slow circling and lifting movement that turned his palms forward as if to signify an opening and extending of his embrace. It was a gesture of readiness, of welcome, and of relaxed acceptance" (34). With this movement, he invites the boy, "the stranger god," and the disease into himself simultaneously.

As Aschenbach drinks in Tadzio and the vulgar music of the street singer, the narrator comments that "passion cripples the ability to select" (Mann 1989, 77).[17] The longer he extends his stay, the more Aschenbach loses his ability to discriminate and exclude, a condition that will lead to his "taking in" the bacillus along with the delightful visions of his beloved. Before he is infected by the disease, Aschenbach is infected by a person, indicating the failure of the notion of self as a fenced-off cordon. Here, and throughout the story, Mann implies that Aschenbach plays an essential part in his own destruction. The "stranger god" and the comma bacillus may come from India; his beloved may come from Poland, but ultimately it is he who invites them in; he who seeks them out. His grim and dogged choice to sacrifice life for art, the very structure of his own consciousness, brings him to the city, to the boy, and to the disease, so that his death in Venice becomes a carefully orchestrated collaboration of the foreign and the *heimisch*.

Foreign Bodies: The Politics of Disease

Behind these tropes of disease in the novel lies a political map of colonial Europe. Satisfied that cholera is an Eastern disease, Robert Koch describes its two means of *Einschleppung* (importation) in terms that emphasize the contrast between ancient and modern communication with the Orient: the traditional overland trading route, through Persia; and the modern shipping route, via the Red Sea, Suez Canal, and Mediterranean. He notes that from Bombay, one can sail to Italy in sixteen days, and he expresses particular concern about "ships for mass transportation such as those carrying troops, pilgrims, workers, or emigrants" (Koch 1987, 168). Echoing Koch, Mann refers in his notes to the danger of "infested or suspicious [verdächtigen] ships" (DV, 88). Colonialism had made the world smaller, and there would be consequences for the Europeans who had shrunk it.

When Mann outlines the ways that cholera spreads, his notes follow the logic of Koch's article so closely that they might well have been taken from his original study.[18] Once again, however, the Hamburg epidemic gave rise to similar accounts in the press, many of which tied disease to geopolitics. Mann need not have gone directly to Koch. In dramatic tones, the Berliner neuesten Nachrichten pronounced in 1892 that "from the north of Europe, out of Russia, the entry [Einzug] of a terrible scourge threatens the continent and also our German Fatherland at this moment: 'The Cholera.' A nebulous fear envelops the appearance of the cholera specter [des Choleragespenstes] with all the more panic and terror" (27 August 1892).[19] Stressing dangers from the North and East, this writer presents Hamburg as a mirror image of Venice, a port and commercial city, which maintains contacts with the South and East. In Death in Venice, Mann writes that "Europe was shaking in fear lest the specter [Gespenst] should progress [seinen Einzug halten] by land from Russia westward" (DV, 53). His description has its roots both in Koch's findings and in cultural and political myths of the day, myths that predated and influenced the scientist as well.

Underlying these myths about disease was a fear and mistrust of all things foreign. Mann's opening sentence sets the story "in 19—, a year that for months glowered threateningly over our continent," immediately evoking the fear of Germany's European neighbors that preceded World War I (DV, 3). As a young adolescent, Mann would have heard about political and colonial developments from his conservative father. The senator strongly supported Bismarck's policies and once wrote "God preserve the Kaiser and Bismarck" when sixty socialists were elected to the Reichstag (Heilbut, 7). Aschenbach, whose works are acclaimed by the Prussian government, belongs to Mann's father's Bismarckian generation and retains the ethics of bourgeois individualism and propriety that Mann associated with his father.[20] Some twenty years younger than Aschenbach, Mann rejected the fervent nationalism of his father and teachers. His one indirect experience with the

African colonies was a bitter one.[21] In his brief autobiography he reports that Armin Martens, the blond, blue-eyed boy he loved in his youth and the model for Hans Hansen in *Tonio Kröger* "came to a sad end in Africa" (Mann 1968, 17). Mann was writing for a divided German audience, many of whom agreed with Bismarck that colonialism was the wrong course. Aschenbach's longing for "someplace foreign, someplace isolated, but someplace nonetheless easy to get to" thus suggests the ambiguity of Germany's desire for a colonial empire (*DV,* 13). Like the European colonies, Venice is pleasingly exotic and removed, yet far too easy to reach.

In *Death in Venice* Mann emphasizes the disturbing closeness of Europe and Asia, of Venice and India, by using the same word to describe each. *Üppig,* indicating an exotic, overgrown luxuriance, was used by many German writers—including Robert Koch—to describe the tropics. This word recurs throughout Mann's story, tying Aschenbach's initial vision and Koch's 1884 description of the Ganges delta not only to the Italian city but also to the beckoning of death and the nature of art. A list of words in Mann's working notes suggests he gave a great deal of thought to the words he would use for Aschenbach's artistic and libidinal experiences: "Grow, blossom, [rampant], luxuriant lavish, voluptuous, wanton, lulling" (*DV,* 89). Following its appearance in Aschenbach's initial vision, Mann uses the word to describe the condition of the artist: "there is inborn in every artistic disposition an indulgent [*üppiger*] and treacherous tendency to accept injustice when it produces beauty" (*DV,* 17–18, 22). Later, it recurs in the description of "the truth," an image of the Ganges delta that is a variation on Aschenbach's initial vision: "that lushly uninhabitable [*üppig-untauglichen*] primeval world, that wilderness of islands avoided by humankind where tigers lurk in bamboo thickets" (53). Here Mann's compound adjective captures the paradox of the cholera microbe, stressing both its *Heimat* in India and its relation to art. The bacteria, the overgrown landscape, and Aschenbach's writing are all life that causes death, so that the person who reaches out for the one will receive the other. Because Mann uses the same word to describe all three concepts, the contradiction of life that kills life must apply to European art and eroticism as well as to foreign disease.

In the plot, as well, Mann reveals that encounters with the foreign are really encounters with the self. Himself a stranger to Venice, Aschenbach confronts a series of foreigners in the story, culminating in his encounter with "the stranger god" and the foreign disease. *Death in Venice* is the story of a man who *fremd geht* (goes strange) in every sense.[22] The red-haired, snub-nosed stranger who provokes Aschenbach's vision bears "the appearance of a for-

eigner, of a traveler from afar" and is "clearly not of Bavarian stock" (*DV,* 4).
The rogue gondolier is "clearly not of Italian stock" (18). And the offensive
street singer, whose red hair ties him to the first foreigner, "seemed not to be
of Venetian stock," so that the three form a family related through Mann's
descriptions of what they are not (50). Like Aschenbach, they are foreigners
who seem to belong in Venice; like the microbes invading its water, they are
both strange and familiar.

Almost everyone Aschenbach meets in Venice is foreign. In Aschenbach's
perceptions of eastern and southern Europeans, one sees Germany's fears of
its immediate neighbors as they mingle with anxieties about those more
remote. In this respect, *Death in Venice* resembles Mann's *Tonio Kröger* (1903)
in its depiction of a tormented artist who travels to "make contact with life"
(McWilliams, 235). Both present Italians in a negative light, and the idea that
"the sun turns our attention from intellectual to sensuous matters" is common to both (*DV,* 37).[23] In *Death in Venice* the associations of North with
conscience and ingenuousness, and South with corruption and playful mendacity emerge most strongly when the blue-eyed British clerk tells Aschenbach "the truth" about the epidemic. Too ashamed to lie, the clerk possesses
"that steady, trustworthy bearing that stands out as so foreign and so remarkable among the roguishly nimble southerners" (53). The Italians' determination to conceal the cholera, contrasted with the Germans' flight from the city
following reports of it in their newspapers, reinforces the stereotype that
southerners love to lie.

Easterners who remain in the diseased city either through ignorance or
indifference at first seem to fare no better than southerners, becoming associated with the cholera through their very presence. At Aschenbach's expensive
hotel, "the Slavic component seemed to predominate" (*DV,* 21). Besides
Tadzio and his overscrubbed Polish sisters, he notices a Russian family "en-
camped" upon the beach who seem to lack grace, will, and intelligence:
"men with beards and huge teeth; languid women past their prime . . . two
affable, ugly children; and an old maid in a babushka, displaying the affection-
ately servile demeanor of a slave" (26). The "aristocratic" Tadzio is disgusted
by the Russians' simple-minded enjoyment of the beach, and Aschenbach
identifies with him in his distaste.

During the street singer's vulgar and obscene performance, Aschenbach
notes that "the Russians in particular, ensconced in their orchestra seats,
displayed . . . delight over all this southern vivacity and encouraged him with
applause and cheers to ever bolder and more brazen behavior"(*DV,* 49). This

description suggests a collaboration of East with South as disease vectors. Mann again aligns East with South when the narrator voices Italian prejudices in response to the wave of criminal behavior created by the epidemic: "Prostitution and lasciviousness took on brazen and extravagant forms never before seen here and thought to be at home only in the southern parts of the country and in the seraglios of the orient" (55).[24] Whereas Tonio Kröger traveled north, Aschenbach travels north and, like the Poles and Russians, he remains in the diseased city even when he knows its secret. If art, mendacity, and disease reign in the South and East, then they are equally at home in the story's German hero.

The association of racial types with disease, then, does not hold up. Ultimately, *Death in Venice* undermines the stereotypes it incorporates by presenting the concepts associated with the foreign as an integral part of Aschenbach's consciousness. The German artist, like Germany itself, already contains everything associated with the South and the East:

More impetuous and sensuous blood had entered the family line in the previous generation through the writer's mother, the daughter of a Bohemian music director. It was from her that he had in his features the traits of a foreign race. The marriage of sober conscientiousness devoted to service with darker, more fiery impulses engendered an artist and indeed this very special artist. (*DV,* 7)

Aschenbach's fear of the foreign is a fear of himself, a fear that what he has so long repressed will take its revenge. As such, it reflects his nation's fear of the foreign in the colonial age. Mann's story subverts any attempts to project disease, disorder or "sympathy with the abyss" onto a southern or eastern Other in establishing German identity.

Death in Venice depicts the futility of repression in political as well as personal terms. When Jaschu, Tadzio's rough playmate, humiliates his idol in the final scene, Mann writes that "the subservient feelings of the underling turned to vindictive cruelty as he sought to take revenge for a long period of slavery" (*DV,* 62). His description indicates the inevitability of reprisal when a weaker, "aristocratic" ruler holds back a poorly organized but ultimately stronger force. While the wording strongly suggests Aschenbach's sexual repression, the reference to slavery also arouses images of the non-Europeans whose exploitation ensured an inevitable revolt. Repression and oppression, the story warns, can end only in sickness or in violence, and *Death in Venice* conflates anxieties about physiological and political reprisals by creating a violent disease.

From Pestzug to Festzug:
Disease as Myth in the Colonial Age

Throughout the nineteenth century, writers from Western nations had used the tiger to represent the unknown fury of the East. S. Weir Mitchell included a tiger in St. Clair's fantastic narrative of the Cobra City in *Dr. North* (1900), introducing it synecdochically, like Mann, as "two shining eyes." Mitchell's tiger, a "splendid terror," is destroyed by the cobras, who seem guided by St. Clair's strong will and by the western author's wishful thinking. Representing undesirable internal drives, the cobra can be enlisted—like these inner desires—to combat external threats if it is properly controlled. Mitchell's story creates a fantasy in which subservient natives overwhelm ferocious and insubordinate ones. Such images of snake charming convey his hopes that experiences in the colonies will teach westerners to subjugate their dangerous desires and redirect them toward future conquests. Mann's story, in contrast, mocks the very assumption that internal drives or foreign peoples can be controlled or excluded from one's definition of "self." In *Death in Venice*, the tiger wins.

Native to India (not Africa), known for its stealth and the ferocity of its attacks, the Bengal tiger suggested to Europeans of 1911 the oppressed colonials, the foreign bacteria, and the repressed desires waiting to devour them even on their own native soils.[25] Mann's tiger "lurks" (*kauert*) in a bamboo thicket, his glinting eyes barely visible amidst the lush growth; he awaits an opportunity, a moment of weakness, in which to spring.[26] As in Mitchell's image, a brief reference to the tiger's watchful eyes is sufficient to conjure up the fear he inspires. The height of anxiety in the imperial age, the two representations suggest, lies in the feeling of being watched and studied by a hungry and ultimately more powerful life form. The tiger's inevitable attack will be all the more deadly because Aschenbach's "European soul" has suppressed and denied him for so long. He will not be confined to his native habitat; Europe cannot both possess and confine the East.

As a common metaphor in the colonial era, the tiger draws together the different concepts it represents. Many readers have noticed that the "strangers" Aschenbach encounters recall the tiger of his initial vision.[27] The first man is red-haired and snub-nosed, and "his posture conveyed an impression of imperious surveillance [*etwas herrisch Überschauendes*], fortitude, even wildness. His lips seemed insufficient. . . . they were retracted to such an extent that his teeth, revealed as far as the gums, menacingly displayed their entire white length" (*DV,* 4). Both his features and his expression suggest the tiger, which emerges from Aschenbach's mind immediately following his vision of this "imperious" man. The rogue gondolier also bares his teeth and mutters to himself between his teeth, evoking analogous fears. The street singer, red-haired, snub-nosed, and "imperious" like the first man, is "brutal and daring, dangerous and entertaining" (50). By repeatedly describing these figures as "imperious," Mann reveals how Europeans project their own aggressions onto their symbols of foreignness, rewriting their conquest as defense (Brantlinger, 222). Aschenbach, who had planned to travel "not quite all the way to the tigers," finds that again and again the tigers come to him (*DV,* 6).

The tiger returns not only in these portraits of the strangers but also in the description of the disease itself (Parkes, 77). In Mann's account of cholera's journey to Europe, the bacillus becomes a ferocious animal, the verbs accentuating the bacteria's status as a living organism. It had "raged persistently and with unusual ferocity throughout Hindustan" and "had raised its grisly head in Toulon and Málaga" (*DV,* 53–54). More of an *Einmarsch* (invasion) than an *Einschleppung* (importation), cholera's penetration of Europe comes across as an attack from a sentient and extremely angry enemy.

Through its simultaneous associations with the cholera and with "the stranger god," the tiger unites the political, medical, and mythological aspects of the story. Inspired by Euripides' *The Bacchae* and Nietzsche's *The Birth of Tragedy,* Mann shared with Nietzsche "the same (false) assumption, that the homeland [*Heimat*] of the Dionysian cult was Asia" (Dierks, 19).[28] According to Greek mythology, the tiger was sacred to Dionysus; Zeus once sent a tiger to help the god cross the Tigris river in his journey from East to West (Bell, 254; Krotkoff, 448; Parkes, 78). Describing Dionysus' triumphant procession, Nietzsche wrote in *The Birth of Tragedy*: "The chariot of Dionysus is covered with flowers and garlands; panthers and tigers walk under its yoke" (37). Later he invited and challenged his readers, "put on wreaths of ivy, put the thyrsus into your hand, and do not be surprised when tigers and panthers lie down, fawning, at your feet. . . . You shall accompany the Dionysian pageant [*Festzug*] from India to Greece" (124).

Besides suggesting a tiger, Mann's description of cholera's movement to Europe echoes Euripides' account of Dionysus' journey to Greece, particularly in the phrase "shown its grim mask" and in the reference to Persia (Dierks, 22–29). Aschenbach's resistance to the foreign god, as well, links *Death in Venice* to Euripides' tragedy.[29] One hears in the story of Aschenbach Dionysus' warning to Pentheus: "You do not know the limits of your strength. You do not know what you do. You do not know who you are" (Euripides, 177). Both through its origin and through its association with the tiger, Dionysus' *Festzug* (triumphal procession) becomes inseparable from the *Pestzug* (pestilential procession) of the comma bacillus. Mann's phrasing reveals the influence of both Euripides and Nietzsche, stressing the Dionysian goal of breaking down the borders that define individuals. At the same time, however, these images of rupture betray the fear of penetration fostered by germ theory (Dierks, 43–46). Even in the story's most poetic moments, its political and scientific dimensions are inseparable from its mythology.

Nietzsche had associated the *principium individuationis*, the existence of distinct, bounded, individual selfhood, with the Apollinian; the collapse of this principle, with the Dionysian. Until his trip to Venice, Aschenbach has epitomized "this apotheosis of individuation . . . the delimiting of the boundaries of the individual" (Nietzsche, 46). But Aschenbach has found that although "Apollo wants to grant repose to individual beings precisely by drawing boundaries between them," the state of individuation is actually "the origin and primal cause of all suffering, . . . something objectionable in itself" (72–73). In Dionysian tragedy, the greatest fear of Europeans in the age of germ theory and colonialism is realized as "the gulfs between man and man give way to an overwhelming feeling of unity leading back to the very heart of nature" (59). *Death in Venice* is just such a tragedy, culminating in the dissolution of Apollinian boundaries.

In the story's climax, Aschenbach's Dionysian experience, the latent imagery of piercing and violation takes over the narrative. Mann's description of Dionysus in his notes as "a foreigner pressing powerfully inward from without" (*ein Fremder, von draußen gewaltsam Eindringender*) suggests that from the outset, he conceived of the god and the bacteria as analogous symbols of an extrinsic, penetrating force (Dierks, 208). His words depict a rape in which the German hero is humiliated by being forced to assume the female role. The aging artist has lived too long with his membrane intact, and his senescent deflowering will be an excruciating experience.

Mann emphasizes the collapse of borders as the essence of Aschenbach's dream, implying that his suffering has its source in his long-standing resistance to the Dionysian. The images of his dream, Mann writes, "burst in upon him from outside [*brachen von außen herein*], violently crushing his resistance, his deep, intellectual resistance, passing through easily and leaving his whole being, the culmination of a lifetime of effort, ravaged and annihilated [*vernichtet*]" (*DV,* 56). Struggling pitifully, Aschenbach attempts to block the invasion even in his dream: "great was his loathing, great his fear, sincere his resolve to defend his own against the foreign invader [*bis zuletzt das Seine zu schützen gegen den Fremden*], the enemy of self-controlled and dignified intellect" (57). As the passage is written, "the foreign invader" can refer equally to the god, to Aschenbach's repressed libido, or to the disease, all of which Mann conflates in the references to "*den Fremden*" as a piercing and avenging force. The brutal sexuality of the Bacchantes, working toward "an unfettered rite of copulation," expresses itself as a violent process of mutual penetration: the celebrants "pierced each other's flesh with their pointed staves and then licked the bleeding limbs" (*DV,* 57). Literally "a mixing with no regard for borders" (*grenzenlose Vermischung*), the Dionysian experience mocks the very ideas of boundaries and of individual identity demanded by the new science (Mann 1989, 90).[30]

This terrifying scene of violation, which suggests the entry of germs into the human body, sets the stage for Aschenbach's invasion by cholera bacilli. His infection is now inevitable since he has no boundaries left.[31] He awakens "shattered," incapable of defense even against the obsequious barber, and is now fully prepared to take into himself the overripe strawberries laced with comma bacillus (*DV,* 57). Representing the humiliating failure of all those who protect themselves with imaginary borders, Aschenbach's Dionysian experience also indicates Germany's need to recast its identity in relation to the rest of the world in an age in which traditional national boundaries have lost their meaning.

The Dionysian breakdown of selfhood, then, is intimately related to the preoccupation with borders created both by bacteriology and by colonialism. As Aschenbach pursues Tadzio through the "silent labyrinth" and "deep into the maze in the heart of the diseased city," Mann's image simultaneously suggests the ancient Minotaur, the origin of art, the protagonist's repressed libido, and the inevitable decay of empires, all of which Aschenbach has worked a lifetime to deny and conceal (*DV,* 46, 59). At the center of the labyrinth, of course, lies death, Nietzsche's truth of Silenas. This is the "abyss" that through works like "Ein Elender" (A man of misery) Aschenbach has tried to overcome. It is Nietzsche who has given Aschenbach his title, if not his moral system: "Oh, wretched, ephemeral race [*elendes Eintagsgeschlecht*], . . . What is best of all is utterly beyond your reach: not to be born, not to *be,* to be *nothing* [*nicht zu sein, nichts zu sein*]. But the second best for you is—to die soon" (Nietzsche, 42). The aging writer has dedicated his life to resisting this beckoning void, only to discover that he always carried it within him.

The idea that the same horrible absence of truth lies at the center of European minds, morals, and politics ties *Death in Venice* to Joseph Conrad's *Heart of Darkness,* both of which express and question the imperial mentality.[32] Like Mitchell's Cobra City episode, both novellas represent internal, psychological dangers through images of danger in foreign lands. Unlike Mitchell's story, however, they both question the legitimacy of their own comparisons. Mann's novella explores the soul of an artist more than that of an economic system, but both works depict a voyage in which a northerner travels south and an "inflated ego acquires a taste for the fruits of chaos" (McIntyre, 219). Both Mann and Conrad use an outer landscape to represent an inner, unconscious one, and both protagonists catch a "foreign" disease that is "the manifestation and corollary of an inner wastage" (223). In both stories, what is dangerous is what is "submerged," and both end with concealment (Vidan, 274). *Heart of Darkness*, in fact, suggests that European imperialism is a disease from which Africa is suffering. "Business" in the Congo, like Aschenbach's art, is a process that consumes and lays waste (McIntyre, 227). Conrad's decision to give his character a German name meaning "short" (and both Kurtz and Aschenbach come up "short" in many senses) ensures that "the embodiment of a European empire in general starts out as a specific example of the Wilhelmine colonial spirit" (McIntyre, 222). While Kurtz represents all of Europe, his initial motivation is the German "colonial fever" of the 1880s. Mann admired Conrad greatly later in his life but had not read *Heart of Darkness* before he wrote *Death in Venice* (Heilbut, 13; McIntyre, 233). Rather than the results of direct influence, then, the striking parallels between these novellas must be read as related responses to European imperialism with its fears of disease and reprisal and questions about the Europeans' relation to their colonial subjects.

Mann's work, perhaps even more than Conrad's, presents the corruption, the disease, and the violence associated with the tropics as forces already operative within the protagonist.[33] Despite Mann's reliance on Nietzsche in his representation of the Dionysian, *Death in Venice* refutes Nietzsche's early assertion that "the courage of the Greek results from his struggle against his Asianness" (*DV*, 147).[34] Instead, the story reveals that the lust, mendacity, and bloodthirstiness projected onto Africa and Asia by Europeans are integral parts of Aschenbach's "European soul." *Death in Venice* unmasks fear of the oppressed as fear of the repressed; both lie in wait like tigers, and both consume like diseases.

Conclusion: Meaning through Connections

Reflecting on the period in which he wrote *Death in Venice*, Mann confesses: "I love this word: relationship [*Beziehung*]. . . . The meaningful, that is nothing further than what is rich in relationships" (Mann 1968, 41).[35] He relied on *Beziehungen* to write the story, whose elements were already provided to him by his own trip to Venice in 1911: "the cholera, the honest clerk in the travel agency . . . everything was given; it really needed only to be employed to demonstrate its remarkable ability to be interpreted compositionally [*Deutungsfähigkeit*]" (42).[36] In the bacterial and colonial age, in which an infinite number of new connections were established worldwide, *Beziehungen* became dangerous in new ways. *Death in Venice*, owing its own existence to *Beziehungen*, reveals the futility of denying one's essential openness, either on a personal or a national level, and basing one's identity on artificial and indefensible boundaries.

According to Mann, "*Death in Venice* was executed in absolute accordance with the full realization of the bourgeois era's problem of individualism, a problem that was leading to catastrophe" (*DV,* 111). The concept of the intact individual, which had been the basis of cell theory and had served cultural needs for reform when Virchow and Mitchell were performing their research in the 1850s, no longer fulfilled cultural demands in 1911. Germany, which had sought to define itself though introverted examinations of its "origins" as it unified and expanded in the nineteenth century, found that in an imperial age it could do so only in relation to its neighbors. The face that "glower[s] threateningly" in Mann's first sentence reminds the reader, as the coming war would prove, that *Beziehungen* create anxiety. Only when ignored, however, can they kill.

Aschenbach's moral system, based on the command *Durchhalten* (literally, hold through), expresses an obsolescent siege mentality.[37] Like the nationalist politics it reflects, it will die in the trenches in the coming war. In an age of colonies and germs, one can create one's identity not in terms of barriers, but only in terms of *Beziehungen*, a fact that Bismarck knew all too well. Both Aschenbach and the society that created him combined an "entire being [*Wesen*] bent on fame" with a policy of exclusion, projecting undesirable elements of their own psyches onto the "foreign" forces they were determined to subjugate (*DV,* 7). As Mann's and Schnitzler's works suggest, attempting to define oneself in opposition to any undesirable Other by constructing a mental barrier will only leave one "shattered," without any identity at all, when one is finally forced to admit that the barrier is an illusion. Mann's artistic *Beziehungen*, which create meaning from myth, politics, and disease, rise up to mock those who deny their own *Beziehungen* and their affinity to "foreign" forces.

Conclusion

Identity in the Age of AIDS

In the West, we have built our systems of knowledge and our concepts of ourselves upon the boundaries essential for our vision. To know, since the time of Aristotle, has meant the ability to sort ideas and objects into categories; to be has meant to be different, to define oneself by drawing a boundary between oneself and others. So entrenched are these notions of self and epistemology that we wonder whether, in the absence of borders, knowledge and identity could exist at all.

Such a world view leads understandably to an anxiety about connectedness, for if one's self-concept relies on boundaries, any sort of penetration or communication becomes a threat. Germ theory, itself intimately related to imperialistic concepts of nationhood, has provided a means of expressing all fears about the breaching of boundaries, reinforcing with very real biological "evidence" the long-standing suspicion that penetration means death. But need we impose on ourselves, on our nations, and on our ways of thinking the borders our retinas seek? In construing our compulsion to exclude and divide as "natural," we create a culture of denial in which our notions of identity, at odds with twentieth-century biological and economic reality, must ultimately collapse. It is fundamentally illogical to define oneself with borders in a world in which everyone is connected.

The nineteenth-century notions of the independent, distinctly bounded cell, individual, and nation began to crumble with the advent of imperialism. The imperialist fantasy is to penetrate without being penetrated, to influence without being influenced. If one opens one's borders, however, to "take in" raw materials and to impose one's own cultural order on what one perceives as alien chaos, the ensuing diffusion must proceed in both directions, and inevitably, one will take in more than oil, ivory, and tea. Hoping to get something for nothing, to annex vast new territories without being altered in the process, the imperialist lives a contradiction, conceiving of the colonies as "self" and "not-self" simultaneously. An almost schizophrenic split occurs in which the crimes, the diseases, and the terrifying otherness of the colonial possessions are at once admitted and denied, accepted as a necessary evil to conduct business but painstakingly excluded from the mother country. The resulting society, which relies economically on the very connections it denies socially, will be unstable. Its citizens are open to blackmail and to colonial "diseases" in every sense, for the only really threatening connections are those that are ignored.

With the twentieth century drawing to a close, we are still living in the imperial age, an age in which the purely local no longer exists. The desires to expand, control, and steal have rendered the fantasy of impermeable borders not only obsolete but also dangerous in an era of increasing mobility. In the past decade, three devastating cholera epidemics have illustrated the ability of political conflicts, mass communications, and increased human contact to spread disease in a global age.

In 1991–92, about four hundred thousand people sickened and four thousand died of cholera in Latin America (Brooke 1992, 4). As in Robert Koch's day, people contracted the disease when they drank water contaminated with fecal matter or ate uncooked fruits, vegetables, or fish that had been in contact with unclean water. An Asian ship is believed to have triggered the epidemic when it dumped "infected ballast" into Chimbote Harbor (Suro, 33). Using the same word as Thomas Mann and his contemporaries, journalist James Brooke describes "the *specter* of cholera hanging over the Dickensian slums of Latin America" and compares sanitary conditions in Lima to those in nineteenth-century London (Brooke 1991b, 2, my italics). In Peru, where over 80 percent of the cases occurred, less than half of the people have access to piped water or sewer systems (Lazo, 16). At first, Peru and its neighbors responded by trying to "contain" the cholera, but tightening national boundaries made little sense when sixty thousand people a day cross the Ecuadorian border. The half million tourists who visit Peru each year were encouraged to come anyway; only "indigenous people living under poor conditions," assured one official, were at risk (Brooke 1991a, 3).

Bacteria, however, move as freely as people in the jet age. On 14 February 1992, an Aerolineas Argentinas flight from Buenos Aires landed in Los Angeles with five passengers showing symptoms of cholera (Nash, 6). By the end of the five-day incubation period, one passenger had died, eight had developed cholera, and fifty-seven had experienced cholera-like symptoms. The plane, it turned out, had stopped in Lima to load the passengers' food, and a shrimp salad served for lunch was suspected to have distributed the bacteria. While the media stressed that in the United States, sophisticated water treatment systems would preclude a major outbreak, it was apparent how easily microorganisms could cross politically and economically defined borders (Mydans, 12).

The border between the United States and Mexico, always a porous screen between the wealthy and the poor, provides no protection against diseases common to all. Recently, *colonias* have sprung up along the Río Grande in the El Paso area, communities on American soil that because of a zoning "loophole" are not connected to nearby water or sewage systems. While insisting that cholera in these *colonias* "does not threaten the American population at large," Roberto Suro calls them "ground zero in the US for a cholera epidemic" (Suro, 33). In the El Paso area alone, he points out, there are forty million northbound border crossings a year, and many immigrants carry fruits and vegetables in with them. Since the Peruvian epidemic has long since reached Mexico, cholera—always preying on the poor—could establish new "colonies" in the United States. Suro, like Virchow, blames "lax development laws" for the prevalence of the disease in the *colonias*, and he urges political action to prevent a serious epidemic.

Questioning our stubborn and increasingly harmful belief in national boundaries, Julia Epstein writes, "borders *produce*, it is thought, clarity and autonomy. Yet their current splintering under demographic, environmental, and political pressures make cartography appear to be an outmoded skill" (Epstein, 185). The hideous ethnically motivated wars of the 1990s and the cholera epidemics they have created have shown that in more ways than one, borders can kill. In April 1991, after uprisings against Sadam Hussein failed, 750,000 Kurds fled to Iran; 300,000, to Turkey, and another 300,000 massed along the Iraqi-Turkish border, forbidden to cross. The United States declined to interfere militarily; Hussein called attempts to establish a safe haven a "conspiracy," and the Turkish government refused to open the border. With no shelter, food, water, sanitation, or communications, "so densely packed on the sides of mountains that there [was] scarcely room for them to sit down," many Kurds sickened and died (Sciolino, 1).

Three years later, however, the use of modern communications may have caused the cholera that killed thousands. In Rwanda, as Tutsi rebels were about to overcome their Hutu opponents, Radio Mille Collines made broadcasts urging the Hutu to flee for their lives. Within days, a million refugees headed for Zaire, where they settled in camps with no food or sanitation and fell victim to cholera when forced to drink contaminated water (Hanson, 49).

When the desperate refugees tried to return home, they found themselves trapped. Zaire had closed the border because stockpiles of weapons lay along the last fifty yards of road before the cross-point. Together, the panic-inducing broadcasts and the sealed border allowed an epidemic to develop that killed more people than had died in the original massacres (Hanson, 49).

Thus in the twentieth century as in the nineteenth, cholera has refused to recognize the false boundaries we have erected. As Schnitzler demonstrated so aptly in *Reigen*, our biological sameness, our common susceptibility to disease and sexual desire, mocks the social and political borders we have drawn to define ourselves. The AIDS virus does not distinguish African from American, heterosexual from homosexual, rich from poor; the tragedy is that it has taken this devastating and unmistakable evidence for us to admit our common humanity.

Unfortunately, responses to AIDS thus far have borne an eerie resemblance to those directed against colonial diseases a hundred years ago. Koch's notion of a *Heimat* for each microorganism continues to thrive in discussions about the origin of AIDS in Central Africa. Cholera flourishes in Lima just as it does in Calcutta, and AIDS flourishes in New York City as it does in Zaire. What is the value of imposing on a microorganism that can live anywhere, in anyone, a label of *African* or *Asian,* reflecting geographical boundaries that do not restrict it? As we write a "mystery" of AIDS based on a long-standing "mystery" of Africa, we merely reveal self-deluding wishes for containment, for "the metaphors of mystery and otherness produce the desire for control" (Epstein, 165). Such labeling only stimulates our self-destructive desire to uphold the borders that microbes deny.

The "hungry life" that Cajal feared is today the desire and anger of the Third World, and we continue to define our diseases in light of the "hungry life" we imagine is stalking us, lurking just beyond borders that are ever easier to cross. Cajal's and Doyle's tales of biological warfare, particularly Cajal's title "For a Secret Offense, a Secret Revenge," retain their force when one considers our contemporary arsenals of biological weapons. And we still have tendencies, like Koch, to conceive of Africa and Asia as a vast laboratory, a place where people conduct experiments on themselves and one need only step in to record the data.

How does one best combat disease in a world in which everyone is connected? Koch's strategy of Identification, Segregation, and *Vernichtung* (of the parasites, not of the carriers) seems inhumane today. There are many, though, who would advocate it to stop the spread of AIDS. The key to selecting a strategy lies in the way one conceives of the relationship between the agent and the carrier of the disease. If one accepts the traditional notion of a "constitutional" factor, depicted so powerfully in Mann's *Death in Venice*, then one will inevitably focus on the carrier, for he or she is a disease waiting to happen. Such myths live on in our determination to associate diseases only with particular groups. Despite the overwhelming evidence for heterosexual transmission, for instance, AIDS is still considered by many to be a "gay" disease. To save ourselves from the twentieth century's viruses, we must abandon any such illusory divisions, directing our attention instead to the ways in which we are interrelated. If we continue to believe that connections to others diminish our sense of self, eventually our ideology will kill us.

Historian of science Evelyn Fox Keller has hypothesized that our ideal of scientific objectivity reflects a carefully cultivated masculine personality type that conceives of connectedness as loss of control. "A science that advertises itself as revealing a reality in which subject and object are unmistakably distinct," she argues, "may perhaps offer special comfort to those who, as individuals (be they male or female), retain particular anxiety about the loss of autonomy" (Keller, 89–90). Cultural theorist Donna Haraway describes a similar attitude in Western society, both inspired by and inspiring the scientific one: "the self is the One who is not dominated. . . who knows that by the experience of domination, which gives the lie to the autonomy of the self" (Haraway, 177). The scientist, that is, is trained to think like the imperialist: to penetrate without being penetrated, to influence without being influenced.

Such an attitude undermines our ability to understand and resist disease. "Seeing" epidemics today means tracing lines of communication more than resolving the membranes of microorganisms. Arguing that isolation and knowledge are mutually incompatible, Donna Haraway writes: "one cannot 'be' either a cell or molecule . . . if one intends to see and see from these positions critically. . . . Self-identity is a bad visual system" (Haraway, 192).

With AIDS, our visual system has supplied its own boundaries, created through centuries of cultural instruction on how to see. Social theorist Simon Watney finds that people's fear of AIDS is intimately related to their horror of sodomy and homosexuality, and he proposes that "AIDS has been mobilized to a prior agenda of issues concerning the kind of society we wish to inhabit" (Watney, 3). How people feel about AIDS depends on how they feel about their own sexuality. The panic that both AIDS and gay people inspire results from their subversion of socially constructed categories defining who is safe and who is vulnerable; who is good and who is evil; who is male and who is female. Arguing that "homosexuality problematizes the casual identification of primary power with the figure of the biological male as masterful penetrator," Watney speculates that hatred of homosexuality—and hence the tendency to blame the gay community for AIDS—may be rooted in misogyny, a "hatred of what is projected as 'passive' and therefore female" (28, 50). Westerners have responded to AIDS as we have because our concept of identity is grounded in male sexuality, construing receptiveness as weakness and penetrability as pathology.

To what degree, though, is influence control? Need it be threatening to conceive of oneself as linked to others? Must the identity, freedom, and the value of an individual be diminished in a world in which all people are connected? To a sexually active woman, especially one who has borne children, the idea that taking in another body disrupts identity is puzzling, even amusing.

Having traced the Western concept of selfhood over more than two millennia, philosopher Charles Taylor reaches a conclusion strikingly similar to Claude Bernard's physiological view: "one is a self only among other selves. A self can never be described without reference to those who surround it" (Taylor, 35). Biological and economic links among human beings are an undeniable fact, and the comedy and tragedy of our fact-worshipping epistemology has been its refusal to incorporate these bonds. "The enormous irony in pollution narratives about HIV-positive bodies as containers that need to be contained," writes Julia Epstein, "is that they presuppose the inevitability of contact with the Other" (Epstein, 182). While biological metaphors once served imperialism, urging citizens to guard their borders all the more zealously against the foreign "germs" to which they had exposed themselves, biological reality today should inspire us to abandon our anachronistic notions of boundaries, so that we may begin to build a new concept of identity upon the connections we once struggled to deny. With all the devastation it is causing, AIDS offers us an opportunity to move beyond obsolete notions of difference, greatly increasing our ability to cope with future diseases.

In this study, I have explored nineteenth-century conceptions of disease and selfhood because notions of boundaries, along with the imperial thinking that reinforces them, persist in our own culture. By examining the roots of our personal, political, and medical reliance on "membranes," I have aimed to show both why we have clung to these "membranes" in defining our identities and why it is now so essential to dispense with them. I do not condemn science, nor do I condemn the scientific writers of a hundred years ago for holding the same imperial views as their contemporaries. Instead, I propose that we begin to reconstruct our identities in a manner more appropriate to an era of retroviruses and global communications.

In the human brain, thought occurs because of neurons' dynamism and plasticity, their ability to form new connections and associations. Neurons take their identities not so much from their structures, from their all-important membrane, as from their functions, in terms of the cells to which they are connected and the nature of the communication between them. In the same manner, people and nations can define themselves in terms of connections and relationships, so that contact enriches rather than threatens identity.

Evelyn Fox Keller believes acknowledging such relationships would improve science as well, proposing that "autonomy needs to be reconceived as a dynamic condition enhanced rather than threatened by connectedness to others" (Keller, 73). Just as germ theory once reinforced our fears of being colonized, our greater knowledge of microbiology today may help to alleviate these fears. An enormous variety of bacteria "colonize" the human body at birth, but the vast majority are beneficial. Penetration, intermingling, coexistence, and symbiosis are facts of life, while hermetic boundaries are not. "Life is a window of vulnerability," writes Donna Haraway, and "the perfection of the fully defended, 'victorious' self is a chilling fantasy" (Haraway, 224). Germ theory and imperial politics once served one another in articulating fears of invasion; hopefully new knowledge of the body and its diseases will serve a new ideology celebrating global interconnections.

One. *Virchow and Koch*

1. In "Reshaping the Self: Popular Religion, Medicine, and Madness in *Vormärz* Germany," Ann Goldberg shows how middle-class doctors in the early nineteenth century imposed their bourgeois ideal of selfhood on peasants suffering from "religious madness," classifying them as clinically insane and interring them in their new asylums. Goldberg writes that "the self that comes through in the popular experience of madness is one of non-boundedness, where the person is vulnerable to invasion from a host of external forces. . . . The person at the mercy of such forces was also someone who fundamentally lacked responsibility. . . . This person contrasted radically from the self which physicians experienced and expected as a sign of health, namely a modern, secular, and individualist self—unitary, self-bounded, internalized, responsible, and cut off from direct divine intervention" (9).

2. All references to the *Dictionary of Scientific Biography* are denoted *DSB* in the text.

3. "Une réunion d'individus distincts"; "la masse tissulaire tout entière des végétaux n'est qu'une agglomération, plus ou moins considérable, de plus petits végétaux globuleux, univésiculaires, ayant chacun leur principe vital d'action, d'organisation et de reproduction." My translation.

4. L. S. Jacyna points out that early-nineteenth-century physiologists had a pragmatic as well as a philosophical investment in their quest for universal structural principles. To make physiology a respectable science, like physics, they believed it must likewise be founded on universal laws (Jacyna, 41–48).

5. The political documents quoted in this section are from the Virchow Nachlaß, Archiv der Berlin-Brandenburgische Akademie der Wissenschaften, Jägerstr. 22, Berlin. As many of the documents and newspaper articles lack titles, authors, and dates, they will be referred to by their file numbers in the Nachlaß. All translations of these documents are my own. Here the source is Nachlaß 2767, 6th Session of the House of Representatives, 17 November (year not indicated): "Die deutsche Politik Preußens [wird] nur dann wirklich zur Sicherheit des Staates beitragen, wenn sie sich auf der Entwicklung der Freiheit stützt. . . . Wir wünschen nicht, daß in der Selbstverwaltung so hohe Stellen geschaffen werden, eine Art Oberpräsidium, sondern von unten aus, aus den kleinen Kreisen des Volkes soll die Selbstverwaltung geschaffen werden."

6. "Sie [wollten] den Staat möglichst benutzen als eine große Polizeianstalt, um das Geschick jedes einzelnen Bürgers zu bestimmen." All translations of Virchow's essays are my own except for those included in the Rather anthology.

7. Nachlaß 2751, Wilhelm Georg, "Eine Unterredung mit Geheimrath Vir-

chow," *Neueste Nachrichten* (Braunschweig), 7 August 1898: "Wenn Herr von Bismarck den betreffenden Bericht wirklich gelesen hätte, so wisse er nicht, was er von seiner Wahrheitsliebe denken solle."

8. Nachlaß 2751, *Mitteldeutsche Volkszeitung*, 15 June 1865: "Ein Mann wie er, der in seinem ärztlichen Berufe jeden Tag dem Tod ins Antlitzt sehen muß, braucht nicht erst durch Unterwerfung unter ein dummes und brutales Vorurtheil zu beweisen, daß er Muth hat. Wer gefaßt sein muß, täglich, stündlich dem Typhus, der Cholera, den Blattern und wie alle diese Geißeln der Menschheit heißen, die Hand zu geben, braucht wahrlich nicht sich vor die Mündung einer Pistole oder die Spitze eines Degens zu stellen, um der Welt zu zeigen, daß er ein Mann ist."

9. "Vergessen wir gerade in diesem Kriege nicht, daß wir mit demjenigen Volke kämpfen, welches nach dem unsrigen die größten Opfer für die Befreiung der Menschheit gebracht hat."

10. "Als Naturforscher kann ich nur Republikaner sein." All translations of Mazzolini's text are my own.

11. "Eine Zelle . . . ja, das ist eben eine Person und zwar eine thätige, eine active Person"; "führte ich aus einer Schrift Schelling's über das Leben und seine Erscheinung ein altes Citat von dem Wesen der Pflanze an: Intus habitat, sibi soli prospicit, sibi soli vivit, nihil foras judicat aut agit"; "Eine solche Betrachtung ist kein Mysticismus, sondern reiner Realismus."

12. Because "altered conditions" can refer either to a physiological or a social environment, Virchow's definition has a provocative double resonance. Julia Epstein states that Virchow's concept of pathology "compellingly articulates" her own view of disease as "the intersection between medicine and storytelling," since the notion of disease always contains within itself a culturally defined norm. Virchow's words provide the title of her insightful study of culture and disease (Epstein, 9).

13. "Denn das lezte Ziel der cellularpathologischen Untersuchung ist die Localisation der Krankheit"; "[diese Gewebsveränderungen] zeigen abschliessend, wo die Angriffspunkte für die virulenten Stoffe liegen."

14. "Stellte ich die lebende Zelle als das eigentliche Krankheitswesen auf oder . . . ich definierte die kranke Zelle als das pathologische Wesen."

15. "Was das Individuum im Grossen, das und fast mehr noch als das ist die Zelle im Kleinen"; "Jede Zelle ist als solche eine geschlossene Einheit, die in sich selbst den Grund, das Princip ihres Lebens aufgenommen hat, die in sich selbst die Gesetze ihrer Existenz trägt, und die gegenüber der übrigen Welt eine bestimmte Autonomie besitzt."

16. "Ein Historiker ist sehr geneigt, in der Abstraktion seines Studierzimmers die einzelnen lebenden Menschen zu vergessen, aus denen sich ein Staat oder ein Volk zusammensetzen. . . . Und doch ist alle Action in den Theilen und das Leben des Volkes ist nichts als die Summe des Lebens der einzelnen Bürger. So ist es auch in dem kleinen Staate, den der Leib jeder Pflanze und jedes Thieres darstellt."

17. "Despotische bzw. oligarchische Auffassung des Organismus insofern sie die Aristokratie und die Hierarchie von Blut und Nerven vertreten."

18. "Die Eiterung ist nicht mehr ein Heilbestreben des Organismus, um dieses oder jenes Loch auszufüllen; die Eiterkörperchen nicht mehr die Gensdarmen, welche der Polizeistaat beordert, diesen oder jenen ohne Paß eingedrungenen Fremdling über die Grenze zu escortieren; das Narbengewebe bildet nicht mehr die Gefängnismauern, in welche ein solcher Fremdling eingeschlossen wird, wenn es dem Polizei-Organismus eben so gefällt."

19. "Das Leben besteht im Wechsel, aber es würde aufhören, Leben zu sein, wenn dieser Wechsel nicht gewisse Grenzen hätte. Diese Grenzen setzen bestimmte Moderations- und Regulations-Einrichtungen voraus, sowohl in der einfachen Zelle, als in dem zusammengesetzten Zellen-Organismus. In der Zelle haben wir die Membran und den Kern als Moderatoren und Regulatoren kennen gelernt."

20. "La pathologie cellulaire a vécu. Notre corps n'est plus cette 'république de cellules vivant chaquune d'une vie propre' . . . C'était la République chère au professeur allemand Virchow. Détronée, votre république cellulaire, grand Maître. . . . elle succomba sous le verdict de la mode . . . parasitaire. A bas les cellules, vivent ces êtres indépendants, infiniment petits, mais prolifiques, . . . venant du dehors, pénetrant comme des soudaniens dans l'organisme, le ravageant par le droit d'invasion de conquête."

21. "[Die Zellen] sind doch noch da und sie sind . . . immer noch die Hauptsache"; "Zuerst die Entdeckung des Parasiten, dann die Erforschung seiner Lebensweise, dann die Frage: wie erzeugt er die Krankheit?"

22. Nachlaß 3004, *Hamburger Fremdenblatt*, 11 May 1891, "Sagen Sie doch, was die wissenschaftliche Bedeutung ist!" "nun erst rief Virchow: 'Alles Phrase!' Aber die Rechte jauchzte Herrn Graf Beifall zu." The *Leipziger Zeitung*, 12. May 1891, gives the Count's reply: "Die Phrase haben große Autoritäten ausgesprochen, und ich befinde mich also mit meiner Auffassung in guter Gesellschaft."

23. "Der Unterschied ist nur der, daß bei den epidemischen die Krankheitsursachen das Individuum aufsuchen, bei den endemischen die Krankheitsursachen, örtlich gebunden, von dem Individuum aufgesucht werden." Translations of Henle's essay are my own.

24. "Die Materie der Kontagien [ist] nicht nur eine organische, sondern auch eine *belebte*, und zwar mit individuellem Leben begabte, die zu dem kranken Körper im Verhältnisse eines *parasitischen Organismus* steht."

25. "Hier würde also durch den Dorn nicht die Krankheit, auch nicht ein Produkt derselben, sondern der Reiz, der sie hervorbrachte, übertragen. . . . Nicht die Krankheit ist der Parasit, sondern der Dorn."

26. "Au début de tout recherche il faut avoir une idée préconçue pour guide." Translations of Pasteur's *Oeuvres* are mine.

27. "Les ferments proprement dits sont les êtres vivants, . . . des germes d'orga-

nismes microscopiques abondent à la surface de tous les objets, dans l'atmosphère et dans les eaux."

28. "Le corps humain dans l'état de santé est fermé à tous ces organismes."

29. "Les trois maladies dont je viens de parler: charbon, putridité du sang, choléra des poules, existent renfermées à l'état de germes dans une foule de vases de mon laboratoire."

30. "Le corps de l'homme et celui des animaux peuvent donner asile à certains êtres microscopiques."

31. Ignaz Semmelweis in Vienna and Oliver Wendell Holmes in Boston had argued very convincingly in the 1840s that puerperal fever was spread from one patient to another by doctors who did not wash their hands. Although some physicians still disagreed with them in 1879, it was one of the earliest diseases widely believed to be contagious.

32. "Es ist doch eine wunderbare Sache, wenn man Menschen, die unrettbar dem Tode verfallen sind, diesem Schicksal entreißen kann. Da macht es wirklich Freude, Arzt zu sein." All translations of Genschorek's biography are mine.

33. "Ihre Gestalt ist so charakteristisch, daß das Auffinden eines einzigen Parasiten genügt, um die Krankheit mit Sicherheit zu diagnostizieren." All translations of Koch's essays are my own except for those included in the Carter anthology.

34. Comparing Koch's work to Pasteur's, Thomas Brock finds that "Pasteur and the French school developed treatments for *individuals*, whereas Koch and the German school developed approaches for the control of infectious diseases in *populations*. The strong central government that dominated Germany at that time was probably a major factor in the success of this approach" (Brock, 293).

35. "Die 'Kolonialschwärmer' seien von einem wahren 'Kolonialfieber-Bazillus' befallen."

36. "Es ist aber recht Schade, daß die europäische Kultur so unbarmherzig alles wegfegt, was das Land früher so interessant machte."

37. "Für die Bekämpfung der Malaria ist es von grösster Bedeutung, auf solche Weise sich schnell über das vorhandensein und die Stärke des Feindes orientieren zu können"; "Allmählich wird man dann immer mehr Plätze besetzen und die Operationsbasis ausdehnen können."

38. "In Muansa liegen die Häuser der Europäer mitten unter den Hütten der Eingeborenen. Das ist ein schwerer Fehler, denn so sind die Europäer, trotz aller Sorgfalt, die sie auf die Hygiene im eigenen Hause verwenden, derselben Gefahr ausgesetzt wie die Eingeborenen. Es muß deshalb dafür gesorgt werden, daß die Europäischen Niederlassungen von den Wohnplätzen der Eingeborenen räumlich weit getrennt werden."

39. "Es handelt sich hier also gewissermaßen um ein durch Zufall herbeigeführtes Experiment am Menschen, welches den Mangel des Tierexperiments in diesem Falle ersetzt."

40. "Kaum waren sie wieder zu Kräften gekommen, so gaben sie das Farmerleben

auf und reisten mit dem nächsten Dampfer nach Europa zurück"; "Ich bin davon überzeugt, daß wir unseres Kolonialbesitzes nicht eher froh werden, als bis es uns gelingt, Herr dieser Krankheit zu werden"; "[wenn wir] vollständig Herren dieser Krankheit werden, dies [würde] gleichbedeutend sein mit der friedlichen Eroberung der schönsten und fruchtbarsten Länder der Erde!"

41. "Unser Versuch beweist aber ferner, dass wir mit unserem Untersuchungs-verfahren in der That alle Parasiten aufgefunden und mit unserem Behandlungsver-fahren auch wirklich vernichtet haben."

42. "Jeder Mensch, welcher die Krankheitserreger in sich trägt, [ist] eine Gefahr für seine gesunde Umgebung."

43. "Früher verhielt man sich mehr *defensiv*. . . . Wir sind von diesem defensiven Standpunkte ganz abgegangen und haben die *Offensive* ergriffen." Koch then con-tinues with the text quoted in the epigraph: "Wir brauchen nur ein Blutpräparat anzufertigen und mikroskopisch zu untersuchen, dann finden wir die Malariapara-siten darin und haben damit den unumstößlichen Beweis dafür, daß der betreffende Mensch den Infektionsstoff in sich birgt. . . . Werden nun alle Parasitenträger an einem Orte von ihren Malariaparasiten befreit, dann ist derselbe malariafrei gemacht. . . . Wir müssen im Stande sein, erstens den Infektionsstoff leicht und mit Sicherheit aufzufinden, und zweitens, ihn zu vernichten."

44. "Die Typhuskranken unter solche Verhältnisse zu bringen, dass von ihnen eine Infektion nicht mehr ausgehen konnte."

45. "Daß in den Häusern die Dejektionen der Kranken und die beschmutzte Wäsche vernichtet oder sicher desinfiziert wird, bleibt mehr oder weniger dem guten Willen der Leute überlassen."

46. "Eine sachgemäße Desinfektion nach polizeilicher oder hausärztlicher Vor-schrift."

Two. S. Weir Mitchell

1. Mitchell's works of fiction are identified, where necessary, by abbreviations of their titles: *The Autobiography of a Quack and Other Stories,* "AQ"; *Roland Blake, RB*; *Characteristics, C*; *Dr. North and his Friends, DN*; and *Constance Trescot, CT*. Mitchell's scientific essays will be referred to by publication date.

2. Mitchell's autobiography, an unpublished typescript, can be found at the Ar-chive of the College of Physicians in Philadelphia, Pa., Box 16, Series 7.1. References to the autobiography (A) indicate pages in this typescript.

3. Mitchell's letters from Europe 1850–51 can also be found at the Archive of the College of Physicians in Philadelphia, Pa., Box 4, Series 3.4.

4. In 1895 Mitchell advised the graduating class of Radcliffe College to discipline their senses until they became "watchful sentinels." As an example, he proudly re-called an occasion on which he had smelled smallpox on a lady's maid at a French railway station because "my nose was on guard" (Mitchell, 1896, 17–18).

5. Compare Louis Pasteur's statement quoted in chap. 1, n. 29: "The three diseases of which I have just spoken . . . all exist in the state of germs enclosed in a bunch of flasks in my laboratory."

6. He continually fainted at operations, confessing in his autobiography that "surgery was horrible to me." Breast amputations, in particular, appalled him: "The terribleness of the woman held by strong men, the screams, the flying blood jets and the struggle were things to remember" (A 94).

7. In his 1860 article, Mitchell explains: "I finally gave up the attempt [of "tempting" the snakes with food], and contented myself with feeding, by force, such of them as seemed feeble and badly nourished. For this purpose, I used milk and insects, which I placed in their throats, while they were properly pinioned" (Mitchell 1860, 4). In 1904, reviewing the logic of his rest cure, he wrote, "with this combination of seclusion, massage, and electricity, I could overfeed the patient until I had brought her into a state of entire health" (1904, 4–5).

8. Mitchell's original notes on the cases he treated at Turner's Lane Hospital in 1863–64 can be found in the Archive at the Philadelphia College of Physicians. I refer here to the cases of William Armlein (Series 1.1) and Hy. Clark (Series 1.3).

9. Mitchell's ethic of resistance and struggle often suggests the puritanical religious model of Bunyan's *Pilgrim's Progress* in which the individual achieves salvation through allegorical battles against his own sin, externalized as monsters he must fight or outwit. When North calls spiritualism a "slough of mental disaster for feebler minds," he recalls Bunyan's Slough of Despond, a strong symbol to American readers of how one might become "bogged down" in one's own weakness (*DN,* 97).

10. In *Injuries of Nerves*, Mitchell proposes that individual uniqueness manifests itself even at the cellular level: "the cell-life of one man so differs from that of another as thus to present us with varied phenomena under what seems to be equality of conditions" (33).

11. Oberndorf proposes that Mitchell was "probably fearful of revealing the weaknesses of the entrenched favored class into which he was born and inferentially also of himself" (Oberndorf, xi).

12. In his autobiography and letters from Europe, one sees Mitchell's political views developing as he reacts to the instability of 1851. He was deeply moved when he saw Austrian soldiers shoot an Italian peasant for smuggling arms, and he despised King Bomba of Naples, "ruling tyrannically a people who hated him," too fat to arise without help when he knelt before the Host (A 114, 118). After walking through Paris and thinking about the French Revolution, he wrote to his mother, "Blood, blood. It is so all over Paris, no spot that knew not death" (13 December 1850). Reflecting on all that he had seen in Europe, he wrote to his parents, "All this teaches one to love and honor our own free home where passports are not and honesty is. I am more a democrat than ever. I have always been for free trade. I am now yet more so and as for monarchies I begin to think regicide a noble virtue" (Earnest, 30).

13. David Rein proposes that Mitchell "emphasized the many outside forces that

acted upon an individual and made his actions, to a large extent, the outcome of causes he could not control" (Rein, 59). In Mitchell's writing, however, this external pressure is always a *limited* monarchy, and he is never a determinist in the sense that Zola is, believing that people act merely in response to environmental forces and physiological drives. For Mitchell, human behavior is never fully determined by these forces.

14. The protagonist of Gilman's story tells readers, "John says if I don't pick up faster he shall send me to Weir Mitchell in the fall" (Gilman, 18). Gilman herself "almost lost her mind" under Mitchell's treatment, which she underwent to cure extreme depression after childbirth (Hedges, 46–47). *The Yellow Wallpaper* depicts the struggle of a woman to conceive of her own selfhood when she is forbidden to work, confined to bed, and made to feel guilty for rejecting an identity that is imposed upon her. Mitchell's statement, "Of late I find it better to teach the girl to creep, which is an easy and natural mode of training for the walk," has eerie repercussions in the story (Mitchell 1880, 131).

15. Earnest believes that this "model" patient was Mitchell's own sister, who continued, after his wife's death from diphtheria, to manage his household and care for his young children even when she herself was dying of cancer and was in extreme pain (Earnest, 64).

16. When one especially stubborn patient refused to get out of bed, Mitchell threatened to get into bed with her unless she arose. He began undressing until, defeated, she finally got up (Rein, 46, 48). He wrote in *Fat and Blood*, "The man who resolves to send any nervous woman to bed must be quite sure that she will obey him when the time comes for her to get up" (58).

17. Mitchell boasts of how he exposed one woman who had supposedly lost her appetite when he spotted soot marks on her feet and crumbs in her bed. When he whipped back the pillow, he discovered a cache of food. "Well, now I am caught," she admitted. "The game I have played on you I have played with others, and in my restricted life I have found it very amusing. . . . I went on experimenting until I hit on the starvation idea" (Mitchell 1881, 85–86).

18. With an irony missing from Mitchell's works, Friedrich Nietzsche writes in *Ecce Homo* (which appeared shortly after *Doctor and Patient*), "Has my answer been heard to the question how one *cures* a woman—'redeems' her? One gives her a child" (267).

Three. Santiago Ramón y Cajal

1. Under the Spanish system of dual last names, the neurobiologist would properly be called Ramón y Cajal. Most of the literature about him, both in Spanish and in English, however, refers to him as Cajal, and I have followed this practice.

2. Among the scholars who conceive of Cajal's work as a unified effort are Pedro Laín Entralgo and Gregorio Marañón, who see it as united by the theme of the cell as

individual, and Helene Tzitskas, who sees it as united by the theme of individual will as a regenerative force.

3. Dale Pratt, in "Literary Images of Spanish Science Since 1868," points out the centrality of the visual sense in Cajal's literary and scientific writing. Pratt proposes that being able to see for oneself was for Cajal always the most convincing evidence, and in his writing Cajal tries to let others see what he sees (147). In "Stimulants of the Spirit: Metaphors and the Science of Santiago Ramón y Cajal," Pratt writes that in Cajal's rhetoric, "the key lies in the visual sense," many images drawing their persuasive power merely by referring to the visual (16). Ultimately, Cajal's talent lay not just in visualizing cells under the microscope but in "painting verbal pictures" of what he saw (14).

4. "Denso vivero microbiano, tierra de promisión de todos los agentes patógenos. . . . un medio obstinadamente hostil, en que todo es enemigo, porque todo es vida." Except where otherwise indicated, all translations of Cajal's scientific essays are my own.

5. "Envuelve al individuo, le persigue sin descanso . . . introduciéndose tan fácilmente en el organismo."

6. See also Benítez, 25–29. D. J. O'Connor calls Cajal's biological adventure novel "a 'poetic' account of the cell theory . . . and its relation to the concept of personal identity" (O'Connor, 101).

7. Max von Forschung's life caricatures that of Robert Koch, who also identified numerous microbes, made legendary trips to Africa to search for more, and became involved with a younger woman late in life (after Cajal had written the story of Forschung). Cajal mentions Koch in the story, however, as a distinct personality.

8. All translations of the stories in *Cuentos de vacaciones* are my own. Here the original reads, "la gallarda y animosa colaboradora daba a luz otro microbio, es decir, un niño robusto y hermoso, como incubado al fin por el ardiente sol de Palestina . . . No hay que decir que el retoño recibió el nombre de Max, y el microbio el de *bacillus Sandersonni*."

9. Pratt proposes that Forschung's seismograph turns the adultery into written language, for the lines to the scientist are like "words on a page" (Pratt 1995, 108).

10. Cajal's representation of Koch's views in this case is puzzling, since Koch at this stage in his career believed that the bovine tuberculosis bacillus could infect human beings. In 1908, Koch created an uproar by asserting that it could not, since massive government programs had been initiated in England and the United States for the pasteurization of milk based on the premise of human vulnerability to the bovine bacillus (Brock, 279–84).

11. "Millones de seres diminutos, de invisibles envenenadores"; "el invisible enemigo de la raza humana"; "los soldados destinados a ampararnos contra la formidable gavilla de microbios envenenadores, que nos acechan traidoramente ocultos en lo invisible"; "el hombre se defiende sólo del enemigo que conoce."

12. "Sino como un ser vivo, con propia autonomía, asociado a otros seres tan diminutos como él."

13. "Cada elemento es un cantón fisiológico absolutamente autónomo."

14. "Han conservado, y acaso perfeccionado, el hábito de cazar cuerpos extraños"; "autonomía vital."

15. "Uno de los más interesantes problemas de la Anatomía es la determinación del modo como las células de los centros se relacionan entre sí. . . . . ¿Se realiza esta conexión por contigüidad, es decir, por simples contactos entre expansiones celulares, o más bien por medio de anastomosis?"

16. "¿Tocan realmente el protoplasma desnudo de la célula o existe entre ambos factores de la sinapsis membranas limitantes?"

17. "El sarampión poético"; "Huyamos del pesimismo como de virus mortal." These phrases are from Cajal's prologue to the second edition (1898) and postscript (1899), respectively, and are not included in the 1953 English translation. My translation.

18. "La idea del alma es un parásito ténaz. . . . el bacilo espiritual . . . goza de poderosa toxicidad."

19. "Hegel, el prodigioso sofista que paralizó con la toxina de la *Idea* el análisis filosófico positivo iniciado por Kant, sucumbiera envenenado por el bacilo vírgula del cólera."

20. "Enfermizos y peligrosos romanticismos"; "desaparecido el hipnotizador, cesó el encanto."

21. "La mujer . . . 'posee un *yo* más débil que el del hombre;' un *yo* que se siente flaco y busca instintivamente la fuerza de la voluntad."

22. The psychologists August Forel and Hippolyte Bernheim, both of whom believed that responsiveness to suggestion occurred to some degree in all people, will be discussed in chapter 5.

23. "Pilas nerviosas de gran capacidad y tensión;" "magnéticos efluvios;" "voluntad férrea e incontrastable."

24. "Tibia, movediza y frívola atmósfera moral formada por borrosas y contradictorias sugestiones de padres, maestros, y amigos"

25. "El auxiliar más eficaz del ortopedista mental es la crasa ignorancia del vulgo acerca del poder soberano de la sugestión."

26. "Limpiar la herrumbre de la herencia y la rutina . . . [e] imponer ideas y sentimientos conformes con los fines de la sociedad. . . . reeducar la voluntad."

27. "Transformados en autómatas, en máquinas morales"; "En un pueblo de santos, ¿qué podía valer la honradez?"

28. "La posibilidad de reeducar el pueblo mediante la sugestión es un hecho firmemente establecido."

29. "Seducidos por la presunta necesidad de una estructura continua, *suponían* luego la existencia de una red anastomótica entre las dendritas y los cilindro-ejes."

30. "Para ciertos espíritus la teoría reticular ofrece seducciones y comodidades explicativas extraordinarias."

31. "Tomemos ejemplo de la Naturaleza. . . . ese incontrastable afán de los gérmenes por fundir dos existencias en el ardiente beso de la fecundación . . . sólo hay en el mundo dos realidades serias . . . *luchar para vivir y vivir para amar.*" Note that Cajal uses the same word, *incontrastable,* for Mirahonda's forceful will and for the "life force" at the cellular level.

32. "La superstición popular había bordado sobre aquel fondo de trágicas realidades sombrías y fatídicas leyendas."

33. "El foco de infección, puramente local, aquí creado fue importado por la familia inglesa."

34. "Simple consecuencia de condiciones naturales del terreno y del ambiente, fáciles de descartar con un poco de ciencia y buena voluntad."

35. "En ellas no han tomado parte Dios ni el diablo, sino el microbio, un demonio invisible. . . . los microbios de hoy son los diablos de ayer."

36. Dale Pratt points out the complexity of Cajal's decision to describe human behavior in terms of the activity of individual cells. Cajal's extraordinary description of the lovers' kiss from the perspective of their cells draws the reader's attention to science as a new and powerful language with which to explore human consciousness. Although certainly not an idealist (he rejected any notion of a human soul independent of cellular life), Cajal is not quite a determinist either. He does believe that the action of individual cells ultimately determines human behavior, but he describes the cells in anthropomorphic terms, making his maneuver more metaphoric than reductionist. The comparison of cells to conscious individuals remains a metaphor, however, an amusing possibility rather than a serious explanation (Pratt 1995, 96–107).

37. "El diccionario de la emoción es más pobre que el de las ideas."

38. "Se ha quedado Ud. un poco *esférico*, a semejanza del *amibo* cloroformizado que retrae sus seudopodos."

39. "Quel est le vrai moi, celui qui agit ou celui qui résiste?" My translation.

40. "Un sanatorio incomparable para los extravíos de la atención y los desmayos de la voluntad."

41. "La plasticidad de las células está casi del todo suspendida"; "Todo hombre puede ser . . . escultor de su propio cerebro."

42. "Tan rico en *colaterales* nerviosas como preñado de imágenes melancólicas"; "sin distinguir el genio del microbio, se complace en destruír la vida con la vida"; "¿por qué has creado los enemigos de la vida, las insidiosas y crueles bacterias patógenas?"

43. "No veía los objetos más grandes, sino más detallados"; "los detritus de la vida alta y baja"; "asistir a la disolución de un mundo cuyos elementos hubieran retrogradado al caos primitivo."

44. "Habían desaparecido, como por arte mágico, las diferencias de alcurnia, de raza y de profesión."

45. "El arte resiste menos al análisis que la Naturaleza."
46. "En todas las cosas hay algo bello y atrayente. Todo es cuestión de colocarse en el adecuado punto de vista."
47. "Desempeñan trascendental misión en la economía de la Naturaleza. . . . Merced a su capacidad para vegetar en los organismos débiles y degenerados, corrigen la disonancia, imperfección o incongruencia de las formas superiores."
48. "Nadaban y se refocilaban lindamente, bien ajenos de presumir eran blanco de obstinada observación."
49. Pratt points out the tension between Cajal's desire for a scientific language like a mirror that would reflect the outer world clearly but never refer back to itself and his knowledge as a good rhetorician that language would always play a part in developing scientific ideas (Pratt 1995, 120, 142–58).
50. "Es lo mismo que si en una batalla entre dos ejércitos, a pretexto de auxiliar a los más débiles, un tercero en discordia acabase con los unos y con los otros."
51. Pratt writes that Cajal's "descriptive passages are not tropes in themselves, but use tropes to stimulate visually oriented thinking" (Pratt 1993, 13).
52. "Las células son individuos vivos asociados entre sí para formar el organismo;" "El organismo es como un pueblo, cuyos individuos se renuevan muchas veces durante la vida de la colectividad;" "su profesión orgánica y su título."
53. Pratt writes that in Cajal's eyes, "Spanish society need[ed] invigorated 'cells' (especially better 'neurons' in the legislative brain) to function for the collective good" (Pratt 1995, 122).
54. "Sin querer columbro siempre, a través de cada moneda recibida, la faz curtida y sudorosa del campesino, quien, en definitiva, sufraga nuestros lujos académicos y científicos."
55. "Cada descubrimiento debido al extranjero era algo así como un ultraje a nuestra bandera vergonzosamente tolerado." This statement is taken from Cajal's prologue to the second edition and is not included in the 1953 English translation. My translation.
56. "Sólo la ciencia hace soportable, y hasta deseable, el dominio. . . . Sabia y prudente política es, al ocupar un país, que el médico y el naturalista formen la vanguardia del administrador y del soldado."
57. "Ensanchar la geografía moral de la raza con estas radiantes islas de la inteligencia."

Four. Arthur Conan Doyle

1. Stephen Arata argues that Bram Stoker's *Dracula* (1897) is a "narrative of reverse colonization" in which foreign invaders like Dracula colonize a mother country perceived as vulnerable and weak. According to Arata, "The fear is that what has been represented as the 'civilized' world is on the point of being colonized by 'primitive' forces. . . . a terrifying reversal has occurred: the colonizer finds himself in the position

of the colonized, the exploiter becomes exploited, the victimizer victimized. Such fears are linked to a perceived decline—racial, moral, spiritual—which makes the nation vulnerable to attack from more vigorous, 'primitive' peoples" (Arata, 623). Arata mentions Doyle's *The Sign of Four* as an example of this tendency. Patrick Brantlinger writes of the popularity of "invasion scare" novels after 1871. Holmes's adventures, like Stoker's *Dracula*, can easily be placed in this genre (Brantlinger, 33).

2. All references to the Holmes stories by volume and page number are to *Sherlock Holmes: The Complete Novels and Stories*.

3. Carlo Ginzburg compares Holmes's deductive method to Freud's psychoanalysis and Morelli's method of identifying painters' works through apparently insignificant details, and he assesses the detective's strategy as essentially a medical one. As detectives, Freud, Morelli, and Holmes read subtle signs that provide hints about individual "cases" and variations. Created by three doctors, these three epistemological systems "attribut[e] identity through characteristics which [are] trivial and beyond conscious control" (Ginzburg, 104).

4. In its description of the 1857 mutiny, *The Sign of Four* epitomizes the projection present in Victorian mutiny novels. As Patrick Brantlinger describes it, "in the basic fantasy . . . the imperialist dominators become victims and the dominated, villains. Imagining the Mutiny in this way totally displaced guilt and projected repressed, sadistic impulses onto demonicized Indian characters" (Brantlinger, 222).

5. Patrick Brantlinger argues that upper-class Victorians associated colonial rebellions with working-class discontent. The dream of a "docile" Eastern workforce at first appealed to their nostalgic longings for "pliable" workers in the face of their own increasingly vociferous working class. When the easterners proved not so docile as they had hoped, colonial protests recalled the anger of workers at home (Brantlinger, 34–35, 183).

6. In Freudian theory, a box as a dream symbol represents female genitalia.

7. Pierre Nordon writes that the Holmes stories often voice "the only reproach levelled at the aristocracy by their admirers the middle-classes; they sometimes fail to set a good example" (Nordon, 255).

8. As a physician, Doyle did not study hypnotism to the extent that Mitchell, Cajal, or Schnitzler did; and I have encountered no record of his having used it in his practice. He would have been familiar with it, however, through his medical training and avid reading.

9. "Er, der das geheimnisvolle Leben des Milzbrandbacillus entschleiert" (Koch 1898, 315).

10. Such an intensification of blackness is biologically possible but highly unlikely. Doyle is invoking a cultural myth that even if a light-skinned "black" person succeeds in "passing" and marries a "white" person, the truth of his or her racial origins will "out" in their "coal-black" children (Sander Gilman, personal communication). Ge-

netically, skin color is "multifactorially determined," so that "a 'dark' person and a 'white' mate cannot have a baby much darker than the dark parent, contrary to the myth that black ancestry on only one side of the family can result in a 'black' baby, even though both parents are light-skinned" (Fraser, 132).

11. I am indebted to Katherine Arens for this socio-political reading of the counterfeiting motif.

Five. Arthur Schnitzler

1. "Refiérome a la condición campechana y esencialmente igualitaria del microbio. Para las bacterias patógenas, hombres y animales, ricos y pobres representan meros terrenos de cultivo y albergues por igual provechosos y codiciables. Era de ver con qué inconsciencia respiraba cierta dama linajuda el bacilo gripal recién expulsado del pecho de golfa descocada y harapienta. Descendiendo de lujoso coche y en el momento de penetrar en el Ministerio de la Gobernación, vióse a un arrogante y soberbio ex ministro aspirar con fruición el bacilo de la tuberculosis, momentos antes aventado por el ulcerado pulmón de furibundo anarquista. . . . ¡Desolador era el espectáculo! ¡Enfrente de los enemigos invisibles, en todas partes, como únicas armas, la desidia, la indiferencia y la indefensión más absolutas!"

2. Schnitzler, Freud's junior by six years, studied medicine with the same professors, particularly the anatomist Theodor Meynert, and lived only minutes from Freud in Vienna (Hausner, 48). The writer and psychoanalyst did not meet intentionally, however, until 1922. Schnitzler's psychology, as it emerges from his novels, stories, and plays, does resemble Freud's in its stress on unconscious, irrational, and destructive drives. Schnitzler has been associated with Freud in his tendency to depict "the way people lose themselves in their drives [*die Verlorenheit des Menschen an den Trieb*]" (Delius, 108). Schnitzler, however, disagreed with many of the central points of psychoanalysis. An important exception to this concentration on the Schnitzler-Freud relationship is Katherine Arens's "Characterology: Hapsburg Empire to Third Reich," which analyzes Schnitzler's *Der Geist im Wort und Der Geist in der Tat* (1927) and *Leutnant Gustl* (1900) in the light of early-twentieth-century debates on natural selection versus the inheritance of acquired characters. My thanks to Arens for her valuable advice in the preparation of this chapter.

3. All translations of Schnitzler's medical writings are my own. Here the original reads: "eine der *wertvollsten therapeutischen Errungenschaften* unseres Jahrhunderts" and "etwas *für die Menschheit Entwürdigendes*."

4. "Die Pädagogik ist Suggestion, die großen Männer waren eigentlich Suggerenten. Die Religionsstifter haben suggeriert, und ganze Völker waren ihre Medien. Die unwillkürliche Tyrannei, die der bedeutende Geist über den kleineren ausübt, ist Suggestion, und wenn wir uns vornehmen, um fünf Uhr früh aufzustehen und uns tatsächlich nicht verschlafen, so haben wir eine Autosuggestion ausgeführt."

5. "[Ich] werde denken, daß ich in der hypnotischen Suggestion zugleich ein Mittel in der Hand habe, gewisse allgemeine neurotische Zustände, als deren Symptom die Aphonie gelten kann, günstig zu beeinflussen."

6. "Jeder spielt seine Rolle mit den Eigenschaften, die er besitzt, mit den Fähigkeiten, über die er verfügt."

7. "Eine der wichtigsten Fragen auf dem Gebiete der Syphilis, die nicht nur medizinische, sondern auch soziale Interessen aufs nächste berührt." In Schnitzler's time, Ernest Finger (1856–1939) was the leading syphilologist in Vienna. An active experimenter interested in bacteriology and in other new approaches to venereal diseases, Finger succeeded in producing syphilis in monkeys while attempting to identify the syphilis microbe (Lesky, 315–21).

8. "Daß die Lues im allgemeinen viel *längere* Zeit, und sorgfältiger zu behandeln sei, als es für gewöhnlich geschieht"; "kann dem eingehenden Studium aller Ärzte aufs wärmste empfohlen werden."

9. "Vorläufig steht es noch immer fest, daß die Lues nicht nur 'gern' sondern . . . 'am liebsten' durch außerehelichen geschlechtlichen Umgang erworben wird."

10. Quotations of Schnitzler's "The Sensitive One" are taken from *Die erhählenden Schriften*. All translations of this story are my own. "Ich bin gepinselt, elektrisiert, geätzt, massiert worden—massiert am ganzen Körper wegen zweier kleiner Stimmbänder, die nicht ordentlich schließen wollten."

11. "Mancher hatte schon gesagt: Ach, mein Fräulein, Sie sind eben nervös, es wäre gut, wenn Sie heirateten; und andere drückten sich ungeheuer vorsichtig aus und sprachen von einer durchgreifenden Änderung der Lebensweise; und einige waren riesig verschmitzt und sagten: Fräulein, waren Sie denn noch nie verliebt . . . Und andere waren wieder frech und sagten: Wissen Sie, was Sie brauchten?"

12. Schnitzler suspected that repressed sexuality played a role in aphonia, commenting at the conclusion of one case study that "maybe marriage does more than hypnosis can" ("*vielleicht tut die Ehe mehr, als die Hypnose vermochte*"; *Schnitzler 1988b*, 202).

13. "Denk dir nur, glauben, daß man von einem jungen Mädchen angebetet wurde, und erfahren, daß sie einen—eingenommen hat. Er mußte sich ja selber nach Empfang dieses Briefes widerwärtig und unheimlich vorkommen."

14. Gustl's name is short for Augustus, a Viennese clown. I am indebted to Katherine Arens for this observation and for the idea that Gustl is a bounded entity without content.

15. I am indebted to Tomás Casas-Arruti for this observation on Cajal's passage.

16. Annette Delius points out that both language and desire take their course in the play independent of the characters (Delius, 110).

17. I thank Katherine Arens for making me aware of this point.

18. The soldier is suggesting (not asking) that they address each other with the informal "you": "*Sagen wir uns du.*" Marie's response, "*Wir sein noch nicht so gute Bekannte,*" (literally, we are not yet such good acquaintances) is even more reserved in

the original German than in the English translation (Schnitzler 1983, 72). Eric Bentley's translation, however, preserves Schnitzler's plays on "knowing" and "knowledge," which echo throughout the scene.

19. In *Beyond the Pleasure Principle,* Sigmund Freud uses the *fort-da* game, in which a toddler repeatedly throws away an object that is always brought back to him, to introduce his notion of an aggressive or destructive drive. Freud believes that the game repeats the departures of the mother, so painful to the child. When the child reenacts them symbolically, he or she gains some control over them.

20. In Ibsen's *Ghosts,* as well, the author's representation of syphilis emphasizes its tendency to destroy the subsequent generation of the bourgeois family. Ibsen, however, never associates the disease with lower-class women or points to any social group as a reservoir of it.

21. "Ein Empörter stand auf und schrie: das ist Freiheitsberaubung. Die Freiheit, die Luft zu verpesten, sollte einem geraubt werden." My translation.

22. This attitude accounts for many of his objections to Freudian psychoanalysis. In 1921–26, almost thirty years after he wrote *Reigen,* Schnitzler criticized psychoanalysis in a series of notes, objecting to its determinism and its tendency to generalize from pathological cases. Schnitzler disagreed particularly with the division (*Trennung*) of the psyche into an ego, a superego, and an id, a move that he called "clever but artificial" (*geistreich aber künstlich*) (Segar, 118–20).

23. According to Horst Thomé, Schnitzler may have been influenced in this belief by Theodor Fechner's and Ernst Mach's idea of a fragmented self, or the notion that "The self is no ontologically distinct unity" (*Das Ich ist keine ontologisch distinkte Einheit*) (Thomé, 63).

24. This passage does not appear in Pollock's translation: "Pour lesquels le bourgeois est toujours un peu un ennemi, et qui sont féroces lorsqu'ils peuvent se venger sur lui de leur infériorité." My translation.

25. Pollock's translation ("we set the ball rolling . . . and it runs back to bruise our own shins" [Brieux 1913, 253]) is here very loose and does not capture the power of the original: Cette victime, transformée en fléau, est le symbole du mal créé par nous et qui retombe sur nous." My translation.

Six. Thomas Mann

1. I give the original German here because it is interesting to compare Koch's wording to Mann's: "Eine üppige Vegetation und ein reiches Thierleben hat sich in diesem unbewohnten Landstrich entwickelt, der für den Menschen nicht allein wegen der Überschwemmungen und wegen der zahlreichen Tiger unzugänglich ist, sondern hauptsächlich wegen der perniciösen Fieber gemieden wird, welche jeden befallen, der sich auch nur ganz kurze Zeit dort aufhält" (Koch 1884, 500).

2. Due to spatial limitations, I will quote the German text only where the original words convey a broader range of meaning than the English translation and where it is

essential to know the connotations of German words in order to recognize the affinity to bacteriological discourse. I prefer Koelb's translation of the novel to H. T. Lowe-Porter's because it is more direct and literal and brings out the strong sexual implications of Mann's phrasing, although it occasionally undercuts Mann's intentional ambiguity. Here the original reads: "Seine Begierde ward sehend. . . . er sah, sah eine Landschaft, ein tropisches Sumpfgebiet unter dickdunstigem Himmel, feucht, üppig und ungeheuer, eine Art Urweltwildnis. . . . sah zwischen den knotigen Rohr-stämmen des Bambusdickichts die Lichter eines kauernden Tigers funkeln—und fühlte sein Herz pochen vor Entsetzen und rätselhaftem Verlangen" (Mann 1989, 84). Lowe-Porter's translation of the famous sentence introducing Aschenbach's vision, "desire projected itself visually," preserves the endless interpretations invited by the original phrase, which literally declares, "desire became seeing."

3. Mann, like many Europeans in the colonial age, had had the tiger in mind for some time as a literary symbol; when Tonio Kröger sails to Denmark, a seasick, homesick Bengal tiger in the hold emits miserable sounds suggestive of Kröger's own repressed longings.

4. Ford Parkes proposes that in Aschenbach's first fantasy, "everything in the vision ultimately points to the tiger" and that the tiger image subsequently permeates the story (Parkes, 75). Parkes, along with Eugene McNamara and Hertha Krotkoff, believes the tiger represents the internal forces Aschenbach is repressing, concluding that "the author uses the tiger to portray the latent Dionysian side of Aschenbach's character" (79). Stephen Arata's insightful thoughts on reverse colonization in *Dracula* (see chap. 4, n. 1) can be equally applied to Mann's story, which appeared fourteen years after Stoker's novel but incorporates the same fears.

5. Manfred Dierks, André von Gronicka, David Luke, and T. J. Reed all comment on the close affinity of the cholera epidemic and the Dionysian forces in *Death in Venice*, analyzing the way the story creates effects on realistic and symbolic / mythological levels simultaneously. "Iridescent interweaving" is Luke's phrase for Mann's technique, a translation of Mann's own metaphorical description, *changieren*.

6. André Cadieux, A. E. Dyson, and Hertha Krotkoff all point out that the conflicts and suffering depicted in *Death in Venice* have their source in Aschenbach's own mind.

7. T. J. Reed, using this passage to demonstrate Mann's intentional creation of multiple layers of meaning in the story, writes that Mann's descriptions of the cholera provide a "coincidence between the external cause and a mythologically understood inner cause" (Reed, 173).

8. Koelb's translation of Mann's working notes for the novel, compiled in German by T. J. Reed (Mann 1983) appears in the 1994 Norton edition. Here the original reads, "zahlreiche Bakterien, darunter die spezifischen Erreger." My translation. In this case, Koelb's translation, "countless bacteria, among them those that carry the specific virus," is misleading, since the bacteria do not carry a virus; they themselves produce the toxin that causes the disease (*DV,* 84).

9. All contemporaneous statements about the 1892 cholera epidemic and Pettenkofer's subsequent experiment are taken from the Zeitungsausschnittsammlung 3006, Rudolf Virchow Nachlaß, Archiv der Berlin-Brandenburgische Akademie der Wissenschaften, Berlin. Unless otherwise indicated, these articles have no titles or authors, and all translations of these articles are my own. Here the original reads: "Wie die Cholera in ihrem indischen Vaterlande geboren wurde, . . . ist unerklärlich. . . . Das aber ist sicher, daß sich bei uns die Krankheit nur durch Ansteckung verbreitet, niemals von selbst entsteht."

10. "Man hüte sich vor rohem Obst und Gemüse, das ja vielfach auch leider in noch unreifem Zustande genossen wird."

11. "Die Fleete in Hamburg sind schlimmer als die Kanäle in Venedig, doch ist auch Venedig eine von Seuchen und allen Krankheiten bevorzugte Stadt."

12. "Der einzelne, das Individuum, wurde sich bewußt, daß es ein Glied inmitten einer großen Gemeinschaft ist, dessen Ergehen zu schützen auch seine Sorge und Pflicht sein mußte. Früher, als man die Cholera auf in der Luft oder im Boden ruhende, nicht greifbare Ursachen zurückführte, konnte von einer Verantwortlichkeit des einzelnen nicht in dem Sinne und dem Maße die Rede sein wie jetzt."

13. Koch and other bacteriologists have been accused of neglecting the role of individual disposition in the development of contagious diseases, but Koch's biographer Wolfgang Genschorek protests that "the accusation occasionally raised against Robert Koch, that he underrated the role of disposition, is completely unfounded." ("Der zuweilen gegen Robert Koch erhobene Vorwurf, er habe die Rolle der Disposition unterschätzt, ist völlig unbegründet." Genschorek, 146. My translation).

14. "Die Bacillen seien also . . . die Ursache der Krankheit, ohne die Krankheit selbst oder das Wesen der Krankheit auszumachen."

15. In 1880, for the first time, Robert Koch systematically tested chemicals widely used in Europe as disinfectants to see whether they actually killed bacteria. Most did not. Among those that proved ineffective was carbolic acid, which until then had been used by Joseph Lister in his antiseptic surgery (Brock, 106–12).

16. "Das alte Sprichwort bleibt, ganz wörtlich genommen, völlig in Geltung: was der Mensch braucht, muß er haben."

17. My translation. The German reads, "die Leidenschaft lähmt den wählerischen Sinn." Koelb's translation, "passion numbs good taste," is appropriate in context but is much more specific than the original and eliminates the ambiguity in Mann's phrasing.

18. Koch's 1884 article reads: "The further course of the disease, beyond the borders of India, was originally to the north, toward the center of Asia. From there it went toward Persia and then further to southern Europe. However, commerce [*Handelsverkehr*] no longer moves by caravans [*Karawanenwege*] through Persia; rather it moves by sea lanes [*Seewege*] through the Red Sea and the Suez Canal. . . . In my opinion, however, the sea passage [*Seeweg*] from India, especially from Bombay, which is the main embarkation port through the Red Sea, will become more dangerous year by year" (Koch 1987, 168). Mann's working notes closely resemble this

passage: "The rapid increase and acceleration of transport [*Verkehr*] since the introduction of steamboats explains the extensive spread [*Verschleppung*] of the disease since
the nineteenth century. . . . [Only] two *paths* [*Wege*] especially important *for the spread*:
The first one through central Asia following the main roads of the caravan trade
[*Karawanenverkehr*] to European Russia. *The second by the sea route to Mediterranean
harbors*. Danger from sea trade [*Schiffsverkehr*] very much in the foreground" (*DV,* 85).

19. "Vom Norden Europas, von Rußland aus, droht dem Kontinente und auch
unserem deutschen Vaterlande in diesem Augenblicke die Gefahr des Einzugs einer
schweren Geißel: 'Der Cholera.' . . . eine unklare Furcht umschwebt mit desto
panischerem Schrecken das Erscheinen des Choleragespenstes."

20. Aschenbach, who became Gustav von Aschenbach on his fiftieth birthday, is
over fifty when the story takes place. If the year is 1911 and he is fifty-five, he would
have been born in 1856, making him about twenty years older than the author.

21. Anthony Heilbut writes that as a young adult, Mann was "immune to Bismarckian chauvanism" and "despised the conventional nationalism of his Bismarckian instructors" (Heilbut, 24, 28).

22. In contemporary German, *fremd gehen*, literally, "to go strange," means to have
an extramarital affair.

23. J. R. McWilliams, comparing *Death in Venice* to *Tonio Kröger*, believes that
both stories show "the same abhorrence of Italians and their lack of conscience"
(McWilliams, 235).

24. Manfred Dierks believes that in 1911, in Mann's literary system, "the aesthetic-
individualistic antithesis 'North/South' transforms itself into the culturally grounded
East/West antithesis, which opposes 'Europe' with 'Asia'" ("die ästhetizistisch-
individualistische Antithese 'Norden-Süden' geht über in den kulturtypischen Ost-
West Gegensatz, der 'Europa' mit 'Asien' konfrontiert"). Venice, both Southern and
Eastern, serves as a "city of opposites in which the 'Southern' becomes permeable to
the Oriental" ("Gegensatzstadt in der das 'Südliche' für das Morgenländische durch-
lässig wird" [Dierks, 56–57]). My translation.

25. Eugene McNamara proposes that Mann's tiger represents Aschenbach's
"long-repressed animal nature, coiling for its spring" so that "the tiger lies in wait
within the bamboo thickets of the secret self" (McNamara, 234). Hertha Krotkoff
quotes C. G. Jung's *Psychology of the Unconscious*, reading the tiger as a symbol "of an
uneducated, undifferentiated, and un-humanized piece of libido, which still possesses
the compulsive character of a drive, and has not been tamed by domestication"
("[eines] nicht erzogenen, nicht differenzierten und nicht-vermenschlichten Stückes
Libido, welches noch zwangsartigen Triebcharacter besitzt, also nicht durch Domes-
tikation gezähmt ist.") She concludes, "We can thus identify the bamboo thicket as
the unconscious; the lurking tiger as the hidden dynamic content of the unconscious"
("können wir das Bambusdickicht als das Unbewußtsein, den kauernden Tiger als
den im Unbewußten versteckten dynamischen Inhalt werten" [Krotkoff, 447–48]).
My translation.

26. In Koch's description the tigers are simply present; in Mann's they *kauern*, crouching or cowering, half-hidden. The verb appears on two other occasions in the story, once describing the second-class passengers waiting to board the boat to Venice, and once describing a beggar who holds out his hat to Aschenbach. Mann's painstaking attention to his choice of words suggests a link between *kauern* and people of lower social classes, "foreign" to the bourgeois protagonist and very likely to the bourgeois reader as well. From the 1880s onward, such people became suspect of harboring not only dangerous passions but also dangerous bacilli, and analogous fears were applied to the natives of the colonies, whose bodies and whose lands concealed angry life. It is thus not surprising that the epidemic produces "a certain demoralization of the lower levels of society. It encouraged those antisocial forces that shun the light, and they manifested themselves as immoderate, shameless, and increasingly criminal behavior" (*DV,* 55).

27. Isadore Traschen points out that the "strangers" all resemble the tiger, and he proposes that the snub nose, suggesting the nose of a skull, is an image of death. (Traschen, 168)

28. "D[ie] gemeinsame (falsche) Annahme, die Heimat des Dionysos-Kults sei Asien." (Dierks, 19. My translation.)

29. A. E. Dyson believes the common moral of *The Bacchae* and *Death in Venice* is that "a man cannot really exile the more dangerous parts of his nature" (Dyson, 12).

30. Koelb's translation of "grenzenlose Vermischung" as "an unfettered rite of copulation" (*DV,* 57) does justice to the powerful sexuality of Mann's passage but detracts from the possibility for multiple readings, focusing on only one type of mingling.

31. Manfred Dierks writes that after the Dionysian experience, "now the mythic gains dominance over the realistic; Aschenbach's infection by cholera occurs as if coincidentally" "Über die Realschicht dominiert jetzt die mythische; die Cholera-infection geschieht wie beiläufig" (Dierks, 27; *DV* 140).

32. Allan J. McIntyre and Ivo Vidan compare *Death in Venice* and *Heart of Darkness* and reveal striking thematic and structural parallels. Vidan writes that the texts "thematically coincide as if they represented one narrative in two different codes" (Vidan, 276).

33. Ford Parkes and J. R. McWilliams both stress that Aschenbach's initial vision depends more on internal than on external forces. McWilliams writes that "what Aschenbach sees is not dependent on an external stimulus, but is rather the result of forces at work within his mind" (McWilliams, 237). Isadore Traschen believes that the "strangers" Aschenbach encounters are "the shifting shapes of his unconscious" (Traschen, 170).

34. Manfred Dierks writes that "Aschenbach deceived himself (as did Nietzsche) about such a victory over his 'Asianness,' which was really innate in him" ("Aschenbach täuschte sich [wie Nietzsche] in einem solchen Sieg über seinen 'Asiatismus,' der ihm eingeboren war," Dierks, 58). My translation.

35. "Ich liebe dies Wort: Beziehung. . . . Das Bedeutende, das ist nichts weiter als das Beziehungsreiche." My translation.

36. "Die Cholera, der ehrliche Clerc im Reisebureau . . . alles war gegeben, war eigentlich nur einzustellen und erwies dabei aufs verwunderlichste seine kompositionelle Deutungsfähigkeit" My translation.

37. It is interesting to compare Aschenbach's motto, *Durchhalten*, which might be translated as "hold through," "hold out," or "hold on," with those of another Prussian workaholic, Robert Koch: *Nunquam otiosus* (Never restful) and *Nicht locker lassen* (Never loosen up) (Brock, 11).

Ackerknecht, Erwin H. "Anticontagionism between 1821 and 1867." *Bulletin of the History of Medicine* 22 (1948): 562–93.

——. *Rudolf Virchow: Doctor, Statesman, Anthropologist.* Madison: University of Wisconsin Press, 1953.

Alexander, Theodor W. "The Author's Debt to the Physician: Aphonia in the Works of Arthur Schnitzler." *Journal of the International Arthur Schnitzler Research Association* 4, no. 4 (1965): 4–15.

Alter, Maria P. "Schnitzler's Physician: An Existential Character." *Modern Austrian Literature* 4, no. 3 (1971): 7–23.

Arata, Stephen D. "The Occidental Tourist: *Dracula* and the Anxiety of Reverse Colonization." *Victorian Studies* 33 (1990): 621–45.

Arens, Katherine. "Characterology: Hapsburg Empire to Third Reich." *Literature and Medicine* 8 (1989): 128–55.

Bell, Joseph. "Mr. Sherlock Holmes." In *A Study in Scarlet,* by Arthur Conan Doyle. London: Ward, Lock, and Bowden, 1893.

Bell, Robert E. *A Dictionary of Classical Mythology: Symbols, Attributes, and Associations.* Santa Barbara, Calif: ABC-Clio, 1982.

Benítez, Rubén. "La novela científica en España: Ramón y Cajal y el Conde de Gimeno." *Revista de estudios hispánicos* [Puerto Rico] 6 (1979): 25–39.

Bernard, Claude. *An Introduction to the Study of Experimental Medicine.* Translated by Henry Copely Greene. N.p.: Schuman, 1949.

Bernheim, Hippolyte. *Bernheim's New Studies in Hypnotism.* Translated by Richard S. Sandor. New York: International University Press, 1980.

——. *Suggestive Therapeutics: A Treatise on the Nature and Uses of Hypnotism.* Translated by Christian A. Herter. Westport, Conn: Associated Booksellers, 1957.

Bichat, Xavier. *General Anatomy Applied to Physiology and the Practice of Medicine.* Translated by Constant Coffyn. 2 vols. London: Highley, 1824.

——. *Physiological Researches on Life and Death.* Translated by F. Gold. Boston: Richardson and Lord, 1827.

Blasius, Dr. Untitled article. *Berliner neuesten Nachrichten,* 27 August 1892.

Brantlinger, Patrick. *Rule of Darkness: British Literature and Imperialism 1830–1914.* Ithaca: Cornell University Press, 1988.

Brieux, Eugène. *Les Avariés.* In *Théatre complet de Brieux.* 9 vols. Paris: Dellamain Boutelleau, 1938.

——. *Three Plays by Brieux.* Translated by John Pollock. 7th ed. New York: Brentano, 1913.

Brock, Thomas. *Robert Koch: A Life in Medicine and Bacteriology*. Madison, Wis.: Science Tech Publishers; Berlin: Springer, 1988.

Brooke, James. "Feeding on Nineteenth-Century Conditions, Cholera Spreads in Latin America." *New York Times*, 21 April 1991.

——. "How the Cholera Scare is Waking Latin America." *New York Times*, 8 March 1992.

——. "Peru's Neighbors Halt Food Imports." *New York Times*, 15 February 1991.

Burr, Anna Robeson. *Weir Mitchell: His Life and Letters*. New York: Duffield, 1929.

Carr, John Dickson. *The Life of Sir Arthur Conan Doyle*. New York: Harper, 1949.

Carter, K. Codell. Introduction to *Essays of Robert Koch*, by Robert Koch. Contributions in Medical Studies, no. 20. New York; Westport, Conn.: Greenwood Press, 1987.

Corbin, Alain. *The Foul and the Fragrant: Odor and the French Social Imagination*. Translated by Miriam L. Kochan and Roy Porter. Cambridge: Harvard University Press, 1986.

——. "L'hérédosyphilis ou l'impossible rédemption: Contribution à l'histoire de l'hérédité morbide." *Romantisme* 31 (1981): 131–49.

——. *Women for Hire: Prostitution and Sexuality in France after 1850*. Translated by Alan Sheridan. Cambridge: Harvard University Press, 1990.

Couch, Lotte S. "Der 'Reigen': Schnitzler und Sigmund Freud." *Österreich in Geschichte und Literatur* 16 (1972): 217–27.

Delius, Annette. "Schnitzlers 'Reigen' und der 'Reigen'-Prozeß: Verständliche und manipulierte Misverständnisse in· der Rezeption." *Deutschunterricht* 28, no. 2 (1976): 98–115.

Dictionary of Scientific Biography. Edited by Charles Coulston Gillispie. New York: Scribner, 1970–1980.

Dierks, Manfred. "Nietzsche's *Birth of Tragedy* and Mann's *Death in Venice*." In *Death in Venice*, by Thomas Mann. Edited and translated by Clayton Koelb. New York: Norton, 1994.

——. *Studien zu Mythos und Psychologie bei Thomas Mann*. Thomas Mann Studien. Bern: Francke, 1972.

Doyle, Sir Arthur Conan. "Dr. Koch and His Cure." *Review of Reviews* 2 (1890): 552–56.

——. *Sherlock Holmes: The Complete Novels and Stories*. 2 vols. New York: Bantam, 1986.

Dubos, René. *Louis Pasteur: Free Lance of Science*. New York: DaCapo, 1960.

Duchesneau, François. *Genèse de la théorie cellulaire*. Montréal: Vrin, 1987.

Dyson, A. E. "The Stranger God: 'Death in Venice.'" *Critical Quarterly* 13 (1971): 5–20.

Earnest, Ernest Penney. *S. Weir Mitchell: Novelist and Physician*. Philadelphia: University of Pennsylvania Press, 1950.

Ellenberger, Henri F. *The Discovery of the Unconscious: The History and Evolution of Dynamic Psychiatry.* New York: Basic Books, 1970.

Epstein, Julia. *Altered Conditions: Disease, Medicine, and Storytelling.* New York: Routledge, 1995.

Euripides. *The Bacchae.* In *The Complete Greek Tragedies.* Edited by David Grene and Richmond Lattimore. 5 vols. Chicago: University of Chicago Press, Phoenix Books, 1968.

Farrell, Kirby. "Heroism, Culture, and Dread in *The Sign of Four.*" *Studies in the Novel* 16 (1984): 32–51.

Ford, Brian J. *The Revealing Lens: Mankind and the Microscope.* London: Harrap, 1973.

——. *Single Lens: The Story of the Simple Microscope.* New York: Harper, 1985.

Forel, August. *Hypnotism, or Suggestion and Psychotherapy: A Study of the Psychological, Psycho-physiological, and Therapeutic Aspects of Hynotism.* Translated by H. W. Armit. New York: Rebman, 1907.

Foucault, Michel. *The Birth of the Clinic: The Archaeology of Medical Perception.* Translated by A. M. Sheridan Smith. New York: Vintage Books, 1975.

Fraser, F. Clarke, and James J. Nora. *Genetics of Man.* 2nd ed. Philadelphia: Lea and Febiger, 1986.

Freud, Sigmund. *Beyond the Pleasure Principle.* Edited and translated by James Strachey. New York: Norton, 1975.

Genschorek, Wolfgang. *Robert Koch: Selbstloser Kampf gegen Seuchen und Infektionskrankheiten.* 7th ed. Leipzig: Hirzel, 1987.

Georg, Wilhelm. "Eine Unterredung mit Geheimrath Virchow." *Neueste Nachrichten* [Braunschweig]. 7 August 1898.

Gilman, Charlotte Perkins. *The Yellow Wallpaper.* New York: Feminist Press, 1973.

Ginzburg, Carlo. "Clues: Morelli, Freud, and Sherlock Holmes." In *The Sign of Three: Dupin, Holmes, Peirce.* Edited by Umberto Eco and Thomas A. Sebeok. Bloomington: University of Indiana Press, 1983.

Goldberg, Ann. "Reshaping the Self: Popular Religion, Medicine, and Madness in Vormärz Germany." Paper presented at the German Studies Association Meeting, Chicago, September 1995.

Granjel, Luis S. *Baroja y otras figuras del noventiocho.* Madrid: Guadarrama, 1960.

von Gronicka, André. " 'Myth Plus Psychology': A Style Analysis of *Death in Venice.*" In *Death in Venice,* by Thomas Mann. Edited and translated by Clayton Koelb. New York: Norton, 1994.

Hanson, Christopher. "Courting Disaster." *Columbia Journalism Review* 33 (1994): 49.

Haraway, Donna. *Simians, Cyborgs, and Women: The Reinvention of Nature.* New York: Routledge, 1991.

Hausner, Henry H. "Die Beziehungen zwischen Arthur Schnitzler und Sigmund Freud." *Modern Austrian Literature* 3, no.2 (1970): 48–61.

Hedges, Elaine R. Afterword to *The Yellow Wallpaper*, by Charlotte Perkins Gilman. New York: Feminist Press, 1973.

Heilbut, Anthony. *Thomas Mann: Eros and Literature*. New York: Knopf, 1996.

Henle, Jakob. *Von den Miasmen und Kontagien und von den miasmatisch-kontagiösen Krankheiten*. Klassiker der Medizin, no. 3. Leipzig: Barth, 1910.

Jacyna, L. S. "The Romantic Programme and the Reception of Cell Theory in Britain." *Journal of the History of Biology* 17 (1984): 13–48.

Keller, Evelyn Fox. *Reflections on Gender and Science*. New Haven: Yale University Press, 1985.

Koch, Robert. "Ärztliche Beobachtungen in den Tropen." *Verhandlungen der Deutschen Kolonialgesellschaft*. Abteilung Berlin-Charlottenburg. Berlin: Reimer, 1898.

———. *Die Bekämpfung des Typhus*. Berlin: Hirschwald, 1903.

———. "Conferenz zur Erörterung der Cholerafrage." *Berliner klinische Wochenschrift* 21 (1884): 477–83; 493–502.

———. "Ergebnisse der vom deutschen Reich ausgesandten Malaria Expedition." *Verhandlungen der Deutschen Kolonialgesellschaft*. Abteilung Berlin-Charlottenburg. Berlin: Reimer, 1900.

———. *Essays of Robert Koch*. Translated by K. Codell Carter. Contributions in Medical Studies, no. 20. Westport, Conn: Greenwood Press, 1987.

———. *Gesammelte Werke*. 2 vols. Leipzig: Thieme, 1912.

———. *Über meine Schlafkrankheitsexpedition*. Berlin: Reimer, 1908.

———. *Wie schützen wir uns vor Erkrankungen der Atmungs-Organe?* Berlin: Steinitz, 1902.

Krotkoff, Hertha. "Zur Symbolik in Thomas Manns 'Tod in Venedig.'" *Modern Language Notes* 82 (1967): 445–53.

de Kruif, Paul. *Microbe Hunters*. New York: Harcourt, Brace, and World, 1953.

Laín Entralgo, Pedro. "Estudios y apuntes sobre Ramón y Cajal." In *España como problema*. Madrid: Aguilar, 1957.

LaTour, Bruno. *The Pasteurization of France*. Translated by Alan Sheridan and John Law. Cambridge: Harvard University Press, 1988.

Lazo, Oswaldo. "Two Faces of Poverty." *World Health* 94 (1994): 16–17.

Lehnert, Herbert. "Thomas Mann's Interpretations of *Der Tod in Venedig* and Their Reliability." *Rice University Studies* 50, no. 4 (1964): 41–60.

Lesky, Erna. *The Vienna Medical School of the Nineteenth Century*. Translated by L. Williams and I. S. Levij. Baltimore: Johns Hopkins University Press, 1976.

Lewy Rodríguez, Enriqueta. *El Madrid de Cajal*. Madrid: Artes Gráficas Municipales, 1985.

Liebow, Ely. *Dr. Joe Bell: Model for Sherlock Holmes*. Bowling Green, Ohio: Popular Press, 1982.

Loewy, Arthur D. "Ramón y Cajal and Methods of Neuroanatomical Research." *Perspectives in Biology and Medicine* 15 (1971): 7–36.

López Piñero, José María. *Las publicaciones valencianas de Cajal.* Valencia: Secretariado de Publicaciones, Universidad de Valencia, 1983.

Lovering, Joseph P. *S. Weir Mitchell.* New York: Twayne, 1971.

Luke, David. "Thomas Mann's 'Iridescent Interweaving.'" In *Death in Venice,* by Thomas Mann. Edited and translated by Clayton Koelb. New York: Norton, 1994.

Mann, Thomas. *Death in Venice.* Edited and translated by Clayton Koelb. New York: Norton, 1994.

———. *Death in Venice and Seven Other Stories.* Translated by H. T. Lowe-Porter. New York: Vintage Books, 1963.

———. "Lebensabriß." In *Autobiographisches.* Frankfurt am Main: Fischer, 1968.

———. *Der Tod in Venedig und andere Erzählungen.* Frankfurt am Main: Fischer, 1989.

———. *Thomas Mann: "Der Tod in Venedig": Text, Materialen, Kommentar.* Edited by T. J. Reed. München: Hanser, 1983.

Marañón, Gregorio. *Cajal: Su tiempo y el nuestro.* 2nd ed. Santander: Zuñiga, 1950.

Marcuse, Ludwig. "Der 'Reigen'-Prozeß: Sex, Politik und Kunst 1920 in Berlin." *Monat* 14, no. 168 (1962): 48–55 and no. 169 (1962): 34–46.

Mazzolini, Renato G. *Politisch-biologische Analogien im Frühwerk Rudolf Virchows.* Translated by Klaus-Peter Tieck. Marburg: Basilisken-Presse, 1988.

McIntyre, Allan J. "Psychology and Symbol: Correspondences between *Heart of Darkness* and *Death in Venice.*" *Hartford Studies in Literature* 7 (1975): 216–35.

McNamara, Eugene. "'Death in Venice': The Disguised Self." *College English* 24 (1962): 233–34.

McWilliams, J. R. "The Failure of a Repression: Thomas Mann's *Tod in Venedig.*" *German Life and Letters* 20 (1966): 233–41.

Mettenry, Lawrence C., Jr. Introduction to *Injuries of Nerves and Their Consequences,* by S. Weir Mitchell. 1872. American Academy of Neurology Reprint Series. New York: Dover, 1965.

Mitchell, John Kearsley. *Five Essays by John Kearsley Mitchell.* Edited by S. Weir Mitchell. Philadelphia: Lippincott, 1859.

Mitchell, S. Weir. "Address on the Opening of the Institute of Hygiene of the University of Pennsylvania." 1892. Papers. College of Physicians, Philadelphia, Pa.

———. "Address to the Students of Radcliffe College." 17 January 1895. Cambridge: N.p., 1896.

———. Autobiography. Papers. College of Physicians, Philadelphia, Pa.

———. *The Autobiography of a Quack and Other Stories.* New York: Century, 1915.

———. *Characteristics.* New York: Century, 1907.

———. "Clinical Lecture on Nervousness in the Male." *Medical News and Library* 3 (1877): 177–84.

———. *Constance Trescot: A Novel.* New York: Century, 1905.

———. *Doctor North and His Friends.* New York: Century, 1905.

———. *Doctor and Patient.* 5th ed. Philadelphia: Lippincott, 1904.

———. "The Evolution of the Rest Treatment." *Journal of Nervous and Mental Disease* 31 (1904): 368–73.

———. "Experimental Contributions to the Toxicology of Rattlesnake Venom." *New York Medical Journal* 6, no. 4 (1868): 289–322.

———. *Fat and Blood: An Essay on the Treatment of Certain Forms of Neurasthenia and Hysteria.* 3rd ed. Philadelphia: Lippincott, 1884.

———. *In War Time.* New York: Century, 1902.

———. *Injuries of Nerves and Their Consequences.* 1872. American Academy of Neurology Reprint Series. New York: Dover, 1965.

———. *Lectures on Diseases of the Nervous System, Especially in Women.* Philadelphia: Lea, 1881.

———. "Man, the Individual." 1902. Papers. College of Physicians, Philadelphia, Pa.

———. *Mary Reynolds: A Case of Double Consciousness.* Philadelphia: Dornan, 1889.

———. "On the Modern Methods of Studying Poisons." *Atlantic Monthly* 22 (1868): 294–302.

———. "Paralysis from Peripheral Irritation." *New York Medical Journal.* 1866.

———. "The Poison of the Rattlesnake." *Atlantic Monthly* 21 (1868): 452–61.

———. "Researches upon the Venom of Rattlesnakes." *Smithsonian* 12 (1860): 1–46.

———. *Roland Blake.* New York: Century, 1909.

———. *On the Treatment of Rattlesnake Bites with Experimental Criticisms upon the Various Remedies Now in Use.* Philadelphia: Lippincott, 1861.

———. "The Treatment by Rest, Seclusion, Etc. in Relation to Psychotherapy." *Journal of the American Medical Association* 50 (1908): 2033–37.

———. "The True and False Palsies of Hysteria." *Medical News and Abstract* 38 (1880): 65–71; 129–36.

———. *Wear and Tear, or Hints for the Overworked.* Philadelphia: Lippincott, 1874.

Mitchell, S. Weir, George R. Morehouse, and William W. Keen. *Gunshot Wounds and Other Injuries of Nerves.* Philadelphia: Lippincott, 1864.

Mitchell, S. Weir, and Edward T. Reichert. "Preliminary Report on the Venoms of Serpents." *Medical News,* 28 April 1883.

Mydans, Seth. "Cholera Kills One and Fells Many on Flight. *New York Times,* 21 February 1992.

Nash, Nathaniel C. "Latin Nations Feud over Cholera Outbreak." *New York Times,* 10 March 1992.

Nehring, Wolfgang. "Schnitzler, Freud's Alter Ego?" *Modern Austrian Literature* 10, no. 3–4 (1977): 179–94.

Nietzsche, Friedrich. *The Birth of Tragedy and the Case of Wagner.* Edited and translated by Walter Kaufmann. New York: Vintage Books, 1967.

———. *On the Genealogy of Morals and Ecce Homo.* Edited and translated by Walter Kaufmann. New York: Vintage Books, 1969.

Nordon, Pierre. *Conan Doyle: A Biography.* Translated by Frances Partridge. London: Murray, 1966.

Oberndorf, C. P. Introduction to *S. Weir Mitchell as a Psychiatric Novelist*, by David Rein. New York: International University Press, 1952.

O'Connor, D. J. "Science, Literature, and Self-Censorship: Ramón y Cajal's *Cuentos de Vacaciones.*" *Ideologies and Literature* 1, no. 3 (1985): 98–122.

Parkes, Ford B. "The Image of the Tiger in Thomas Mann's *Tod in Venedig.*" *Studies in Twentieth-Century Literature* 3 (1978): 73–82.

Pasteur, Louis. *Oeuvres de Pasteur.* Edited by Pasteur Vallery-Radot. 7 vols. Paris: Masson, 1922–39.

———. *Studies on Fermentation: The Diseases of Beer, Their Causes, and the Means of Preventing Them.* Translated by Frank Faulkner and D. Constable Robb. London: Macmillan, 1879.

Perrín, Tomás G. "Cajal como español." *Abside* 22 (1958): 191–216.

Poirier, Suzanne. "The Physician and Authority: Portraits by Four Physician Writers." *Literature and Medicine* 2 (1983): 21–40.

———. "The Weir Mitchell Rest Cure: Doctor and Patients." *Women's Studies* 10 (1983): 15–40.

Pratt, Dale. "Literary Images of Spanish Science Since 1868." Ph.D. diss., Cornell University, 1995.

———. "Stimulants of the Spirit: Metaphors and the Science of Ramón y Cajal." Unpublished manuscript.

Quétel, Claude. *History of Syphilis.* Translated by Judith Braddock and Brian Pike. Baltimore: Johns Hopkins University Press, 1990.

Ramón y Cajal, Santiago. "Algunas conjeturas sobre el mecanismo anatómico de la ideación, asociación, y atención." *Revista de medicina y cirugía prácticas* (1895): 3–14.

———. "Conexión general de los elementos nerviosos." In *Trabajos escogidos 1880–1890.* Madrid: N.p., 1924.

———. "The Croonian Lecture: La Fine Structure des Centres Nerveux." *Proceedings of the Royal Society* 55 (1894): 444–68.

———. *Cuentos de vacaciones.* 5th ed. Madrid: Espasa-Calpe, 1964.

———. *Degeneration and Regeneration of the Nervous System.* 2 vols. Translated by Raoul M. May. 1913. Reprint. New York: Hafner, 1959.

———. "Dolores del parto considerablemente atenuados por la sugestión hipnótica." In *Trabajos escogidos 1880–1890.* Madrid: N.p., 1924.

———. *Elementos de histología normal y de técnica micrográfica.* 4th ed. Madrid: Moya, 1904.

———. "Estructura de los centros nerviosos de las aves." In *Trabajos escogidos 1880–1890.* Madrid: N.p. 1924.

———. "Estudios sobre el microbio vírgula del cólera y las inoculaciones profilácticas." In *Trabajos escogidos 1880–1890.* Madrid: N.p., 1924.

——. *Estudios sobre la degeneración y la regeneración del sistema nervioso.* 2 vols. Madrid: Moya, 1913.

——. *Histology of the Nervous System of Man and Vertebrates.* 2 vols. Translated by Neely Swanson and Larry W. Swanson. New York; Oxford: Oxford University Press, 1995.

——. "Neuronismo o reticularismo?: Las pruebas objetivas de la unidad anatómica de las células nerviosas." *Archivos de neurobiología* 13 (1933): 217–90.

——. *Precepts and Counsels on Scientific Investigation (Stimulants of the Spirit).* Edited by Cyril B. Courville. Translated by J. M. Sánchez Pérez. Mountain View, Calif.: Pacific Press, 1953.

——. Prólogo to *Desinfección doméstica: Aislamiento y desinfección simplificados,* by D. Carlos Vicente y Charpentier. Madrid: Fortanet, 1901.

——. Prólogo to *Informe de la Comisión del Instituto Nacional de Higiene de Alfonso XIII Enviada a las Posesiones Españolas del Golfo de Guinea para el Estudio de la Enfermedad del Sueño y de las Condiciones Sanitarias de la Colonia.* Madrid: Blass, 1910.

——. "Ramón y Cajal and Methods of Neuroanatomical Research." Edited and translated by Arthur D. Loewy. *Perspectives in Biology and Medicine* 15 (1971): 7–36.

——. *Recollections of My Life.* Translated by E. Horne Craigie. Cambridge: MIT Press, 1989.

——. *Reglas y consejos sobre investigación científica (Los tónicos de la voluntad).* 12th ed. Madrid: Espasa Calpe, 1991.

——. "El renacimiento de la doctrina neuronal." *Gaceta médica catalana* 31 (1907): 121–33.

——. *Textura del sistema nervioso del hombre y de los vertebrados.* 2 vols. Madrid: Moya, 1899.

Rather, L. J. Introduction to *Cellular Pathology as Based upon Physiological and Pathological Histology,* by Rudolf Virchow. Translated by Frank Chance. 1859. Reprint. New York: Dover, 1971.

Reed, T. J. "The Art of Ambivalence." In *Death in Venice,* by Thomas Mann. Edited and translated by Clayton Koelb. New York: Norton, 1994.

Rein, David. *S. Weir Mitchell as a Psychiatric Novelist.* New York: International Press, 1952.

Ribot, Théodule. *Diseases of the Will.* Translated by Merwin Marie Snell. Chicago: Open Court, 1894.

——. *Les Maladies de la volonté.* Paris: Baillière, 1883.

Riley, James C. *The Eighteenth-Century Campaign to Avoid Disease.* New York: St. Martin's, 1987.

Rothfield, Lawrence. *Vital Signs: Medical Realism in Nineteenth-Century Fiction.* Princeton: Princeton University Press, 1992.

Said, Edward. *Culture and Imperialism.* New York: Knopf, 1993.

Schinnerer, Otto P. "The History of Schnitzler's Reigen." *PMLA* 46 (1931): 839–59.

Schlein, Rena R. "Arthur Schnitzler: Author-Scientist." *Journal of the International Arthur Schnitzler Research Foundation* 1, no. 2 (1967): 28–37.

Schneider, Gerd K. "The Reception of Arthur Schnitzler's *Reigen* in the Old Country and the New World: A Study in Cultural Differences." *Modern Austrian Literature* 19, no. 3–4 (1986): 75–90.

Schnitzler, Arthur. *Die erzählenden Schriften*. Frankfurt: Fischer, 1961.

———. *Leutnant Gustl und andere Erzählungen*. In *Das erzählerische Werk*. 7 vols. Frankfurt am Main: Fischer, 1988.

———. *Medizinische Schriften*. Edited by Horst Thomé. Vienna: Zsolnay, 1988.

———. *Plays and Stories*. Edited by Egon Schwarz. New York: Continuum, 1994.

———. *Reigen und andere Dramen*. In *Das dramatische Werk*. 8 vols. Frankfurt am Main: Fischer, 1983.

Schwann, Theodor. *Microscopical Researches into the Accordance in the Structure and Growth of Animals and Plants*. Translated by Henry Smith. 1847. Reprint. New York: Kraus, 1969.

Sciolino, Elaine. "Kurds Will Die in Vast Numbers without Swift Aid, Agencies Say." *New York Times,* 10 April 1991.

Segar, Kenneth. "Determinism and Character: Arthur Schnitzler's *Traumnovelle* and his Unpublished Critique of Psychoanalysis." *Oxford German Studies* 8 (1973): 114–27.

Simon, W. M. *Germany in the Age of Bismark*. London: Allen and Unwin, 1968.

Sulloway, Frank J. *Freud, Biologist of the Mind: Beyond the Psychoanalytic Legend*. New York: Basic Books, 1979.

Suro, Roberto. "The Cholera Watch." *New York Times Magazine,* 22 March 1992.

Taylor, Charles. *Sources of the Self: The Making of Modern Identity*. Cambridge: Harvard University Press, 1989.

Thomé, Horst. "Kernlosigkeit und Pose: Zur Rekonstruktion von Schnitzlers Psychologie." *Text und Kontext* 20 (1984): 62–87.

Traschen, Isadore. "The Uses of Myth in 'Death in Venice.' " *Modern Fiction Studies* 11 (1965): 165–79.

Turpin, P. J. F. *Organographie Végétale*. Paris: Belin, 1827.

Tzitsikas, Helene. *Santiago Ramón y Cajal: Obra literaria*. Colección studium, no. 53. México: De Andrea, 1965.

Urban, Bernd. "Schnitzler and Freud as Doubles: Poetic Intuition and Early Research on Hysteria." *Psychoanalytic Review* 65 (1978): 131–65.

Vicente y Charpentier, D. Carlos. *Desinfección doméstica: Aislamiento y desinfección simplificados*. Madrid: Fortanet, 1901.

Vidan, Ivo. "Conrad and Thomas Mann." In *Contexts for Conrad*. Edited by Keith Carabine, Owen Knowles, and Wieslaw Krajka. Boulder: East European Monographs, 1993.

Virchow, Rudolf. "Alter und Neuer Vitalismus." *Archiv für pathologische Anatomie und Physiologie und für klinische Medizin* 9 (1856): 1–55.

——. *Cellular Pathology as Based upon Physiological and Pathological Histology*. Translated by Frank Chance. 1859. Reprint. New York: Dover, 1971.

——. *Collected Essays on Public Health and Epidemiology*. 1879. Edited by L. J. Rather. 2 vols. Canton, Mass.: Science History Publications, 1985.

——. "Die Epidemien von 1848." *Archiv für pathologische Anatomie und Physiologie und für klinische Medizin* 3 (1851): 3–11.

——. "Der Kampf der Zellen und der Bakterien." *Archiv für pathologische Anatomie und Physiologie und für klinische Medizin* 101 (1885): 1–13.

——. "Krankheitswesen und Krankheitsursachen." *Archiv für pathologische Anatomie und Physiologie und für klinische Medizin* 79 (1880): 1–18; 185–228.

——. "Der Krieg und die Wissenschaft." *Archiv für pathologische Anatomie und Physiologie und für klinische Medizin* 51 (1870): 1–6.

——. "Mittheilungen über die in Oberschlesien herrschende Typhus-Epidemie." *Archiv für pathologische Anatomie und Physiologie und für klinische Medizin* 2 (1849): 143–322.

——. *Sozialismus und Reaktion*. Berlin: Barthel, 1878.

——. "Der Stand der Cellularpathologie." *Archiv für pathologische Anatomie und Physiologie und für klinische Medizin* 126 (1891): 1–10.

——. *Über die Heilkräfte des Organismus*. Berlin: Lüderitz, 1875.

——. "Über die Reform der pathologischen und therapeutischen Anschauungen durch die mikroskopischen Untersuchungen." *Archiv für pathologische Anatomie und Physiologie und für klinische Medizin* 1 (1847): 207–255.

——. "Über die Standpunkte der wissenschaftlichen Medizin." *Archiv für pathologische Anatomie und Physiologie und für klinische Medizin* 1 (1847): 3–19.

Watney, Simon. *Policing Desire: Pornography, AIDS, and the Media*. 2nd ed. Minneapolis: University of Minnesota Press, 1989.

Wehler, Hans-Ulrich. *Bismark und der Imperialismus*. Frankfurt: Suhrkamp, 1984.

INDEX

Ackerknecht, Irwin, 11
Agassiz, Louis, 43
AIDS: anxiety about, 172; origins of, 171;
and social boundaries, 7, 172–73; transmission of, 172–73
amoebae, 71–72, 80
analogies. *See* metaphors
anarchy, 56
animal magnetism, 38, 41. *See also* hypnotism
anthrax, 29, 93, 110
anti-contagionism, 10–11. *See also* miasma
theory
anxieties: imperial, 162, 164; sexual, 7–8,
50, 101–2, 123, 156, 164
aphonia, 126, 129–30, 188n. 12
Apollo, 164
Arata, Stephen, 185–86n. 1
Arens, Katherine, 187n. 2, 188nn. 14, 17
Aristotle, 65, 168
authority, physician's, 49, 57, 60
Azorín, 88

Bacteria. *See* microbes
Baroja, Pío, 88
Bell, Joseph, 92–94, 100
Bernard, Claude, 43–44, 58, 84, 110
Bernheim, Hippolyte, 75, 121–25, 127,
132, 134
Beziehungen, 141, 166–67
Bichat, Xavier, 11–12
The Birth of Tragedy (Nietzsche), 163–66
Bismarck, Otto von, 16–17, 158–59,
167
blackmail, 169; in literature, 112, 114–16
Bloemfontein, 92
Boer War, 92, 94, 102
borders. *See* boundaries
boundaries: collapse of, 164; to define life
forms, 8; disciplinary, 2; national, 169–

70; penetration of, 101–2, 156–57, 164–
65, 168, 174; and personal identity, 2, 5,
41, 61, 120, 130–34, 149, 156–57, 164–
68; social basis of, 83, 119, 145; and
visual system, 1, 82–84
Boyle, Robert, 9
Brantlinger, Patrick, 98, 186nn. 1, 4, 5
Brieux, Eugène, 135, 139, 146
Brock, Thomas, 178n. 34
Brouardel, Paul, 10
Bunyan, John, 180n. 9

Cadwalader, Mary, 53
Cajal. *See* Ramón y Cajal, Santiago
capitalism, 54
cells: connections between, 65, 73, 89; vs.
crystals, 14, 71; independence of, 14, 21,
64, 71–73; as individuals, 18, 21, 86;
membranes of, 23, 71, 73; physiology of,
23
cell theory: and culture, 9, 15; definition
of, 4; development of, 14
cellular pathology, 15, 21, 24, 65
centralized power, 17, 19, 22, 54, 76, 86,
89; and public health policy, 35, 178n. 34
changieren, 150
character, individual, 47–48, 54
Charcot, Jean Martin, 121, 123, 125
childbed fever. *See* puerperal fever
cholera: bacillus identification, 33, 66, 93–
94, 148, 152; in Egypt (1883–84), 32–
33; in Hamburg (1892), 152–53; origins
of, 149, 152; in Peru (1991), 169; in
Rwanda (1994), 170–71; in Spain
(1885), 66; spread of, 151–53, 158, 163,
169
circulation, social and physical, 136–37,
147
Civil War, American, 46–47, 51
class. *See* social class

Library of Congress Cataloging-in-Publication Data

Otis, Laura, 1961–
  Membranes: metaphors of invasion in nineteenth-century
literature, science, and politics / Laura Otis.
    p.   cm. — (Medicine and culture)
  Includes bibliographical references and index.
  ISBN 0-8018-5996-4 (alk. paper)
    1. Literature and science.   2. Literature, Modern—19th century—
History and criticism.   3. Identity in literature.   4. Self in
literature.   5. Physicians as authors.   6. Biology—Social aspects.
7. Cytology.   I. Title.   II. Series.
PN55.O87   1999
809'.93356—dc21   98-29763
                                                           CIP